GARRY SOBERS

GARRY SOBERS

My Autobiography

With Bob Harris

headline

First published in 2002
by HEADLINE BOOK PUBLISHING

10 9 8 7 6 5 4 3 2 1

Cataloguing in Publication Data is available
from the British Library.

ISBN 0 7553 1006 3

Typeset by
Letterpart Limited, Reigate, Surrey

Printed and bound in Great Britain by
Clays Ltd, St Ives plc

HEADLINE BOOK PUBLISHING
A division of Hodder Headline
338 Euston Road
LONDON NW1 3BH

www.headline.co.uk
www.hodderheadline.com

Contents

Acknowledgements

Sir Garfield Sobers and Bob Harris would like to thank Ralph Taylor and all the staff at the Ormond Beach Hotel and Spa in Barbados for their help and hospitality; Ian Marshall and Jo Roberts-Miller at Headline; the Barbados Board of Tourism; Richard Branson and Virgin Atlantic; Morris Greenidge; and Jackie White.

Prologue

For most of my international Test career I was playing for two – myself and my great friend Collie Smith who died one Saturday night in England in a car I was driving.

He was one of Jamaica's favourite sons, a wonderful cricketer whom the people loved with all their hearts, and I felt a lot of apprehension when I returned for my first game back at Sabina Park in Kingston after his tragic death. I worried about how they would react towards me on a ground that I had always loved and where I had made a world record score against Pakistan exactly two years earlier to the month.

I couldn't have been more mistaken in my fears. The Jamaican people understood the grief I felt and mourned with me. While it was so melancholic that you could feel the sadness in the atmosphere, there was not a scrap of animosity towards me from anyone, not even his family. All the people at that famous ground made me feel at home and welcome. But deep down inside, in the back of my own mind, was the thought that missing from this Test match was one of the sons of their soil to whom they looked up. Collie would have been among the top players in the world had he not been taken away by that fatal accident.

Arriving back at Collie's home ground brought it all back to me. On 6 September 1959, I met up with Collie and Jamaica's medium-fast bowler Tom Dewdney after our respective Lancashire League games to travel through the night to London to play in a charity match the next day.

Collie, or O'Neill Gordon Smith to give him his full name, was my closest friend and my best adviser. He was three years older than me and already a very fine cricketer who seemed destined to become even better. He was more than just an accomplished batsman, having scored big 100s against England and Australia. He was also developing into a very good off-spin bowler. I am serious when I say that he had the potential to be a top class all-rounder, probably one of the world's best.

We shared a room on our first tour of England in 1957 and again in Pakistan when his wise words helped me overcome the dreadful umpiring decisions I was receiving. He was full of fun but he was also a religious man. We called him the 'Wayside Preacher' because he liked to read the lesson in church.

While I was playing for Radcliffe in the Lancashire League, he was a sensation for Burnley and just a couple of months earlier had scored a remarkable triple 100 against Lowerhouse in a one-day game.

There should have been four of us making the journey south on that fateful night. We were waiting for Roy Gilchrist but after an hour or more we gave up and decided to make our way to London without him. Such is the fickle finger of fate. Had we left on time or had we waited a little longer who knows what might have happened. But there is no turning the clock back.

We were all in good humour because, although leaving late, it meant that we would avoid the heaviest of the London-bound traffic. Collie drove first, passed the wheel to Tom and then it was my turn. Tom switched to the front passenger seat to keep me company. Collie wanted to sleep in the back.

I had just taken the wheel and we were on the A34 near Stone in Staffordshire at around 4.45 a.m. approaching a bend when, suddenly,

I was confronted with two dazzling headlights coming straight towards me leaving no time to react. Then everything went black.

That was all I remembered about the collision. It was only later I learned that I had run head-on into a 10-ton cattle truck. I suppose I was unconscious for a short while. The next thing I remember was getting up and hearing Tom making a lot of noise. He was hysterical and clearly in a lot of pain. Collie was lying on the ground and I asked him with some trepidation, 'How are you little man?'

He responded straightaway, 'I'm all right, Mun – go look after the big boy.'

I went back to Tom and tried to help him and quieten him down until the ambulance arrived to take us to hospital in Stone. I had a dislocated bone in my wrist that was pressing on a nerve, a cut eye and a severed nerve in a finger on my left hand.

At the hospital, Tom and Collie were away from me being looked after in separate rooms. The first thing I did each morning when I woke up was to ask about Collie. I was horrified when I heard that there was damage to his spinal cord and he had lapsed into unconsciousness. Three days after the crash he was dead.

I was devastated. I could not believe it had happened. It just took everything out of me. I was stunned at how life could suddenly change and, of course, there was the inevitable question – why him of all people? It changed my life completely. Later, I was charged with driving without due care and attention and was fined £10, adding to the burden of responsibility that I already felt.

After I came out of hospital, I was due to return home to the Caribbean to play against England but there was nothing that could take what had happened off my mind. I went to stay with friends in London and spent some time with them. Then I met with Dr C.B. 'Bertie' Clarke, the former West Indies leg spinner, and he said we had better start working to get me mentally and physically ready for the Test series ahead. He took me to the Middlesex indoor nets and Alf Gover and Stanley Goodrich from Jamaica bowled to me until I recovered my fitness.

But it didn't concern me at all. In the frame of mind I was in, I just didn't care. The events of that late summer morning were still fresh in my mind and I thought about them every minute of the day and night. Cricket was a distant second at the time.

Collie, although not much older than me, was a restraining influence and would always be the one to say when it was time to go home. We were keen to establish ourselves in the game and did not drink a lot in those early days, but with him not around I began drinking more. I was fortunate that it did not affect my cricket. I lived more by night than I had before, not wanting to go to bed to think or dream.

I was deeply depressed. I wasn't going to jump under a bus, commit suicide or anything like that but in my own way it was as if I was trying to destroy myself. Life had suddenly become too short and I was going to give whatever was left of it all I had. Collie was such a good Christian man. His death showed me how quickly it could all end, even for him, how easy it was for life to vanish.

He was so jovial and such a good fellow; we hit it off straightaway. It was wonderful rooming with him, and we quickly became firm friends. We were good company for each other. We would lie on our beds talking through the night, confiding in each other. We were so close, like brothers.

Although he was not a drinker, he used to keep a bottle of the 150 per cent proof rum to rub into his muscles. He had me doing it too. When his Jamaican friends came to our room visiting, they used to drink it!

At that time, the nightlife hadn't claimed me that much although I was always something of a night owl. As a teenager, I regularly attended midnight movies. After his death, I used to stay up all night and drink. It didn't touch me. So much that was going on in my head was stronger than alcohol, it had no effect. Sometimes I would drink from one day to the next without even sleeping. Scotch or brandy, whatever was there.

After a while, I realised that the West Indies had lost Collie who could have been a great cricketer and I would be letting my country down if I disappeared into the mists of an alcoholic haze. It suddenly struck me forcibly that I no longer had to play for Garfield Sobers. I had to do two men's jobs – Collie's and mine. The decision helped me put my life back together and I willingly took the burden on my shoulders. I started to bat and bowl for Collie and for myself, and that probably improved my cricket to the level I reached during my career!

Two or three months after the accident, I went back to the West Indies to start 1960 off with the series against England in January. I was young but by then I had an old head on my shoulders. I had always mixed with much older people and I would listen to their experiences and learn from them. That helped me and, combined with the added responsibility, I'm sure made me the cricketer I became. If I was going to be a West Indian cricketer, I had to find a way to do his job and mine. It was Garfield Sobers and Collie Smith playing as one.

I had no outside help in putting my head back together. There was no consultancy. It was something I had to do myself.

I'm sure Collie would have been pleased with my decision and with the cricket that followed for, to some extent, I think I succeeded in my aims. My first innings of the series was in Bridgetown at the Kensington Oval exactly four months to the day after the crash. I remembered Collie with every run I scored and there were 226 of them before Fred Trueman clean bowled me.

It was the start of a new life and a few weeks later I paid my respects to my best friend again when I scored 147 at his home ground. He has stayed with me ever since. He has always been there and always will be there because he was such a wonderful person and such a good friend.

Jamaica was always good to me both before and afterwards, and I will always thank them for that. It is no coincidence that many of my best innings came at Collie's favourite ground.

CHAPTER ONE

Twelve-fingered symphony

There are those who claim I was destined to do well in life because I arrived in this world with two extra fingers, as though there was something mystic about it. I wasn't bothered. They didn't inhibit me in any way at all and I never worried about them. The condition is rare but there are still people in the Caribbean who have this unusual feature. In fact, I met a West Indian quite recently who had an extra finger on each hand, just as I did.

I don't know how it came about and I was neither embarrassed nor excited by it but the other kids would say that I was so good at cricket because I had six fingers on each hand. Certainly I didn't think there was anything mystic about it although some of the crueller boys would call me a freak.

The first extra finger fell off quite early, when I was nine or ten, and I played my first colonial game with 11 fingers! I took the second off when I was 14 or 15 and playing serious cricket. The first of the spare fingers came off with the help of a piece of cat gut wrapped around the base and a sharp tug, something like the old-fashioned way of removing a child's milk tooth. The other came off with the help of a sharp knife.

I was born Garfield St Aubrun Sobers on 28 July 1936 in what is now Walcott's Avenue in the Bay Land area of the parish of St Michael in Barbados. In those days the street had no name at all. It was my parents who originated from Chelsea Road, which tends to be called my birthplace. It is also said that I was born at 3.30 a.m. but I couldn't tell you; I never troubled to go into it that deeply.

My father, Shamont, was a seaman working in the Canadian merchant navy on what were known as the lady boats. All of this particular company's boats were called *The Lady* something, and were named after notable British naval officers. I recall *The Lady Hawkins*, *The Lady Rodney* and *The Lady Nelson*. They docked in Barbados every couple of weeks.

I cannot remember that much about my father. I was very young, just five, when he died at sea. He was serving on *The Lady Hawkins* when it was sunk by the Germans on 11 January 1942. I remember a messenger coming to our house and my mother Thelma sobbing and crying. She told us that his boat had been torpedoed but it wasn't definite that he'd been drowned; there were some survivors. That gave her some little hope but after a few days and then the weeks passed, we came to realise that Dad would never be coming back. That was a very sad day for my mother. I didn't really know how to react because I was so young and had seen so little of him while he was away at sea.

It left my mother with the huge responsibility of bringing up a big family on her own. There was my eldest brother George, who was 11 at the time, followed by sisters Greta and Elise, then Gerry, me and Saul, or Cecil as he was christened. There was another child in there somewhere but he died shortly after birth and I never knew much about him.

George had just started at Combermere High School when our father died and, unfortunately, it meant that any hopes he had of staying on for further education were dashed. He had to leave when he was 15 and he went to work for the island's electrical company. When he was old enough, he followed our father to sea to help support the family. It was necessary because the pension my mother received from the Canadian shipping company was not enough to support her and six kids.

My mother was such a wonderful person. She did whatever she had to do and looked after us tremendously well. We went to school, we were clean, we had shoes on our feet and food in our bellies. We even had a maid in the early days to help with the household chores and to assist my mother in looking after all of us.

Unfortunately, there were no state exams to qualify for senior school then, and if parents wanted to send their children they had to pay. George had thought himself lucky. He was the oldest and was able to go to high school because of my father's wages and a scholarship and he must have been hugely disappointed to have to drop out when he did.

There was no money to send either Gerry, a year my senior, or me to high school. We were sent to Bay Street Boys' School but I don't think it would have made a lot of difference where we'd gone because the dominating factor in our lives, even at that early age, was sport. It was always at the forefront of everything we did.

Although it was sad losing my father when we were so young, leaving such a burden on my mother, it was something of a blessing in disguise as far as I was concerned. I was too young to appreciate the real effect. When he was at home I recall him as being a very strict man and, I suppose, I was a little afraid of him. When we were little boys running around our neighbourhood, as soon as we heard that his boat was in the harbour we would rush back into the house and pretend we had been there the entire time he had been away. If he came home and saw us playing outside it meant that we were going to get flogged. He didn't like us going outside to play with the other children. I was too young to know his reasons and I never bothered inquiring as I grew older. It was nothing to do with religion as far as I knew, and he was a keen enough sportsman. I know that he was a good footballer but I don't know whether he was much of a cricketer. It wasn't the sort of thing to bring up and question my mother about after the tragedy.

My mother never looked at another man once my father was gone. She devoted her life to bringing up her children and it was obvious that it did her no harm. Sadly, she died aged 93 in September 2001, cared for in her last days by our sister Greta. She was a Christian person, a godly person. God was there to help her get through her problems, her suffering, and that is why she lived so long and so happily. We were open house to many people and shared what we had with others. That is the legacy of my mother.

After Dad died we were able to go outside and play. Our mother didn't worry about us as he did. We would go to school neat and tidy, come home and then go out to play behind the house on the Bay Pasture or in the street. It was there that our sports prowess began to develop and blossom.

My earliest memories of cricket are as an eight-year-old playing in the road or on the beach. We would dig up a lump of tar and fashion it into a ball and play what was called Lilliputian cricket, which was one of the favourites because you didn't need a lot of space to play. We even played it in the confines of our little house sometimes, or in the narrow gap between the two houses. The wicket was less than half the normal size and it provided the right sort of entertainment for small boys. What's more, there was no need to prepare wickets as you had to if you wanted to play on one of the fields.

For a bat, we might help ourselves to a piece of wood from someone's palisade and carve it into the right shape; or we would go up to the Wanderers cricket ground on the Bay Pasture at the back of our house and ask them if they had any broken bats, which we would cut down to size.

Sometimes the sun was too hot for the tar ball and it would begin to melt, going oblong when you hit it. When that happened we would take a rock, wrap it in cloth and knit it tight, and use that. It served a purpose but the ideal replacement was a golf ball. They were hard to come by and a lot more dangerous, not only for us but for local property. Windows would break very easily if you struck it too hard!

The Sobers boys were pretty shrewd in those days. We always made sure that we had the cut-down bat, the made-up ball and the stumps. On weekends or during the holidays we would wake up the other fellows as early as 7.30 in the morning to play. Immediately one of us would shout, 'Me first.' Another of us would claim the second batting position and so on, leaving the other kids to fill in later on. They could hardly argue when we owned the cricket gear. After a while, they found that Gerry and I were very difficult to get out. They would threaten to break our bat or to beat us up if we didn't get out and let them have a knock. Even when we moved on to tennis-ball cricket it was the same thing.

Another early memory is putting up the numbers on the Wanderers scoreboard, which I did from the age of about eight. It gave me a ringside seat. I grew up watching all the top players – Frank Worrell, Clyde Walcott, Everton Weekes and Clyde's brother Keith, a tremendous player who many thought was better than Clyde. He was also a great footballer until his eyesight went. Everton played for the army team, Garrison Sports Club, and Frank played for Empire before he went to Jamaica. I saw George Carew, the opening bat for Barbados and West Indies, Roy Marshall and Laurie Johnson who played for Derbyshire in the English summer and then came home to play for Wanderers. It was sheer joy to go to the Bay Pasture every Saturday and watch good cricket.

As we grew, a lot of people would say why don't you go and look for work to help your mother? But cricket was always my focus and took up all my time. It was the top game and at an early age I realised that, if I became good enough, it was the only sport that would allow me to travel and see the world. I was good at football but that was not as well developed as it is today and offered no such opportunities. As a little boy of nine or ten I would read about cricket in the papers, and when the West Indies went to India in 1948 and then to England in 1950 we used to listen in awe to the commentaries on the radio. To a young boy from a humble background, this was something magical. It was a wondrous thing to think that if I could develop my skills enough, I might have that same opportunity.

There was always that chance because all of us in the Sobers family were good at sport, not just cricket but football, table tennis, basketball, tennis . . . whatever it was, we were competent at it. Gerry and I often watched George playing cricket for Combermere in the first and second divisions and he was certainly a player. I didn't see Saul playing very often because I was travelling by the time he came through, but I was told he was a good cricketer and one of the best slip catchers ever seen on the island. He used to field in the slips to Wes Hall and catch everything that came to him.

At school I was little more than an average student. For me, school was a place where you could go to play cricket. My idea was to learn as much as I could so that I didn't look an idiot. There has always been a high literacy rate in Barbados, and Bay Street and St Giles were recognised as the best elementary schools. A lot of the Bay Street boys went on to become notable scholars.

I was a well-behaved boy, well brought up. None of us gave our mother any problems and maybe because of that there were always people outside the family to help and look after us. We did what we thought was right most of the time and I suppose the worst of the boyish things we got up to was to steal some fruit off the trees so that we didn't have to stop playing cricket to go home to eat. We picked mangoes, bananas or the golden apples. It was a lot of fun. We had what you would call truly boy days and whatever boys did then we did it too, pitching marbles, playing cowboys and Indians and police and crooks, or scrumping pears or akees. We had a normal childhood. There was nothing like breaking into houses or sticking someone with a knife. That sort of thing didn't happen in Barbados then. I can only ever remember having one or two fights in my life. I didn't have to fight. Gerry would fight on my behalf on the rare occasions it became necessary.

When Gerry and I played together at Bay Street School, the opposition would be asked by their friends, 'Y'all going to play against those two Chinee boys?' I don't know why we were called that. Maybe it was because our eyes were smaller than most or maybe it was because our complexion was different but we were known as the Chinee Boys by all the other schools. They used to worry that Gerry would destroy them with the bat and that I would bowl them out. There were a lot of good players in our team, including Keith Barker who later lived in England and played league cricket, and John Callender, but Gerry and I were considered the ones to worry about. It was the name Sobers that was mentioned every time a team came to play us.

At the time, I was bowling left-arm orthodox leg-breaks. I was very small so I didn't go through the usual schoolboy dream of being a fast bowler, bowling medium pace trying to be quick. In fact, I was so small they used to call me a runt. It didn't help that I played in short pants up until I started to represent the island.

Apparently it's been written somewhere that, at school, they tried to change me from being naturally left-handed into a right-handed batsman and bowler. That's a myth but it is true that in Barbados a lot of schoolchildren who were left-handed were made to write right-handed and would be smacked with a ruler if they dared to use their left hand.

One of the earliest influences on me was a master at the school, Everton Barrow, who taught us cricket and football. He played for Empire, which was one of our leading clubs where Frank Worrell, Conrad Hunte and Seymour Nurse played their cricket. He used to tell me that when I was older he would introduce me into the Empire club. There was a class system operating at the time; Empire and Spartan were the top teams and all the Combermere High School boys would go to Empire while the Harrison College boys went to Spartan. The boys from Bay Street elementary school had nowhere specific to go.

We joined in the beach cricket, though. Every Sunday morning, boys of all ages from 10 to 24 would gather by the side of the sparkling blue waters of the Caribbean to play. We played with ordinary tennis balls, not the scorched and hardened balls used on some of the other islands. One or two of our guys worked at the tennis courts and would scrounge the old balls that were a bit soft for tennis. They were very good for us. This was where our game really began to develop. Both

Gerry and I were considered exceptional for our age. They simply could not get us out, even the grown men and older boys – and we were still threatened with beatings and being run home if we didn't lose our wickets. We would wait for the right moment, pick up our stumps, bats and balls and run off home with the big fellows shouting and throwing rocks at us. It taught us to run fast as well as play cricket!

It was a lot of fun and a pleasure to play against the older boys because it stretched us and made us improve all the time, but even when we started playing tennis-ball and beach cricket, we still carried on with our Lilliputian cricket, forming a little league among ourselves. This was so successful that we also formed a league with the tennis-ball cricket, preparing our own pitches and dyeing the tennis ball red, to make it look like the real thing. We would have umpires at both ends and play the game just the way it was played at Test level. The only difference was that we did not need pads or gloves because the tennis ball did not hurt when it rapped you on the shins or bounced up to hit the arms or the chest. As youngsters, we preferred the tennis ball and didn't like playing with the hard ball because it hurt too much when you had no protection. We simply could not afford luxuries like pads and gloves.

Most Bajan cricketers – Seymour Nurse, Everton Weekes, Clyde Walcott, Frank Worrell, Conrad Hunte, Cammie Smith and many more – played tennis-ball cricket at a very high level. There were always competitions around Barbados where you played with and against some very good cricketers indeed. I honestly believe that this is how Barbados cricket developed so well. Throughout the West Indies you find that many play off the back foot and on the up because you cannot drive a tennis ball off the front foot – the bounce is too big. That is also why West Indian cricketers have learned how to hook so well – you either drive off the back foot or you play across the line of the ball because it was always bouncing above the height of the stumps. It was difficult to control with a straight bat.

It's said that only the exceptionally good player can stand upright and play with the bat drawn forward. I was one of those fortunate enough to be able to do so. That's where the difference lay between Sir Vivian Richards and me and why it has always been so difficult to compare the two of us as batsmen. Viv was probably the way he was, often hitting across the line, because early on in his career he was brought up in a different way. He came up in another era, playing on lower-bounce wickets and off the front foot. It is difficult to score runs when the ball is keeping low but if you can get across it the way Viv did, you can still do it. Viv went across the line of good-length balls, picking them up just as they bounced, whereas in my era we stood up and pulled, hooked and cut. The good players hit it off the back foot through the covers and that amazed people.

It is all to do with environment. When we were playing in the road, hitting the wooden house on the full was out. Hitting the boards on the bounce was not out, so you had to control it. That process helped tremendously. People who watched my brothers and me between the ages of 12 and 14 were amazed at how we could control the ball and keep it on the ground. They recognised the skill – not necessarily in me. I was acknowledged as a good bat but certainly not the best in the family. If I'm to be honest, I was probably the worst as a youngster.

Two groundsmen at Wanderers were also influential in my development. First, when I was very young, there was Frank Grant, better known to everyone as 'Pitch', and later, Briggs Grandison. Briggs prepared the wickets for Tuesdays and Thursdays for Wanderers and I was one of those who used to help him. In return, we were allowed to play at the ground.

Briggs would sit in front of the pavilion and watch us youngsters play. He seemed to sense that I had some talent and he must have mentioned it to West Indian international Dennis Atkinson, who went on to captain and manage the West Indies. I was watching the Wanderers practise one day when he pointed me out to Dennis, told him that I could bowl accurately and asked him to have a look at me. Dennis called me over and gave me the ball. He must have been impressed because from that evening if I didn't arrive there on time he would ask where I was.

Dennis, an insurance salesman at the Mutual, was able to leave work before all the others and he used to get to the ground early to gain some extra practice. He would arrive around three o'clock while the others didn't get there until four. There were only two nets, one for the first team and the other for the seconds and thirds. It meant that each batsman could have around five or 10 minutes at the most, and often the bowlers didn't have a bat at all. By getting there early, Dennis made sure he had as much practice as he felt he needed. With none of the other players around, he would send for me, 'that little boy', and a couple of the other local boys to bowl to him. It served me well; it was through him that I eventually received recognition.

To make it more interesting and competitive, Dennis would put a shilling on top of the stumps and tell me that if I knocked it off it was mine. That was a lot of money in the early fifties, especially for a young boy who was given four cents a day for his lunch. A penny equalled two cents so a shilling was worth 24 cents. Riches indeed!

Every afternoon, I would bowl to him and then hang around, waiting for Roy and Norman Marshall, Laurie Johnson and the others to arrive, and bowl to them, too. I didn't get too many of those shillings because if I beat the bat it would invariably hit them on the pads. There was no shilling for leg before wicket in the nets! The faster bowlers had more chance of knocking the shilling off the stump. As a spinner, I had to beat the bat and the pad. It wasn't easy, but it was a great incentive. A shilling would buy ice cream, black pudding and souse (pork marinated in vinegar, onions and peppers) plus four or five ham cutters (sandwiches). It made you feel big and important to go to school with a shilling in your pocket. It meant that you could buy all the snowballs (a shaved ice confection) and fishcakes you wanted and you were able to entertain your friends. Four cents would give you bread and fish and a snowball.

My main object was to bowl well enough to be recognised. Dennis, Roy and Norman were all in the Barbados team and were accepted as top players. So many good cricketers played up there on the Bay Pasture for and against Wanderers, they would make the current West

Indies Test team look a joke. The names still roll off the tongue after all of these years. Apart from those three, there was Clyde Walcott, George MacDonald Carew and Everton Weekes. Frank Worrell was around for a while before he went to live in Jamaica. Then there was E.A.V. 'Foffie' Williams, a fast bowler of some quality who had played against the touring England side in 1948, Cecil 'Boogles' Williams, who went to England with the West Indies in 1950, and Charlie Taylor behind the wicket. Tom Pearce was the captain and another who went on to manage many West Indian teams. You could tell how strong Barbados was at that time because no West Indies team left on tour without at least six Bajans in the party.

We used to scrounge proper balls from Wanderers for our own games. When we saw one that had burst out of the seams we would ask if we could have it and take it to the local shoemaker to stitch back in place and shine up. He would give it a nice high seam and boy, oh boy, those balls used to do Dixie. They would move all over the place when you hit the seam. The shoemaker would reshape the ball for nothing if it was too big a job for our ice pick and string. It was very interesting to play with that type of ball because it would always move and I'm sure that it stood me in good stead when I came to play in England on the green wickets.

At first, the other boys used to tease me, saying that I could only play with a tennis ball and that when they bowled at me with the hard ball they would knock me down. We used to play on half a wicket and sometimes the ball would drop on the edge and it would take off. Turf wickets in the Caribbean were always 'elevated' to help the drainage. When the nets were placed halfway down the wicket to allow two batsmen to practise back-to-back at the same time, the edges of the pitch could present a problem – it could be really dangerous if a quickie found the right spot because it would produce a nasty flyer.

Some of the club players would occasionally play with us. There was one fast bowler, Doyle Braddock, whom I used to take it out of when we played with the tennis ball, hitting him all over the place. But when we played with a hard ball, as soon as I went in they brought all the fielders around me close to the bat and told Braddock to knock me down. It was my first experience of sledging. Braddock stormed in, bowling me bouncers and I was pushing them down and crying because of these big fellows telling him to knock me over. But I was getting behind the ball and stopping it. I was determined they weren't going to scare me out and the more I resisted the more bouncers came down and the more water came out of my eyes and ran down my face. I was brought up in a hard school – the school of hard knocks.

In fact, Braddock was a beautiful fast bowler with a perfect action, very much like that of Frank King. It was a delight just to see Frank run up. Even Wes Hall learned from him. Frank was the groundsman at Combermere School when Wes was there and Wes was wicket-keeper to him before he became a fast bowler. You can see a lot of Frank King in Wes, even though King was thin and Wes was muscular. Frank used to glide up in the air, the left foot used to go up and the left arm would go up, the left foot would come down and the right arm would go up, it was like watching poetry in motion.

We played on the Bay Pasture with a select group of players – Charlie and Freddie Daniels, Keith Greenidge, Erlin Lord, the Barkers, Merlin Jones . . . I could go on and call them one after another. They played in trials for Barbados and made runs but couldn't get into the island team. The Barbados Cricket League had so many good players who couldn't get in they could have played the other islands on their own. Playing against all of these, I had to develop if I had anything in me, and I was desperate to improve and progress. It was a good background; I was brought up very well in the game at the highest level and it was the perfect education when I was in my early teens.

While I was growing up and throughout my career I did not watch that much first-class cricket – I had been to the Kensington Oval once before I played there – but when I was scoring at Wanderers or watching cricket somewhere else, I would watch how the batsmen moved. I never watched the sixes or the fours fly to the boundary; I watched how they moved their feet, how they picked up their bat, how they got behind the ball and generally what they did. I would rather see what bowlers were bowling than cheer the boundaries. There were no coaches in those days and you learned by watching. That was my education. It wasn't something I was told to do; it just seemed natural. I watched how batsmen got into position to hit the ball and then I would go into the nets and practise what I had seen. I watched the leg-spinner turning, and saw how the batsman played him allowing for the spin. I watched and practised hard and then I practised some more, so when I was put in the situation and needed to move, I moved.

I was never captain of the school team – that honour went to Gerry. In fact, I never captained any team until I skippered the West Indies. How good was Gerry? He was classed alongside Seymour Nurse with Gerry just having the edge, and we all know what a player Nurse turned out to be. That's how good he was. When the two of them, still schoolboys, played for the Police club, they would attract an extraordinary number of people who turned up just to watch them.

Let's not get away from it. Talk all you like about the problems black players faced in Australia and South Africa but in Barbados in the forties and early fifties, a coloured player had to be three times as good as a white player to play for the island. Fortunately, that was dying out by the time we came through and it did not affect Gerry as much as it had done players before him, and me not at all. There were still lots of white players in the game and they naturally played in their own clubs, namely Wanderers, Pickwick, Carlton, YMPC and Windward in Division Two. But there were also several middle-class black clubs and after the black talent emerged, it was more down to ability rather than colour.

Gerry was just unfortunate because Barbados was so strong in talent. When he came in as a wicket-keeper/opening batsman, he found that Cammie Smith, Conrad Hunte and Roy Marshall were in front of him by virtue of their age. They had already established themselves and it was difficult for him to break in and replace them.

There were two organisations in Barbados, the Barbados Cricket Association and the Barbados Cricket League. During the season, the two played each other and then 20 or so players were selected to take part in two or three trial matches at the Kensington Oval. Gerry would always make 100s in these games and then retire to let others bat, but he just couldn't make it into the island team. After a while he got fed up and went to sea, but even when he came back without having played for months on end, he would go straight into the Barbados Colts team and score runs.

My problem was that the adults were afraid of me playing against the hard ball at a high level when I was so young and small. They were afraid that I might get hurt and be spoilt or put off what they thought was my budding cricketing career. Garnett Ashby came to my rescue and ended my frustrations. He brought a side called Kent down from the country to play a little team from the Bay. I was allowed to enjoy a game against Kent because they were not that highly rated, while I still could not play against the city boys because they were thought to be too good. I scored a few runs and took a few wickets. Garnett liked what he saw and went to speak to Lionel Daniel, a good soccer player who captained leading club Notre Dame and whom he knew was a very close friend of my family. Lionel was a cabinetmaker and joiner by trade and I used to work for him to earn money for Christmas between the ages of 11 and 13. Garnett asked him who the youngster was but Lionel told him to forget it, he couldn't have me because they didn't want me spoiled. Not to be deterred, Garnett came directly to me and asked if I wanted to play some cricket for him in the country. I immediately said, 'Yes, sir,' because I knew they wouldn't play me in the city in case I got hurt. I just wanted to play . . . anywhere. He did the right thing and went straight to my mother to ask her permission but she was not at all happy at the idea of her young son going off every weekend with a stranger.

'You want to carry Garfield on the back of a motorcycle to the country to play cricket against big, able men, and on a Sunday, too?' she said, incredulously. 'I don't see how you could think of asking me such a question. I don't even know you, my gentleman.'

But after talking to my brother George, my schoolteacher Everton Barrow, the groundsman Briggs Grandison and even a local priest to gain support, he went back to my mother who finally relented after five weeks of discussions. She agreed that I could stay with him and his family at weekends if it was what I wanted to do. Garnett would come and pick me up on a Friday night or a Saturday morning on his motorbike and take me up to St Phillip to a place called Penny Hole, now known as Gemswick. I played for Kent and took a lot of wickets, and when they picked the country team to play the city team, I was in the side. Garnett became a close friend and was always there to help and advise.

Playing for Kent opened the door to other opportunities. I was picked to play in a representative match at the Wanderers ground between the BCL and BCA when Captain Wilfred Farmer, who was inspector of police and in charge of their cricket team, was batting. Dennis had already told him about me and pointed me out to him when the game began. Farmer was a good player and a hard hitter of the ball, but when I bowled to him he couldn't get me away at all. There was this skinny little kid in short pants tying him down.

Dennis recommended to Captain Farmer that he should try to enrol me into the police band so that I would qualify for the very good police cricket team. Sure enough, after the game, Captain Farmer pulled me to one side and asked if I could dance or play an instrument. When I told him that I could not, he asked me if I would be interested in learning so that I could join the police team. I agreed because I wanted to play cricket, not because I was interested in music. Only cricket interested me then.

A couple of weeks passed by and then one morning I received a letter asking me to go to see the band leader, Captain Raison, an Englishman. I went to see him on the Monday morning and passed a little exam that was set. I told them I couldn't dance and that meant I couldn't play drums because they said that one went with the other. So they tried to teach me how to 'lip' the bugle and I did that for a couple of weeks. It was enough for me to be picked for the cricket team and my first game was at Empire where I played against a strong team including Foffie Williams. I think Conrad Hunte played, too, along with Clairmonte Depeiza, another Test player.

Police batted first and we went in late in the evening. I can't remember the score but the new ball was taken at 200 and Foffie Williams was bowling to me, at number eight. He couldn't believe that this 14-year-old batsman was getting behind the line of the ball and holding up Empire finishing off the tail. As he walked back to his mark I saw him draw his finger across his throat. I didn't have a clue what he meant but everyone else did and the next ball was a bumper aimed at my head. I tried to evade the rearing ball but it struck me on the jaw. It didn't hurt me that much and I was more frightened than anything else on this fast pitch. I was shy and ashamed that I had been hit, and I left the field with my head bowed. The captain asked me if I was going to go out and bat again later but I told him, 'No sir, my jaw hurts me too much.' I fielded and bowled but didn't bat again in that match.

There were two or three of us from the band in the police side and I told them to tell Captain Raison that I had been struck on the jaw and couldn't blow my bugle so I wouldn't be at band practice on the Monday after the game. I missed that practice and the next and when I went in on the Wednesday, an angry Captain Raison asked me where I had been for the last two days. I told him what had happened and that I had asked one of the boys to let him know. He looked me up and down and told me that he didn't think I was interested enough in the music and that I should leave to make room for someone who was. It was a pity because after being there for four or five weeks I was beginning to enjoy myself.

I don't know where it came from but I was a little presumptuous in those days. I told him I wasn't that interested in the band anyway and I had joined for the chance to play cricket because I couldn't get a game for the Wanderers, Pickwick, Spartan, Empire or any of the other teams in the League.

I told Captain Farmer what had happened and he tried to have me reinstated and was surprised that Captain Raison didn't want to know about apologies or forgiveness. I suspect that Captain Raison was worried that some of the Bay Street Boys Club lads might be having liaisons with his daughter and that I was one of them. I didn't know this until sometime afterwards because I didn't go to the club that often, but I was told that was why I was kicked out of the band.

Captain Farmer, however, would not let it rest there and he wrote to the Barbados Cricket Association and asked if a boy from the Police Boys Club could play for the Police Cricket Club until he was 21. It was not the norm and I doubt whether they would have done it for anyone else. They knew of whom he was talking and said there was no problem. I continued to play for Police from then until I retired from the game at the age of 41. I never played for another club on Barbados.

My days with Police were phenomenal. The wickets in Barbados in those days were so good but, because of the lack of covers, we were brought up on all types of tracks, rain affected, often fast, often good for batting. This is where the skills of good players came in, not on the good wickets but on the bad, rain-soaked wickets. If you can bat on bad wickets, you are showing some signs of technique, ability and skill. Anyone can score runs on good wickets but only good batsmen score runs on bad wickets.

Plenty of other clubs on the island asked me to play for them over the years and I became an honorary member of nearly every club in Barbados, but my club was always Police because it was them and Captain Farmer who gave me my opportunity. They appreciated my loyalty, too, and I remain very good friends with the club. I am the patron of the team and they have done well in the Police World Cup. Whenever I see a policeman on Barbados, he salutes me in recognition of my services to their cricket team.

CHAPTER TWO

On my way

One of the first matches I played for Police was against my neighbourhood club, Wanderers. I batted at seven or eight and when I went in we were being badly beaten. I joined Carl Mullins, one of the most dangerous fast bowlers ever born in the West Indies, and went on to score 113 – my first BCA Division One 100 and it was against Wanderers of all teams. They told me it wasn't nice to do that to the club who had adopted me as a youngster and taught me my cricket. Carl scored 67 and between us we saved the match. It was something I went on to do throughout my career; it was often my role to come in when our backs were against the wall and for me to bat for the team.

I continued to play against not only my old friends but also my family. In one of the trials, Gerry played against me and, to make it worse, when he came in the captain brought me on and I took Gerry's wicket early. Everybody cursed me, saying it was a trial game and I shouldn't have got him out and that I was jealous of him. I said that we were both fighting for a place, him as a batsman and me as a bowler.

What did they want me to do? If he's not going to give me his wicket, why should I give him runs? If he's good enough, he should be able to bat and score runs against me.

I took a few wickets in that game and from that they picked 26 of us to play in the trials at the Oval. There was I at just 15 bowling to the likes of Walcott and Weekes. It was more than awesome but I bowled steady, a good line and length, and they couldn't get me away.

When I was not bowling I was fielding in the covers and I picked off a few of Clyde's shots like they were nothing. He glared at me as if to ask what I thought I was doing. Clyde hit the ball so hard that many fielders would make just a token effort to stop it, but I jumped on it.

Afterwards I went into the dressing room and was gulping down my regular intake of soft drinks when Everton came in.

'Are you Sobers?' he asked, taking a long look at the empty drinks bottles.

'Yes, sir,' I said.

'Well, Soapbox, if you drink any more of those, the ants will follow you home.'

I did reasonably well at the trials, impressing as much with my fielding as my bowling, and after the game when they selected the 12 for Barbados's opening match of the season, I was in. When they picked the 11, I was twelfth man.

In those days, the West Indies had one really good fast bowler and that was Frank King. We were due to play our first game against the touring Indians but before the game, the West Indies Board of Control telephoned the Barbados Cricket Association and asked if they would let Frank stand down to allow him to rest for the Test matches. They agreed and suddenly I was playing in the Barbados side to face the touring Indians at the Oval.

I was still playing in shorts for the trials and they told me during the match that I would have to start wearing long trousers to play with the seniors. The family couldn't afford them and so the Barbados Cricket Association presented me with my first pair of flannels. They also helped with boots, those big, heavy, metal-tipped ones that weighed a ton. Before that, I was wearing little plimsolls; we called them pumps.

There was no dad to buy me kit but there were lots of people who helped in many ways, particularly Goalie Cumberbatch, a neighbour and something of a father figure to me. He was a foreman stevedore by trade but his joy was watching cricket. When I left school at 14, there was talk of me going to work as a cash boy, earning one shilling and six pence a week. I wasn't keen on working for those wages, especially at something I didn't like. Goalie took me out in the boats as a tally clerk when there was a vacancy. It was a job that was in great demand because tally clerks made a lot of money. We used to go out and make a note of the cargo. I would make two or three hundred Barbadian dollars a day and that would see me through for a while.

Both George and Gerry were in the merchant navy by this time and they wanted me to join them, but I didn't want to because it would curtail my cricket. Goalie backed me up, saying that my place was on the cricket fields of Barbados. I decided to stick it out and felt totally justified when I was picked for Barbados and then made my Test debut.

I was so pleased to be given my chance, playing with Weekes, Walcott, Atkinson and Roy Marshall. It was all special but nothing compared to the thrill of being called on to bowl for the first time. That excellent batsman Polly Umrigar – he averaged over 40 in his 59 Test appearances – was at the crease and batting well. I had a touch of nerves as I prepared to bowl to this great Indian cricketer. As I marked my run up, I thought to myself, 'I have bowled to Everton, Frank and Clyde. Polly can't be as terrifying as any of those three.' The thought gave me heart and immediately the ball began to drop right on a spot. The first two overs I bowled were maidens. Polly got a bit fed up with being tied down by this skinny kid and promptly hit me for six on to the top of the Kensington stand. Two balls later I had him with a straight one as he played for the turn that was not there. I didn't turn it much in those days but I varied the flight and the angles. The packed pavilion went up to salute me. I was just 16, it was my first wicket at that level and they loved the romance of it.

I took four wickets in that first innings and three in the second. That was very reassuring because I felt that I had fulfilled my obligations, having been picked as a bowler. To be truthful, I can't remember how many runs I made – I was a few not out in a total of over 600. The 89 overs I bowled and those seven wickets were what mattered to me, and that I hadn't let myself or my island down. I felt good. I had been successful by the grace of the Lord. I felt that I had deserved my place and wasn't just a fill-in. I was indebted to our captain, the late John Goddard, who was not afraid to let this youngster have the ball and bowl so many overs in the match.

After that performance, it was suggested that I might even get a Test call for the Fifth and final Test against the Indians at Sabina Park in Jamaica at the end of March 1953. Sonny Ramadhin had gone sick and it was expected that I would be called in but they picked Alf Scott from Jamaica. I suppose they were trying to save money because they would have had to fly me there while other options were on the spot, including Scott and Reg Scarlett. I missed out that year but I was not going to have to wait long for my Test debut.

I was a regular for Barbados by the spring of the following year when Len Hutton brought the England side to the Caribbean, and had even scored 100 against British Guiana batting at number nine! I played against England for Barbados, took a few wickets but didn't bowl as well as I had against India. There was, however, a strange incident that made the game memorable for me. I was out, bowled by Tony Lock, and on my way back to the pavilion when the crowd started shouting for me to go back. I turned round and found that the square-leg umpire, Clyde Walcott's uncle, had no-balled Tony, presumably for throwing his quick one that had clean bowled me.

During that game, a young fast bowler called Fred Trueman bowled me a bouncer. I ducked, keeping my eye on the ball and the bat in front of me, but the ball didn't get up so I flung the bat upwards and hit myself on the forehead while the ball passed just over the top of the stumps. Fortunately, Fred didn't notice what I had done to myself or I would have had a few choice comments aimed in my direction. He wasn't nicknamed Fiery Fred for nothing; he was very blunt and very aggressive, as I was to discover over the next few years.

I swore there and then that I would never duck another bouncer and I didn't. The policy served me well because I was hit just twice in my long career, once by Foffie Williams and the other time by a little fellow named Jefferson who played for Oxford. I played against him at Lord's when he was playing for the MCC and I lost the ball completely in the background and was hit in the mouth. I was never hit above the chest other than on those two occasions. I always said that the bowler would have to kill me before he made me run or back away. I had a bat to protect me and if the bat couldn't protect me because I wasn't good enough, I wasn't worthy to be playing cricket at that level.

After making my Barbados debut because Frank King had been pulled out of the line of fire, I was called upon to make my Test debut against Hutton's England when Alf Valentine was taken ill, and again I took the late call. Now that was something very special for a boy who was still playing cricket in the streets with a tennis ball; I didn't stop until I was 19 or 20 and an established Test player. Sometimes we would play with a hard ball without pads. That made sure you used the bat! Even when I went away to play in England and on tours, I would come back and play beach cricket with a tennis ball.

Playing cricket with a tennis ball and knowing you can't get hurt encourages you to move in behind the ball so that when the hard ball replaces the tennis ball the move is automatic. When you have youngsters starting with a hard ball, they tend to shy away. I saw it in Australia and lots of other places when I was coaching. They back away and wait to see where the ball pitches. If it is outside the off stump, they try to hit it; if it is on the leg side, they run away and try to throw the bat at it. Sadly, some are put off the game forever.

Many years after that first Test in Jamaica, I told the Essex and England all-rounder Trevor Bailey, by that time a friend, that English children should be taught the rudiments of the game with a soft ball. They would learn how to get behind the short ball because it would come up. Trevor started a tennis-ball competition soon afterwards which, I believe, was very successful.

The day I discovered I had been picked to play at Sabina Park, I was playing road cricket with my brothers. Ben Hoyos, secretary of the Barbados Cricket Association, came to tell me. He had received a cable from the West Indies Board requesting that I join the team at the Fourth Test in Trinidad and be prepared to travel to Jamaica to play against England in the Fifth and final Test of the series.

It came out of the blue because I had not performed that well for Barbados against England. You can imagine how the boys reacted to the news that I was to join the West Indies; they were as pleased as if it had been them. My mother was delighted and all my friends came round to congratulate me and tell me what a wonderful opportunity it was. I was overjoyed; it felt like I was walking on air to think that I was going to be in the same dressing room as Weekes, Worrell and Walcott. I may have been small but I was a forthright young man, so I was not scared or in awe, but the feeling was so good I find it as difficult now as I did then to put it into words.

When I joined the team, everyone made me feel welcome. The experienced, established players sat and talked to me and practised with me in the nets. There I was, 17 years and 245 days old, in the thick of the heady atmosphere of Sabina Park, somewhere I had only ever read about, meeting George Headley, Allan Rae and Jeffrey Stollmeyer. In the dressing room I was as quiet as a mouse and they all wanted to know if I was nervous. Of course I was. It was not something I was accustomed to; I had only just started to play cricket as this level. But I wasn't going to tell them how I felt.

Our captain, Jeff Stollmeyer, won the toss and elected to bat. My first thought was what a wonderful opportunity this was going to be to watch the three Ws at first hand in a Test match – not listening on the radio or sitting in the public stand, but there with them in the same dressing room, sitting with them in the pavilion, part of the same team. But that didn't last long. On the first day, 30 March 1954, Trevor Bailey skittled us out for 139, taking 7 wickets for 34 runs, while Fiery Fred took 2 for 39.

I batted at number nine, before Frank King and Sonny Ramadhin, and when I went in it was 110 for 7. When I walked down the steps and through the gate, the Jamaican crowd erupted. I was in another world. I had been sitting there thinking I was settled for at least a day and a half and wondering how many runs we were going to score on this lovely Sabina Park wicket. Jamaican J.K. Holt and Jeff Stollmeyer had opened the batting but in no time at all they were both back in the pavilion to be followed by Weekes and Worrell with the score still on 13! I scored 14 not out in the first innings and 26 in the second innings, caught by Denis Compton off the bowling of Tony Lock and this time there was no reprieve from the umpire.

But, even though the programme described me as a 'useful batsman' with no mention of my bowling, I wasn't in the side as a batsman; I was in as a bowler. The England openers were Len Hutton and Trevor Bailey, who enjoyed the rare experience of opening the bowling and the batting for England on the same day! I watched from my place in the field as they put on 41 before the skipper gave me the ball. In my very first over I had Trevor out, caught behind by Clifford McWatt. I made one turn outside the off stump and Trevor played for the straight one. The crowd exploded again. I was so thrilled to break the partnership, for the team, not so much for me.

It was during that match that I had my first close-up look at Sir Len Hutton, or just plain Len as he was then. I had read about him, of course, and listened to his great performances on the radio. Now here he was playing in the same match and, what's more, I was bowling to him. He was magnificent to watch. He batted throughout the innings and scored 205. He had so much time to play. The Sabina wicket was quick but, in those days, West Indies did not have a battery of fast bowlers, only Frank King and Gerry Gomez, who opened the bowling. Hutton was a joy to watch as England went on to score 414, setting up a 9-wicket win which levelled the series at two-all.

I bowled 28 overs and five balls in my first-ever Test innings and followed up the wicket of Trevor Bailey with those of Johnny Wardle, Tony Lock and Jim Laker for a cost of 75 runs.

I wasn't wasting my time admiring the likes of Hutton, Peter May, Denis Compton and Tom Graveney; I studied them, as I had studied the Wanderers, their style, their technique and their approach to the game. I wanted to learn from them and also I thought that, if I were lucky enough to play against them again, I would be aware of their strengths and any odd weakness. I continued to learn by watching those who had so much more experience than I had at my tender years.

Without a father to turn to and with my older brothers away at sea for long periods, there were a lot of other people whom I admired and a number who helped me although there were no mentors in the true sense of the word; no one replaced my father. As a family, we were not particularly close-knit. We identified with each other but never ran to each other whenever anything went wrong. We were individual, independent people. When I started off, Briggs Grandison, Lionel Daniel, Garnett Ashby, Captain Farmer and, of course, Goalie Cumberbatch were always there to help and I appreciated what they did for me, but I tried to learn about life on my own. Later, when I went to play for Radcliffe in one of the Lancashire Leagues at the age of 21, I spent a lot of time with Frank Worrell and we became very close.

Everton Weekes was my cricketing idol. He and I talked a lot about the game and about people. He was very laid back. He would advise and suggest but in the end he would leave it to me to do what I thought was right. He believed that if you enjoyed doing something and could benefit from it, if it was worthwhile and didn't hurt other people, then it was okay to do — and I did what young boys do. We probably had more freedom than most and we had our girlfriends. There was plenty of rivalry for the girls and being a cricketer and something of a minor celebrity, I had a bit of an advantage. But girls were by the way; they didn't matter when placed next to cricket. If there was a choice between the two, the girl had to go on her way. They knew that. Girls were always going to be there to admire, but you had to get your priorities right. I cannot remember my first childhood sweetheart but I remember my first game of organised cricket.

30

As teenagers, we would sit around and talk, go to the midnight movies or Saturday morning movies, then play cricket and go to the midnight movies again. Maybe later we'd have some corned beef, biscuits and a few beers. I started smoking when I was around 16. I suppose I got through about 20 a day until I learned to control it. It was fashionable and part of growing up. It gave you some false feeling of maturity. There was no question of it being thought of as a health hazard in those days. If I was thinking about a lot of things and needed some comfort, I would smoke a cigarette. Often I would have one while I was waiting to go in to bat. But I am talking about proper tobacco, not the other stuff. We knew nothing about marijuana; it just wasn't around. I didn't know of anyone who used it on any of the islands.

I remember when West Indies were in Australia in 1950–51, I got plastered on Falernum, a kind of sugar-cane liqueur drink we had as a treat on Boxing Day as we listened to the cricket on the radio. Everyone was drinking and I found this sweet stuff went down easily, and I kept drinking it until I realised the room was spinning. That night the bed spun around and I couldn't find a comfortable place.

I never used to drink rum despite its cheapness and availability. I had my first taste of the local drink very late in life. When I started to drink at around 18, I preferred whisky although it was difficult to buy in Barbados because it was expensive. Most of it was brought in duty free by people returning from the UK. I learned a lot more about Scotch and how to drink it when I moved to England. I particularly liked Black Label and White Horse. It wasn't until I retired and returned home to Barbados that I discovered rum.

It's a funny thing in the Caribbean. If you drank four bottles of Black Label, that was all right, but if you drank four snaps of rum and failed in whatever you were doing, you were immediately known as a 'rum drinker', and that was meant as an insult. If you drank Scotch all night nobody would take any notice because it was an expensive and sophisticated drink. Get drunk on rum and people would say, 'What do you expect – he's a rum drinker.' That deterred me from drinking it.

I learned early in life to stay away from certain things; if you didn't, you were pigeon-holed and branded.

In 1955, a strong Australian side toured the West Indies and the great Australian all-rounder Keith Miller predicted that I was going to be a better batsman than bowler, even though I batted down the order.

I was not even selected for the First Test at Sabina Park. Collie Smith had scored 100 in both innings for Jamaica against the tourists and he was also a good off-spinner so it was quite understandable that he was picked in front of me. No one could argue with the decision because the local hero went on to score 44 in the first innings and a century in the second when he was moved up the order to first wicket down. Even so, we lost that match by 9 wickets. Our bowling let us down. Collie bowled just 11 overs despite an Aussie first innings total of over 500.

Collie and I were both selected for the Second Test in Port of Spain, Trinidad. The Australians were popular and had two of the greatest-ever fast bowlers in the side – Ray Lindwall and Keith Miller. What great characters they were! Collie and I were young, new and a little bit shy among these two boisterous teams. We were rooming together and the first night we slipped away early. We were talking in our room when, at around midnight, there was a thumping on our hotel door and an Australian voice barked that he knew we were in there and if we didn't let them in they would break down the door. Nervously we complied and there stood Miller and Lindwall drinks in hand – they had come to have a drink and a chat to make us feel part of what was going on around us. It was a tremendous gesture and typical of these two fine sportsmen.

Most evenings after that they would call in at around 10 o'clock, glasses in hand, and sit down for half an hour's chat. It was during one of these fascinating sessions that Keith said to Collie, 'You scored a hundred in each innings against us in the tour match against Jamaica and another hundred against us in the last Test and everyone loves you and thinks you are a hero in the Caribbean. You'll play in this Test match and you may get a pair and you'll see the change and the difference.'

The conversation must have taken place on the eve of the match for Collie bagged a pair, bowled for a duck by Richie Benaud in the first innings and caught by wicket-keeper Gill Langley off Ron Archer in the second. Was it a clever piece of psychology or just some fatherly advice that happened to come true? Who knows, but the Aussies were clever. I have known them to play opposition players into the Test team by letting them score runs. They knew these players' weaknesses and when they played in Tests the Aussies would search out that vulnerability and have them out cheaply. I don't think that applied to Collie but the conversation must have played on his mind, particularly after his duck in the first innings.

We held on for a draw in a high-scoring match; Clyde Walcott made 100 in each innings while Everton Weekes made 139 and 87 not out. I just failed to reach my 50 in the first innings, caught behind off Lindwall, and was not out for 8 in the second. Like Collie in the First Test, I was hardly used, bowling three overs for 10 runs in a total of 600 while Ramadhin and Valentine bowled 81 between them taking two wickets apiece. Collie bowled 15 overs without success.

I kept my place for the next Test at Bourda in Georgetown, British Guiana, and while I made little impact with the bat – snapped up by Ian Johnson in both innings – I had some reward with the ball. In the Aussies' first innings I took the wickets of Miller, Archer and, ironically, Johnson for just 20 runs off 16 overs. Collie, after his two ducks, was left out but, after another 8-wicket defeat, he was brought back for the Fourth Test at Bridgetown.

Skipper and opener Jeff Stollmeyer had trodden on the ball and twisted his ankle and so was out of the side, triggering a huge debate about who should open. Of the main contenders, J.K. Holt, an established member of the team, was suffering a lack of confidence after being barracked by the crowds for dropping catches; and Clairmonte Depeiza, the wicket-keeper, had failed against the Australians playing for Barbados. No one was quite sure who would be asked to stand up to Miller and Lindwall. Such was the controversy that Jamaican fast bowler Leslie Hylton, in prison waiting to be hanged for murdering his wife, was touted as a possible – when we arrived at the Oval there were banners demanding 'Save Hylton, Hang Holt'. Talk about gallows humour!

As it happened, the problem was put on hold because Australia batted first and piled up another huge total, 668, with Miller and Lindwall both scoring 100s. I had a suspicion that captain Dennis Atkinson was going to ask me and, sure enough, when we came off at the end of the Australian innings, Stollmeyer came up to me and said, 'Son, you're opening the batting with J.K. Holt.' I had reasoned it out. I couldn't see them sending in anyone else – I was a bowler with a little ability as a batsman and they wanted someone to help see off the shine and protect the three Ws. They weren't going to send in Collie because his pair was still in his mind, and they didn't want one of the three Ws risking their wicket in a new-ball attack from Miller and Lindwall. Depeiza was out of the equation because he had had too much work with his wicket-keeping in such a long, demanding innings.

While I was putting on my pads, I went through the situation, as I usually did, telling myself I was not an opening batsman, I was a sacrifice, but this was a team game and I had to go out and do my best for the West Indies. I decided that the worst thing I could do was try to play like an opening batsman. I went out determined to be aggressive and to attack, despite the Aussies having probably the best opening attack in the world at that time. I was interested to see which of the two fields the Australians would use – the Caramody, with all the fielders behind the wicket except for one man in the covers, or the umbrella, with everyone behind the wicket! J.K. Holt took strike from Ray Lindwall and played out a maiden, leaving me to face the fast, dynamic and more unpredictable Keith Miller. I was still determined to go for my shots and take the attack to the Aussies.

The first ball from Miller was outside the leg stump and rather than leave it I thought I had better have a dip at it. Bump! It flew to the fine-leg boundary like a rocket. The second one was short and outside the off stump, and this time I thumped it through the covers. Here was a number nine batsman hitting the famous Keith Miller for two fours off his first two balls – I knew the next one would be short and this time I hit him past point for a third boundary. I took 12 off his first over. My home crowd were whistling and shrieking with delight.

I had won the first round and in the next over Miller pulled out one of his catchers from behind the bat to put one in the covers. It didn't matter. I had the bit between my teeth and I hit him past the cover fielder for three more fours in his second over. Holt had played Lindwall's first two overs for maidens and as the Australian fast bowler walked past me he tapped me on the shoulder and said, 'Sonny, you're doing all right – I should stay down this end!'

I went on to score 43 out of a first-wicket partnership of 52 with 10 fours. Ian Johnson came on to replace the chastened Miller and he brought Jack Hill round to backward square. He flighted one on my pads, I went for the sweep, caught a top edge and put it right down Hill's throat. Afterwards Ian, who went on to become secretary of the Melbourne Cricket Club, would always introduce me as his rabbit, adding that I had kept him in cricket longer than he should have stayed thanks to taking my wicket.

It was a short but sweet innings and there are those on Barbados who still reckon it is the best one they have seen me play! Had I gone out and continually played forward I would have eventually snicked one. As it was, I did my job. I took the shine off the ball and although the three Ws could muster just 75 between them and Collie 2, our captain Dennis Atkinson and Depeiza put on over 300 for the seventh wicket with Dennis scoring a double century before taking five wickets in Australia's second innings.

Depeiza, known as the 'Leaning Tower of Depeiza' because of the way he leant into his forward defensive stroke, was outstanding. He came in at 147 for 6 and was hit all over his body by the Aussie fast bowlers. During the break for tea, John Goddard senior, father of the West Indies Test captain, gave him a piece of foam rubber to strap around his battered chest, probably the first known chest guard in cricket. He was so brave that while skipper Atkinson scored 219, Depeiza was the recipient of the spontaneous collection among the spectators.

We came out of that difficult situation with a draw, which put the Australians somewhat on the back foot, but it made little difference. We were hammered again in the Fifth and final Test back in Kingston, for which the selectors decided to drop Ramadhin and Valentine. I scored 35 not out and 64 while Clyde Walcott scored a century in each innings, but this was not nearly enough. Neil Harvey scored a double hundred and Colin McDonald, Keith Miller, Ron Archer and Richie Benaud all scored centuries in a huge total of 758 for 8. Atkinson bowled 55 overs, Smith 52, Worrell 45 and I bowled 38 with just five wickets to show for it between the four of us. The difference between the two sides lay in the bowling, especially in the quickie department. Frank King was still our only bowler of any pace and he was overworked and rarely supported from the other end.

Despite our heavy series loss, it was a great learning experience for me both on and off the field. At the end of the tour Keith Miller gave me his bat, a 'White Toe', resplendent with a white strip across the bottom. It was a typical gesture from a generous and warm-hearted man. He spent a great deal of time talking to me, telling me of the good things that cricket could offer at this top level and warning of the pitfalls that were strewn along the way to test every player, no matter how good he thought he was. I was to remember his prophetic words around seven months later when I went off to New Zealand on my first overseas tour. Boy was that an eye-opener!

In the build-up to the tour, I was introduced to the interminable inter-island politics that have always blighted West Indian cricket. There were controversies about all sorts of things from the selection of the 19 players to who should be captain. It was always going to be Jeff Stollmeyer and when it became official, Roy Marshall left for England, saying, 'My days with the West Indies are finished.' He just didn't get on with Jeff. Ironically, Stollmeyer was injured during the tour and Dennis Atkinson shouldered the captaincy for all four Tests. Dennis, of course, was a Barbadian and Roy would undoubtedly have stayed and played for him.

There was also a campaign developing to have Frank Worrell

appointed captain. It started in Jamaica and spread to other islands.

I couldn't understand it all and thought what a good thing it was that I would never be captain and have to suffer all that turmoil. I should have listened to Keith Miller because it was heading in my direction.

CHAPTER THREE

Forever England

England played an important part in my development as a cricketer. I made my international debut against Len Hutton's team, lived there for much of my professional cricket life and, fittingly, played my final Test against England at Port of Spain in Trinidad.

As a boy growing up in Barbados, I used to tune in regularly to the BBC World Service to listen to the cricket from England. I loved to hear commentators Rex Alston, Jim Swanton, Peter West and John Arlott painting vivid pictures, not only of the game but also of the wickets, the ground and the atmosphere. I would sit there and visualise the green tops, the ball moving around in the air and off the seam, and wonder just how emerald green the outfields really were. I can still remember Arlott's words, and mimic that distinctive Hampshire burr – 'And here comes the tireless Alec Bedser, shirt tails flapping in the wind; runs in and bowls to the short, stocky Everton Weekes and Weekes is back, playing the ball off the middle of the bat to Peter May at mid-on.' He painted a picture like no other commentator and I would daydream about seeing it for myself.

I really wanted to play in England where the game began and where it all seemed so different. I loved to hear about the ball seaming and cutting and swinging and I wanted to find out about it for myself. Even in those formative years, I thought that England would be a nice place to learn my cricket because it seemed you had to play every ball on its merit and look at it a little bit longer than you did on the glassy wickets of the Caribbean. I felt that if I could play there, I could play anywhere because the ball would do so much and nothing could be taken for granted. All those dreams – then one morning I woke up and found I was in England!

Following the miserable tour to New Zealand in 1955–56, I was depressed and didn't think I had a chance of being selected for the subsequent tour of England. In New Zealand I had made no runs to speak of and taken virtually no wickets. This was the first time I had played outside the West Indies and I couldn't believe the wickets. There were tufts of grass here and tufts of grass there. Our brown, flat, shiny wickets had no grass at all. I took one look and asked myself how I could possibly bat on that? How could I make runs? I was out before I even walked to the crease.

In the meantime, Jim Swanton had brought a tour to the West Indies with the likes of Frank Tyson in the team. They wanted four of the squad to come home from New Zealand to play in an unofficial Test match. Dennis Atkinson, Collie Smith, Everton Weekes and Sonny Ramadhin were asked; I was understandably overlooked. But Dennis was captaining the West Indies in New Zealand and felt he couldn't leave so he told me to go instead.

I was thrilled until I heard just how quick this man Tyson was and how he had twice clean-bowled Clyde Walcott for a duck on his own wicket in Barbados, before the great man had even lifted his bat. I began to wonder whether this was a good idea; maybe those tufty wickets in New Zealand weren't so bad after all!

When I first faced Tyson I was batting high in the order with the reassuring figure of Everton Weekes at the other end. Having come from slow wickets in New Zealand where I hadn't done well, I was wondering how I was going to cope with the pace of this man, pawing the ground in the far distance, starting his run up somewhere by the pavilion steps.

For the first ball I faced, I tried to get forward on the front foot and found that the ball had already gone past when I finally got there. I said to myself, 'What is this?' Everton saw what had happened with my high back lift and quickly came down the wicket to tell me, 'No back lift at all today.' I listened to what he said and the next ball there was no Sobers back lift and the ball thudded into the middle of the bat. Two balls later Tyson bowled me a bouncer, I went to hook but by the time I had the bat in position, Colin Ingleby-Mackenzie had already collected the ball behind the stumps. The next over I watched Everton do the same thing, he got the bat up there all right but the ball had gone and I thought to myself that if Everton couldn't cope, how the hell was I going to! I parried and parried and parried and eventually reached 60 or 70 and felt good.

I had stood up to the pace, acquitted myself well and I even began thinking that I might have a chance to go to England after all, something I doubt would have happened had I stayed on in New Zealand. The trials to pick the squad were held in Trinidad and I scored 100 in the first one. Now I was in with a real chance.

Trials for the West Indies were very much like our trials for the Barbados team; there were players you wanted on the team and players you wanted to knock off. Wes Hall and Frank Mason were competing for one of the places for a fast bowler. At the time Frank was a better bowler than the young, up-and-coming Wes but Everton Weekes and I decided that we would take on Mason and knock him out of the firing line to try to get our fellow Bajan Wes in the team. Poor Frank could not believe what was happening to him as the ball flew to all corners of the boundary. Good balls were hit for four and bad balls for six. By contrast we played a straight bat to everything Wes bowled, saying 'good ball' as we played a half-volley back down the wicket. I was only a youngster, not yet 21, but Everton wanted our fellow islander in the team and coached me in the politics. I was sorry for Frank because he was a darned good bowler but it was Wes who was picked.

We set off for England on a banana boat that I think was called *Golfito*. The bananas used to go on board first and the players afterwards – that's how important we were. Bananas helped support the Caribbean economy, cricket did not.

It took about 10 days to steam to England and for the first couple of days the boys were out on deck but after that you never saw a soul. They were all below being seasick. That's when I discovered that port and brandy is a good drink to settle the stomach. I had a bottle of each and I would make the happy mix first thing every morning. Then I would go for a healthy breakfast of raw eggs in milk while the others turned green at the thought of it. I didn't let them in on the secret.

It wasn't until we went to Australia some years later that I told anyone about it. Seymour Nurse, who was sharing a cabin with me, said one morning, 'Sobey, how come you always fine on the boats and everyone else is sick?'

'Nursery boy,' I said, 'come and see this.'

I showed him the bottles and mixed him a large one. He immediately realised why I was surviving so well.

When we arrived in England, I was one of the first up on deck. The others followed slowly, dragging themselves up for their first taste of fresh air in days. At last I was in England and what's more it was a beautiful day but when I arrived on deck I couldn't believe it – the sun was shining but it was so cold.

It reminded me of what King Dayl had said. He was a West Indian cricket supporter from Barbados, famous for all the wonderful bright suits he wore to the tourists' games at the Kensington Oval. He always used to shout for the opposition, particularly England, when they came to Barbados and as a consequence he was invited by Peter May to Old Trafford for a Test match. When he came back to the West Indies he was interviewed and asked what had struck him most about his first visit to England. He thought for a moment and replied, 'It is the first time in my life I have experienced cold sun!' He had sat in the sun at

Old Trafford and shivered with the cold.

We were met by officials from the MCC and travelled to Lord's, the home of cricket, for a reception. We saw the famed Long Room and the white wicket gate that the players walked through on their way to the wicket, just as so beautifully described by Arlott.

I had never seen such a big dressing room with showers, tubs and a balcony overlooking the ground. We were all excited and watched intently as the ground was being prepared for a game. I stood looking and looking until Everton Weekes came up and asked me what was the matter, what was I looking for. I answered, 'The wicket.' He laughed and told me that I would know where the wicket was when they put the stumps up! I couldn't see the difference between the outfield and the wicket because it was all so green and different from our brown, rolled strips, and from New Zealand's grassy tufts. Again, I couldn't believe we were expected to bat on such a wicket and I was none too happy.

The first game we played was at Eastbourne against a Jim Swanton XI and, to my surprise and delight, the wicket there was brown – but there the similarity ended. This was April in England and Wes Hall was so cold that when he ran up to bowl to Tom Graveney he was still stiff and Tom played him to the boundary twice in the first over. Wes was furious and he started to bowl really quick ones, both to get warm and to gain revenge. Tom was startled by this raw pace so early in the season and didn't want to be hit, so he started backing away. Colin Cowdrey, who was batting with him, also found the pace a bit fierce and snicked one through the slips. I stupidly got my hands to it and boy did it sting in that cold. Wes stalked down the wicket towards me.

'Why didn't you catch it?' he demanded.

'Not with these fingers,' I said, shaking my hands as the ball came back from the boundary. 'Not yet, anyway.'

My fingers were numb and I couldn't feel a thing. He wanted me to catch the ball? He was making a joke!

That was my first impression of England – just how cold it was, even wearing two or three jumpers. The only place for the hands was in the pockets and too bad if you couldn't get them out in time when the ball came your way.

Then we went to Arundel and that was cold, too, with the wicket a little bit greener. This was supposed to be spring and the cricket season but it did not improve. From there we went to Middlesbrough where we were beaten, and beaten badly, by Yorkshire. Freddie Trueman and the boys bowled us out twice and beat us in a day and a half. Freddie and his mates were raving, saying how this West Indies team was not good enough and how England were going to turn us over. Not good enough? This was still April and we were deep in the north in Middlesbrough. They had to be joking.

Gradually the weather warmed up; either that or we became acclimatised. Later in the year we went back to Yorkshire and played in Sheffield, beating them comprehensively. Freddie tells the story:

We had beaten the West Indies in Middlesbrough and beaten them so badly that we knew what was going to happen the next time we met them. The second game was played at Bramall Lane and they batted first and made more than 400 for 6 declared. Then they bowled us out for well under 200 and refused to enforce the follow-on, wanting to rub it in. They batted again and left us around 500 to win. We were 160 for 8 when I went in to bat. I was at the non-striker's end and even I was nervous as Mel Ryan took guard. He couldn't see Wes Hall, he was so far away.

Then suddenly there he was, coming past a pedestrian crossing, into the arena, shirt tail flapping, and the West Indians in the crowd were chanting that they wanted blood. He flashed past me, let go of the first ball and it was with the 'keeper Alexander before Mel had lifted his bat. I thought to myself that they were really out for the kill.

Next ball, Mel actually managed to put bat to ball and shouted, 'Come one.'

'Who? Me?' I answered. 'Wait there.'

When I eventually faced Wes Hall, he came running in and

Mel stopped him just as he was approaching his delivery stride. Turning to the umpire, Mel said to him, 'If all those West Indians behind the wicket don't sit down I am going to appeal against the light.'

England was everything I expected, as was the cricket, although we didn't win a Test. I had a pretty good tour with over 1,000 runs, a few 100s and a few wickets. But while I made my mark individually, and was offered a league job, the team did not perform too well. There was a lot of insularity within the West Indies in those days; politics and inter-island squabbles had played their part within the camp for many years and we had a bit of riffle within the squad.

Things weren't working out too right with the three Ws although Everton Weekes played quite well, despite being troubled with sinusitis. Clyde Walcott was a selector but Frank Worrell wasn't. John Goddard was captain again, making a comeback after being manager in New Zealand having retired from the game. Frank was asked to 'observe'. He told me that he used to observe, they would pick the team and then talk to Frank, with Clyde reminding him that he was not to pick the team, only to offer advice.

Frank was very resentful about this and it showed when they asked Andy Ganteaume, a Trinidadian who played in one Test, scored 112 and never played again, to come out of retirement for the 1957 tour. When Frank was asked whom he would pick between Andy and his fellow Trinidadian Nyron Asgarali, Frank went for Asgarali, citing his league experience in England, but he knew damn well he was wrong and did it deliberately. He did it because Asgarali was a professional and Andy an amateur. His justification was that he was not supposed to tell them whom to select, only to advise.

I gained a lot of experience, playing in all the Tests and 36 out of the 37 tour games, and revelled in playing on English wickets and English grounds, especially when the sun eventually came out. There were, however, some hard lessons to learn. Playing against Somerset, I faced a right-arm over-the-wicket bowler named Bob Lobb who bowled me an inswinger, which I followed down to leg. The next thing I knew my off stump had gone. I had never seen anything like it before in my life. It was totally foreign to me. I realised then that it was going to be a difficult baptism, especially in a team lacking in spirit and losing too often.

It had all looked so easy in that First Test at Edgbaston when I was not even needed to bowl as Sonny Ramadhin spun England out for 186. We totalled 474 with Collie Smith scoring 161, Clyde Walcott 90 and Frank Worrell 81. I made 53. We were quickly brought back to earth as Peter May (285 not out) and Colin Cowdrey (154) put on a record 411, batting for over eight hours. England eventually declared at 583 for 4 before having us on the ropes at 72 for 7 at the close with only Everton Weekes and me into double figures against Fred Trueman, Jim Laker and Tony Lock. Ram bowled 98 overs unchanged and for much of the time watched in frustration as May and Cowdrey stuck their pads down the wicket at him. It was a depressing sight, not that the Birmingham crowd seemed to mind.

Ram was not the same bowler after that session. Skipper John Goddard had kept him on because of injuries to Roy Gilchrist and our emergency opening bowler Frank Worrell. Someone suggested to Goddard that I should take the new ball when it became due but he rejected it and used the old ball for a ridiculous 162 overs.

That game set the trend and we were beaten by an innings in the Second Test at Lord's, Trevor Bailey helping himself to 11 wickets and Colin Cowdrey scoring 152 runs. Again only Everton and I made runs in the second innings. We dropped 12 catches in England's total of 424 – most of them it seemed off wicket-keeper/batsman Godfrey Evans!

Trent Bridge, as I was to discover later, was always a good wicket, more like ours back home. I scored 219 in the county game and probably because of that I opened in the Third Test match with Frank. We put on 80 odd before I was out just short of my half century while Frank batted all through the innings for 191, this despite fielding while England scored over 600. He went straight into the field again and then straight into bat for a second time. No wonder he made just 16 before being bowled by Brian Statham!

We drew the Nottingham Test, although always second best, and were routed by an innings and 5 runs at Headingley and, worse, an innings and 237 runs at The Oval on a pitch described by Everton Weekes as a 'beach'. We were bowled out for 89 and 86. With our backs to the wall I relished the challenge and top scored with 39 and 42 while Asgarali scored a creditable 29 in the first innings but only 7 in the second.

So I had played a series in England as I had always wanted, and enjoyed it a lot, despite the Test results. Now I was looking forward to the less strenuous demands of playing for Radcliffe in the Central Lancashire League. There is no doubt that playing in the League furthered my cricket education. Obviously the players were not as good as at county and Test level but the standard of the wickets brought up the quality of the batting. The wickets were not good and an average bowler could run up, put the ball on the spot and more often than not something would happen. My cricket started to improve, especially my batting as I learned to play each ball on its merit. I would watch bowlers and see what they were doing with the ball. I would watch batsmen's and bowlers' body actions. Playing cricket in England affected my way of thinking. I also learned how to deal with people.

It was made very easy for me because everyone was so friendly. I still believe that you cannot find friendlier people than the Lancastrians. Wherever I went they would pat me on the back, ask me how was I settling in and how was I coping with the weather. I could walk into a pub by myself and instantly find someone to talk to. That is what struck me about the north of England. In London you can stand at the bar all day and there is no one to say hello. In contrast, people in the north open their doors to you and that is why from 1957 up to when I finished in 1975 I played every year in England. I enjoyed every minute playing on English wickets and against English teams.

I remember the warnings I had when I first went to live in England. It was the time of the teddy boys and I was told that their chosen weapon was a razor-sharp flick-knife. I was lodging at the Boar's Head, near to Radcliffe's ground, and when I walked home at night from the bar in our pavilion, the teddy boys in their drainpipe trousers, thick-soled shoes, bright shirts and string ties, with their greased hair, would wave at me and shout hello. I often stopped to ask them what they were doing on the street at 11 o'clock and invite them to come back and have a drink at the pub. We would have a few and then I would go off to bed and they would go home without the slightest hint of trouble.

I became good mates with everyone around the village and I never saw any difference in people's attitudes because of the colour of anyone's skin whether they were white, black or pink. Maybe that was me, but I never had any real racist problems throughout my career. I had a simple philosophy – if you weren't wanted somewhere, you didn't go; if you were wanted, you did. Why go somewhere to create a problem?

Obviously, if you had a name and were a public figure, as I was then, it seemed to help. I always felt that it was up to me to show the people what sort of person I was and then I found that people were generally quite willing to accept me. Word of mouth helps and that is how it worked for me. In England, I was rarely refused entry anywhere, just the odd dancing club.

I had a few friends with whom I liked to socialise or, if I was away from home, there were always West Indian people who would invite me to their homes for some good Caribbean food and hospitality. I enjoyed the social scene of the pubs and clubs in England even though they often wanted to know what a professional sportsman was doing out so late. I also liked to go dancing and to be with my friends to share their experiences.

My first impression of the League was that it was no different from any other cricket. I treated all games the same in those days, as though they were top-class; if I had not done so, I would not have developed the way I did. There were always five or six good players in every league team with four good batsmen and two or three good bowlers along with the professional. Oh yes, there was also always someone who could throw the bat at the ball for quick runs.

The collections around the crowd for a 50 or five wickets also appealed to me, not only to supplement my £500 a season wages but also to help my game. That £500 had to pay for accommodation, digs, clothes and, of course, tax. Playing for the West Indies in 1957 we earned £5 a week, one of those big white £5 notes. There was never much money even in the latter days when they paid you according to how many Test matches you played. I couldn't have survived without the collections, and the extra games as a professional for other sides in different leagues. I would often act as substitute professional in the Lancashire, Bolton or Farmworth Leagues. On Thursday, which was usually a free day, I could always go and guest for someone. That is one reason why I never played in the Lancashire League. Although it paid a lot better, it had too many restrictions with only five or six games allowed for other teams per season. At Radcliffe in the Central Lancashire League, I could play as much as I wanted.

I would even cross the border into Yorkshire to play in their leagues where I would get £25 just for playing in one game, and if I were lucky I would win a collection. They were always substantial for an outsider as the crowd showed their appreciation. Sometimes the collection was as much as £50 and that represented a massive bonus.

Produce an all-round performance and it could provide a lot of money, especially if the team looked as though they were going to win the match because of it. Cricket in the leagues was very, very competitive with local honour at stake.

Frank was shrewd. He used to tell me when I reached 50 not to give away my wicket until I heard that last penny drop in the box. He told me that he used to look around the boundary and he knew where the fellows were with the £5 or £10 donations and he would make sure that the box passed by them first before he lost his wicket. Frank used to work out all these things. He had noticed that when a player was out, the collection would stop.

Another peculiarity of league cricket that Frank pointed out was that when you hit an amateur on the pads right in front, not to bother appealing because it would be not out; but when you hit the professional on the pads, everyone went up and if it was up to your umpire, he would be on his way.

We played and had a bit of fun. We always had a few beers after a game when we would swap stories about the wild Australian Cec Pepper and Clairmonte Depeiza, a fellow Barbadian, two of the great characters gracing the league scene then. Whenever I played against Depeiza I sensed the great rivalry. But that was true throughout the League with, among others, Cec at Oldham, Depeiza at Crompton and Reg Scarlett at Ashington. Roy Gilchrist was at Middleton prior to Basil d'Oliveira and Ray Hogan followed Cec at Oldham.

We used to get together as a group quite often, and the Australians and West Indians would regularly play games on Sundays at places such as Colwyn Bay in Wales. Instead of playing for a fee, we would often ask for a percentage of the gates and sometimes we walked away with £40 or £50 each. This was a good way of subsidising our wages.

I remember once organising two West Indian teams to play at Colwyn Bay and we charged the club £50 per player, to which they were only too happy to agree. When we arrived there was such a huge turnout – six or seven thousand fans turned up – that they rewarded us with £105 each. It was very generous of them. We had agreed to a flat fee and they were not obliged to give us any more. We gave good value; the two teams included Wes Hall, Charlie Griffith, Roy Gilchrist, Rohan Kanhai, Cammie Smith, Lance Gibbs, Seymour Nurse, Basil Butcher and Conrad Hunte. Frank Worrell often used to turn out in those Sunday games, too.

Wherever we went, the league players would have a Cec Pepper story. Unfortunately, not many of them were very clean. On one occasion when he played against us at Radcliffe, there was a tight finish. We needed four to win and Cec pushed one of the youngsters right back on to the boundary. Cec bowled and our batsman had a big sweep at the ball. It went straight towards the youngster who let it go through his hands and his legs and over the boundary for the four we needed. Cec was walking off and going up the steps when some punter said to him, 'Bad luck Mr Pepper. If only he had closed his legs you would have won the match.' To which Cec responded, 'If only his mother had kept her legs closed he wouldn't have been here at all.'

Cec and my great friend Trevor Bailey could never get on, they were on a different planet and the reason why he never played county cricket was probably because of his overripe language. He was certainly good enough as a cricketer but no one wanted to take the chance.

Cec played for the League against the Counties and bowled a succession of balls at Trevor only for the Essex and England man to edge almost every one of them through or to the slips without any going to hand. The frustrated Australian walked down the pitch at the end of the over and spat out, 'You've got more f*****g edges on your bat than a threepenny bit!'

On another occasion, Cec beat the bat several times in a row and he went and told Trevor, 'If I bowled you my nose you still couldn't pick it.'

Cec reckoned that another of the pros, Lou Laza, was afflicted with short arms and long pockets when it came to buying a round of drinks and the two were always having a go at each other. One day I sat down with Lou and a few friends and put a microphone and tape recorder in a bag under the table. As soon as Cec came in we started him off, asking if Lou had bought him a drink. He scowled and said words to the effect that Lou wouldn't buy his own mother a drink, interspersed with the usual expletives. On and on he went but, later, when we told him how foul his language had been, he wouldn't believe it – not even when we played the tape back to him. He swore that it wasn't him. His swearing came naturally, every other word, and sometimes without the other words! But he was a lot of fun.

There are 10,000 more stories like these about Cec still floating around in Lancashire. It has been said that Sir Don Bradman once remarked that had Cec's mouth and his attitude been different, he would have been one of the greatest all-rounders the world has ever seen.

I played for Radcliffe for five years from 1958 to 1962. In 1963 I was in England with the West Indies and in 1964 I joined Norton in the Staffordshire League. I played there in 1965 and 1966 before touring England with the West Indies, and 1967, the third full year of a five-year contract. In 1968, instead of playing a fourth year, Tommy Talbot, President of Norton Cricket Club, sold me to Notts. I was probably the first transferred cricketer. I have no idea what sort of money was paid, but knowing Mr Talbot, I'm sure it was to his benefit!

I also played for Littleborough in the League just before I retired. I had wanted to go back to the Central Lancashire League with my old club, but Radcliffe already had a professional and it was Littleborough who offered me a contract. That was another nice place in a beautiful setting. It was a lovely club and I had a very good friend there, Duncan Carter, who is now a minister in the government in Barbados. He was the professional at Littleborough for many years and stayed on as an amateur to play with me but still doing the bulk of the work.

I have a lot of very fond memories of my time playing in the Leagues. I made many, many friends.

CHAPTER FOUR

To England
with Worrell

The first time I played a series in England was an education on those wickets. As a team, we didn't play to our highest standards because of the dissension in the party due mainly to the usual insularity of those days, just as in 1950. When I listened to reports on the radio, we were always being described as calypso cricketers because of our cavalier style. Our cricket did not really begin to develop until that 1957 tour and, despite the problems, it was a defining point.

When we returned in 1963, Frank Worrell had taken over the team and become the first black man to captain the West Indies, apart from George Headley who had been a stand-in captain during the 1947–48 tour. It was a long time between tours to England, six years in this case, as against every three or four years as it is now.

At one stage, it did not look as though I would be selected. The invitation arrived while I was in Australia, playing in Melbourne for South Australia.

The pay I was offered as a professional cricketer to go on the tour and play almost every day was somewhere around £800, less than I could make playing league cricket once a week. Although we were also given a small daily allowance and our expenses, there were no man-of-the-match awards as there are now and no other perks to bolster the money. I sought advice from Sir Donald Bradman and Richie Benaud who both told me to accept, as did Frank Worrell who wrote to me expressing very strongly the reasons why I should go. He talked about representing my country. Of course he was right and I cabled my acceptance. They certainly had their money's worth out of me on that trip as I played in more matches than anyone else in the 18-strong touring party.

It was a very good tour, spoiled by a controversy over our fast bowler Charlie Griffith that bubbled and boiled from the time we arrived until the time we left. The newspapers, radio, television and even some players reported that Charlie was a chucker and that cast a shadow over the squad. Ironically, the whole controversy had started back home in the Caribbean when one of our own umpires, Cortez Jordan, called him against England. That's why the critics were lying in wait for him when he came on the 1963 tour. It was not to be the last time that this allegation was made against Charlie in his career.

Charlie was a quiet, shy young lad of 24 and he was seriously affected by the strength of the criticism and withdrew even further into his shell. He kept himself to himself and shut himself away in the hotel room he shared with his talkative and outspoken opening bowling partner Wes Hall. But he didn't let it affect his bowling; if anything, it fired him up to even greater efforts. He finished that tour with over 100 wickets at little more than a dozen runs apiece, and he wasn't no-balled by the umpires.

That apart, the 1963 series was good for us. We had some good young players on the trip and some experienced ones from the 1957 tour. There was Rohan Kanhai and me from 1957. Rohan acted as second wicket-keeper. We both had plenty of experience of the conditions after playing in the Leagues, and against the MCC, as had Conrad Hunte who had also been playing in a league set-up at Enfield.

He was one who had failed to make the tour in 1957.

Frank brought the team together and began to mould it into a formidable squad that could account for itself. We won that series 3–1 and it was the first time since 1950 that we had beaten England in a series on their home soil. It was all the more satisfying as England had a very good team, although a few of them were getting on. Both Freddie Trueman and Brian Statham played, long acknowledged as an outstanding opening bowling partnership. There were also a couple of good youngsters who had figured in the minor counties. One was a young opening batsman called Geoffrey Boycott, who could dig in; another was the big hard-hitter Colin Milburn.

Frank was very clever when asked for his impression of Milburn, saying that he thought he was a fairly good, up-and-coming player and one for the future when, in reality, he knew very well that Colin was ready right then. He knew that if Colin played against us, it might have been a very different story. He was not only a very good batsman but scored his runs quickly and could take a match away from you in no time at all. We were very impressed with him and were delighted when he was left out. Not many of the players selected were coping very well with Wes Hall and Charlie Griffith. Colin would have taken them both on and we wanted to keep him as far away from us as we could. We would much rather they brought in Geoffrey if they were going to bring in anyone but as it was they used Micky Stewart, John Edrich, Peter Richardson and Brian Bolus as they rotated their opening bats.

England did not seem to want to play aggressive cricketers in that series but rather preferred to occupy the crease. That negative attitude seemed to permeate the entire squad. Kenny Barrington was an attractive player with all the shots in the world but he was always in and out of the England team. I remember people saying what a good shot maker he was, yet he could never keep his place. He told me how important it was for him to play for England, he was desperate to play for his country and he accepted that he had to change his style. When he did that and scored 20 or 30 in a couple of hours, he kept his place.

So he realised how they wanted him to play and he took the aggression away. He remained a good player, not as beautiful as some, but he always scored runs and he was a delightful person into the bargain. I played a bit of golf with him later on and we always got on very well.

One thing is for sure – he didn't like facing Charlie Griffith. He was a bit hung up on it and it affected him. He wasn't comfortable facing Charlie because he believed he was a chucker and dangerous. He played in a double-wicket competition in Australia and wasn't too happy. He took ill during the competition and didn't play in all the games, including one against Charlie. It transpired later that the chest pains he felt were, in fact, a mild heart attack.

But Ken stood up to Charlie in the '63 series. He made two scores of 50 or more, both in the same match at Lord's when he went on to reach 80 and 60. Charlie took his wicket twice; I took his wicket twice at Edgbaston and three times altogether, as did Lance Gibbs.

Ken loved England and it was symbolic that he should die while on duty with the team he loved. He was assistant manager on the 1981 tour of the West Indies when he suffered a heart attack in the Holiday Inn in Barbados on 14 March, the Saturday night of the Oval Test match.

I did not subscribe to the theory that Charlie Griffith threw because in England they never said anything about his arm but always went on about his foot and his body position. The rules say that for it to be a throw, the arm must straighten at the time of delivery; there is nothing about the foot or the body movement. There is always the freak bowling action that stands apart from others, but that doesn't mean that these bowlers are contravening the laws of the game. It was claimed that when they put the cameras on him he bowled with a straight arm, but this was nonsense to me. How could a man in the field all day know when the cameras were going to be on him and when not? They never really clarified that as far as I was concerned.

Some people in the game seemed to take it personally and that kept the argument raging. There was a game I sat out in Manchester against Lancashire in the '66 series and one of the umpires, Arthur Fagg, called

Charlie for throwing. He had no-balled him nine times, eight for overstepping but the ninth was for throwing. When Fagg was driving home from the game that evening, he heard nothing about it in the cricket reports on the radio. It seemed he expected notoriety and even went so far as to call the radio station to tell them he had no-balled Charlie Griffith for throwing and asked them why it was not reported.

Naturally, Charlie wasn't very happy at the cloud hanging over him but he did his job then and he did it well.

To my mind, we were always favourites to win the '63 series because of the attack we had with Charlie, Wes Hall, Lance Gibbs, me bowling all sorts, and a bit of Frank Worrell thrown in for good measure. The weather was good that summer and we did well, winning at Old Trafford by 10 wickets and drawing at Lord's in an incredibly tight game. England needed 6 to win with the last pair at the wicket and Colin Cowdrey at the non-strike end with a broken arm. Freddie Trueman led England to victory in Birmingham with 12 wickets, before we clinched the series with big wins in Leeds and at The Oval.

Our heroes at Old Trafford were Lance Gibbs with the ball, taking 11 for 157, and Conrad Hunte with an eight-hour 182. Our first innings stood at 501 for 6. I scored 64 and took a couple of wickets in each of England's innings.

The fact that the Second Test at Lord's was drawn doesn't tell half of the story. It was one of the most exciting matches ever played between the two countries. Trueman bowled brilliantly to take 11 wickets while Basil Butcher's second innings 133 gave us something to bowl at. Charlie Griffith took five in England's first innings and three in the second, but star man for the West Indies was Wes Hall who bowled unchanged for almost three and a half hours. In the end, it all came down to a single over, to be bowled by Wes just as it was in the tied Test with Australia in Brisbane. With those six balls to go, there were four results possible – a win either way, a tie or a draw.

England required just 8 runs and there were a couple of singles off the first three balls before Derek Shackleton was run out in a race for the wicket with Frank Worrell. It was a fair race as both of them were born in the same month of the same year, August 1924!

No one knew whether it was all over because the last man due in was Colin Cowdrey who had broken his left wrist earlier in the game. The entire ground broke into tumultuous applause when Cowdrey appeared with his left arm in a sling. Wes couldn't wait to get at him, muttering, 'If he wants to be a hero, I will let him.' But, fortunately, Wes did not have the chance to test Cowdrey's courage because David Allen kept the last two balls out for as thrilling a draw as you could wish to watch.

England had another hero that day in Brian Close who allowed short-pitched balls from Hall and Griffith to strike him on the body, leaving him bruised and battered for the tabloid newspaper pictures the next morning and me wondering what the hell his bat was for. Brian had also taken a lot of blows from Roy Gilchrist on the 1957 tour but not as many as he took in 1976 when he stood up to Michael Holding, Andy Roberts, Wayne Daniel and Vanburn Holder and let it hit him. He had no fear as a batsman, a fielder or as a captain.

There was another fabulous performance by the 32-year-old Fred Trueman in the Edgbaston Test with 7 for 44 in the second innings to skittle us out for 91. I took seven wickets myself in the match but it was not enough to stop England levelling the series with a 217-run victory.

A septic finger meant I arrived at Headingley for the Fourth Test with my arm in a sling and in some pain, but I wasn't going to miss this one. There had been some sharp remarks that neither Rohan Kanhai nor I had scored a century in the series, prompting a few nasty letters. It was something I heard about rather than read and I chose not to worry about it. I had the offending finger lanced and while the swelling went down the pain became worse and the doctors advised me not to play.

There was an instant debate about whether the team would miss Sobers the batsman, Sobers the bowler or Sobers the fielder most when Frank Worrell chipped in and said, 'It would be Sobers the man – and

I want you to play.' How could I refuse? Having persuaded me, Frank did me no favours by winning the toss and electing to bat first and it was not long before I was squeezing on my glove and feeling the searing pain as Trueman's quickest deliveries jarred my bat. But Rohan and I stuck it out, putting on 143, and I reached my first 100 of the tour while Rohan fell short of his by just eight runs.

Finally I was out when I drove Tony Lock hard and straight and the non-strike batsman, Joe Solomon, obligingly jumped out of the way to allow Lock, always a brilliant fielder, to dive into the space he had vacated and take a catch inches from the ground. I suggested to Joe that he might stand his ground in future – but not in quite such polite terms!

Charlie Griffith and Lance Gibbs bowled England out for 174 but instead of enforcing the follow-on, Frank decided to bat again and we rattled up 229 off just 67 overs through Rohan, Basil Butcher and myself. I opened the bowling and cleaned up Micky Stewart for a duck before the close of play and it was all over by lunch on Monday with Lance, Charlie and me bowling England out 221 runs short of their target.

This meant we just had to avoid defeat at The Oval in the Fifth Test and we could declare ourselves world champions. We did better than that, winning by eight wickets, even though umpire Sid Buller drew our fangs when he warned both Charlie and Wes about bowling too many bouncers. Frank didn't agree with the warning but, being the gentleman he was, he acceded – not that it helped England much. The pair took 14 wickets between them while Conrad Hunte scored 80 in the first innings and 108 not out in the second to clinch the series. Fred Trueman bowled just one over before twisting his ankle and limping off.

It was an enjoyable tour apart from a few mindless, anonymous letters that were far from pleasant. They told us to get back into the trees and go home you black this and black that. But we didn't pay that much attention to these cranks because most of us had played in England in the Leagues and we knew what the real English people were like. We showed each other the letters we received and laughed about them, particularly Wes Hall when he saw Charlie's letters! Frank was always the kind of man who could control even the most contentious matters. He had lived in England for a long time.

It couldn't spoil the tour because we weren't going to let one or two little things like that upset us, although we knew that the north, where the colour of a man's skin never made any difference, was very different from some parts of the south. Our problems came mainly when we were in London and the south of England and there was one county game against Surrey at The Oval that was particularly nasty. Frank batted right through; it was one of those occasions when he was determined not to get out because there was so much animosity on the field. It all started when Surrey, having been on top, began to let the game slip. Our supporters, very quiet when Surrey were in the ascendancy, became very loud as we gained control. But it was not only the supporters who were exchanging insults. There was a lot said on the field and Frank became very upset about it. Several of the Surrey team were guilty. I couldn't believe that they were upset simply because of the support we were receiving. Maybe it was just because we had turned the tables on them.

It left us feeling very disappointed and bitter. It was strange. Some of the people who were saying things, we never thought of in that context. While Frank didn't take it well, I have to say that it didn't bother me at all. I was a youngster and I have always believed that if people want to behave in that way, let them. They have their own character to look after and if they want to spoil it through a cricket game, why stop them? In the end, they were the ones who looked and sounded silly. It wasn't going to upset me.

It happened to me in Hampshire in 1966, when I captained the West Indies team. They were on top until Clive Lloyd and I got in and started hitting the bowling about. The crowd didn't like it and started to shout abuse. We were playing shots, as we always did, even in the most difficult situations. Bob Cottam, coming off his short mark, bowled me the fastest bouncer I have ever experienced. It was the only ball in my entire career that I never saw. The thing whistled past me before I could move and when I looked back, Roy Marshall, who was fielding at slip, had his hands to his face. I promptly went down to Bob and told him that I felt sure he must have chucked the ball and that if I ever thought he did it again I would go down the wicket to him with my bat to sort him out and wrap it around his neck.

I was upset because it might have pinned me. I don't mind being pinned if I have the opportunity to see what's going to do it. Roy realised what had happened straightaway. He knew that I was serious and followed up my warning to Bob with one of his own.

At least Bob had the decency to apologise afterwards but it might have been too late by then had he hit me as he intended. He was a good bowler and with Butch White formed a good opening pair but he allowed himself to become upset because Clive and I had taken the match away from his side. As soon as we walked off it was forgotten and we had a drink together. I normally picked up bouncers very early but this one nearly picked me up!

Those were two occasions when I felt very annoyed but, on the whole, the tours to England fulfilled all my expectations with the ball seaming around and little medium-paced bowlers such as Tom Cartwright and Derek Shackleton tying you up in all sorts of tangles. Cartwright was one of the best, having that little bit of extra pace compared with Shackleton, but Shackleton's consistency was legendary. In county cricket he picked up 100 wickets a season for something like 20 seasons. Tom was a real nightmare with his accuracy and his late movement both ways, and there were lots of other bowlers around like him – Jack Favell from Worcestershire, for instance, and Derbyshire's Les Jackson. In fact, every county seemed to have one or two who could move the ball in the air or off the seam with great regularity.

I was playing with Les in a Cavaliers match down in the south of England when he came up to me and said how he wished he could have bowled at me when we were both at our best so that he could have tested himself.

CHAPTER FIVE

The three Ws

The West Indies were thrice blessed when Frank Worrell, Clyde Walcott and Everton Weekes came along in the same era. I was privileged to play alongside all three of the great men. Known worldwide as the three Ws, they were all truly outstanding players.

Throughout the history of cricket, pundits and critics have tried to make comparisons between the three of them, but each had particular, distinctive qualities, which makes that hard to do. All three were world class and any failings can be measured against only the very, very best.

Frank was undoubtedly a great player but between the three of them I reckon Everton was marginally the best. Frank has always been described as elegant, beautiful and very controlled but he was never comfortable with the short-pitched delivery, the quick bouncer. Anything medium paced and just above, he was at home with and would punish, but the really quick stuff from the highest quality fast bowler on a bouncy pitch would cause him difficulties. That doesn't mean he wasn't brave. He once said to me that he didn't mind how fast they bowled at him; once he had covered his face, he reckoned he had enough flesh on his body to take whatever they could throw at him. It needed a bowler of the highest quality and pace to unsettle him, but I thought that was where he fell down a little bit as far as real greatness was concerned. He was very calculating and could read a match and bat on all types of wickets, but I believe that great players always control the game when they are batting, against all types of bowlers. Not taking full control of the short-pitched delivery from the really quick balls counted against him. Everton could do that; it didn't matter what you bowled to him. He had good technique, was a good hooker and had a good defence. That was why, for me, he was just about the best of the three and was probably one of the best batsmen the West Indies ever produced.

Clyde Walcott was also a superb hooker. He had his very own style and was something special on bad wickets, probably because he was tall and a back-foot player who was able to control the ball. He hooked well but he did not have the range of shots nor the full control that Everton showed.

One thing they all had in common was that they were nice people, and to have three players of that calibre in the dressing room was tremendous. They were not only great cricketers but also superb human beings, always willing to help others, particularly the youngsters.

I grew up watching top players at the Wanderers club, feeling my way into cricket and especially admiring the three Ws when they were all young players. Later on, they were not around that much during our domestic cricket season because they were usually away on tour playing in Tests or in the Leagues in England. It was rare for them to play inter-island cricket, but we occasionally caught a glimpse of them. Our season didn't always run from May to December; sometimes it started later, which gave us a better opportunity to watch them. Eventually, I was able to mix with them and talk to them. They were always approachable and I found out what wonderful people they were. There was nothing snobbish about them and they were always ready to offer their help and advice.

I recall when I first went to Jamaica I was shy and would sit in the hotel lounge at nights or in my room watching television. If Clyde and Everton saw me on their way out, they would insist that I join them. More often than not we would go to one of their many friends' homes for a meal and a few drinks. The Jamaicans were always very friendly and welcoming. The important thing was to get away from the hotel room and the game, and get out and meet new people. It helped relieve some of the pressure on a young lad and they were both aware of that.

I had followed Everton's progress from Barbados to the Test team in 1947–48, and seen him at the trials in 1953, but I didn't meet him until I played my first game for Barbados. After that, he often invited me round to his house and we became very close. He would sometimes pick me up in his car and take me home. Joan, his wife, would cook us a meal. Everton gave me my first bat and after he signed for Herbert Sutcliffe's company and was given them free, he would often pass on a couple to me.

There was only one bone of contention between us and that was a slight misunderstanding in our running between the wickets. He was run out on several occasions when we were batting together. There was a particular shot he played to midwicket. He would immediately call for a run and take off down the wicket. I would be watching and occasionally I would start off too late or say 'no' and he would finish up at the wrong end. But, typical of the man, he never showed any resentment or tried to offload the blame on me.

I relished the opportunity to sit down and talk with him when he returned from far-off places. He would regale me with stories, not just of the cricket but of the people and the culture as well. I especially loved to hear about India where he had first gone in 1948. In his early days, it was the tour no one wanted to go on. Players from many of the Test-playing countries simply would not make themselves available because of the heat, the living conditions and the food. He described what the players had to go through and generally how tough and arduous any tour of India was in those pioneering days. By the time I went there in 1958 it had changed a great deal but he prepared me for the tough days – and there were still some of those. Today, India is a superb and fascinating place to visit and now everyone wants to go on that tour.

The poverty, of course, used to strike everyone who went there. Everton told me that often their cricket clothes would mysteriously disappear during the tour and then, on their way out of an area where they had previously played, they would see the fishermen wearing white flannels, shirts and West Indian sweaters.

To me, these were tales of the unknown and they gave me a flavour of what I hoped was to come my way, and encouraged me all the more to make the top grade. The thought of travel excited me intensely. You learn so much from travel and meeting people in their own environment. Everton's traveller's tales not only forewarned me of the problems I could face but excited me about my future.

His experience and wise counsel were invaluable. One example was when we were in the team that toured New Zealand in 1956 along with fellow Bajans Dennis Atkinson, who was captain of the West Indies, former captain John Goddard and Clairmonte Depeiza. I had been close to Dennis since our time together at Wanderers but one day we had serious words, but not so bad because I can't remember what they were about.

Some remark he made had not gone down well with me and I blew my top. Dennis became very upset because he had done so much for me. He went to Everton who told him that if he approached a youngster in that manner he could not expect any other sort of response. Everton came down firmly on my side, not just because it was me but because he had standards in the way he thought players should be handled, especially the seniors with the juniors. After any little spat like that he would work out a compromise to settle things down. Not only did he act as peacemaker but he also found the time to score three successive hundreds in that series.

Everton was the one who stayed in Barbados and when I came back from England he was coaching the island team along with Seymour Nurse and Charlie Griffith. When I had the opportunity to sit down and have a drink and talk to him, I was delighted to discover that the years had not changed him at all. Happily, our friendship has remained intact. We still meet for a game of dominoes – and he is a fair player at that, too.

I hadn't known Frank that well at home. He had played for Barbados in the early forties but by the time I made the step up, he had gone and was playing in Jamaica where he went to university. When I went to play league cricket at Radcliffe in 1958, I became a lot closer to him. He had been the previous professional at the club, spending three or four years there before moving on to play in the Staffordshire League. He lived on Bury Road in Radcliffe and was the only West Indian whom I knew in the area. He and his family were terrific, immediately opening their doors to me. His wife Velda told me straightaway that this was my home and any time I wanted to come just to arrive, no need to call. I took her at her word and used to go there regularly to eat with them and play with their daughter Lana. Frank was a fascinating and intelligent man; he was studying hard at Manchester University for an economics degree at the time. He and I would talk for hours, not just about cricket but about life in general.

Of course, I picked his brains, particularly about playing in the Lancashire League. He would tell me about various players' characteristics, their strengths and their frailties. I suppose the name that cropped up most was that of the outstanding and eccentric Australian all-rounder Cecil Pepper. Cec was playing for Oldham and Frank warned me to watch him if he dropped anything short and not to play across the line because he had perfected the flipper, one of the best I've ever seen.

In my first game for Radcliffe against Oldham I was batting high in the order as the professional. We'd lost a couple of quick wickets so I was in earlier than I had anticipated. It was the tradition that as soon as the professional came in, the opposing skipper would bring on his professional if he bowled and, sure enough, Cec came on straightaway.

He bowled a couple of leg-spinners that came into me and I played them. He bowled another and I played him across to midwicket; then he bowled a googly, which I played down the line. Then, suddenly, he whipped one in short and I was halfway through my shot when I remembered Frank's warning. I dropped my bat, the ball thumped into the middle of it and dropped at my feet. Cec came down the wicket, glared at me and said accusingly, 'You've been talking to that bloody Frank Worrell, haven't you?'

Frank knew his cricket very well. When everyone else was getting excited and things were happening, Frank was an oasis of calm. A typical example was an incident in Adelaide in 1961, during the Fourth Test against Australia when the last Aussie pair, Lindsay Kline and Ken Mackay, batted right through to stumps, defying us for over 90 minutes. Norm O'Neill had been bowling to Kline in the nets before he came out and knocked him over four times out of every six balls, but although all of us tried – Wes Hall, Frank Worrell, me, Lance Gibbs, Alf Valentine and even Joe Solomon – none of us could winkle him out. He finished on 15 not out.

I must say I thought I had finished them off when I took a catch and we all started to walk back to the pavilion, even Frank. No one bothered appealing but the batsmen stood their ground, we stopped, somebody appealed and the umpire said not out. Some of us started to become a little agitated but Frank took charge of the situation, told us to cool down and said that there was still time to get one of them out. He was unruffled and the fact that we were unable to break the partnership left him outwardly untroubled, even though a wrong decision had cost us a victory.

In the famous tied Test in Brisbane, Wes Hall was bowling the last ball with Australia needing one run to win and the last pair at the crease. It could not possibly have been tenser. Frank walked up to Wes and said to him, 'Now Wes, if you bowl a no-ball, you know you will never be able to go back to the West Indies? All of those five and a half million people will want to hang you!'

It was the perfect comment, light-hearted but with an underlying message for Wes to contemplate as he walked back. When he ran in to bowl, he made sure he planted his foot five feet behind the popping crease, just in case they had some belligerent, conniving umpire.

That was the type of man Frank was. He always seemed to have the right word for the right moment. At the time of his death in March 1967 he was working his way back to Barbados. Sadly, he never made it.

I did not see nearly so much of Clyde. He was playing for Guyana and coaching for a sugar factory there when he retired. Clyde came back to Barbados later and worked for the Barbados Shipping and Trading Company, the largest company on the island, and also with the Barbados Cricket Association, eventually becoming president before he moved on once again.

He and I ran into problems on one occasion when he was a selector and I was recovering from a knee operation. I was also in the process of giving up the captaincy and the West Indies teams were being selected to play against Australia in 1972–73 and for the short series in England in 1973. It was all very unfortunate but we got over it, of course. I always found him to be a warm personality and a likeable man.

CHAPTER SIX

1966 and all that

I n all, I had five tours in England and I enjoyed all of them, except for the short tour in 1969, but 1966 was my favourite. I scored over 700 runs as captain with an average of over 100. I also took 20 wickets and plenty of catches. I forced England to change their captain three times in that series. They started off with Mike (M.J.K.) Smith at Old Trafford where we won by an innings; Colin Cowdrey was skipper for the drawn Second Test at Lord's and for their defeats at Nottingham and Headingley; and Brian Close came in to captain England to a big win in the Fifth Test at The Oval.

Ah, Brian Close – now there was a man whom I thought was one of England's best captains. I played both with him and against him and had a lot of respect for the man. I played some odd games with him including a trip to Bermuda with Yorkshire. I guess I was probably the first non Yorkshire-born player to play for the county when they adopted those strict rules, but there was no publicity about it in those days. Yorkshire invited me to go with them and I was very pleased to make the trip. I went almost unnoticed and I made a lot of runs with

Geoffrey Boycott and took a lot of wickets with Freddie Trueman – and it was there that Brian met his wife.

Later, when I went to Notts, I had an even better chance to have a look at Brian Close in action in competitive matches. The thing I admired about him most was that he didn't respect anyone. You had to prove your ability to him in that match, whatever you might have achieved in the past.

We could not have started better than we did at Old Trafford, wrapping up the game in three days and winning by an innings and 40 runs, leaving everyone free to concentrate on the World Cup final at Wembley between England and their old rivals West Germany. We outplayed England completely with Conrad Hunte scoring 135. I came in at number six, adding 161 for a one-innings total of 484.

Any fears we had over Milburn were erased when he was run out for a duck and Lance Gibbs, on one of his favourite Test wickets, took five while David Holford weighed in with three as England were skittled out for 167.

Needless to say we made them follow on and Milburn hit a defiant 94 before being bowled by Lance. Colin Cowdrey was the only one to offer any real resistance after that as Lance took another five wickets and I took three to add to my four catches in the match.

Our concerns over Milburn were realised at Lord's when he struck a magnificent 126 not out in the second innings. In the end, both teams were relieved to draw a game either of us could have lost.

I had some good innings over the years in some difficult situations and on some bad pitches, but my second in this Test was the best. We were really in trouble and there was a lot of nervous chatter in the dressing room when I walked down the steps. England led us by 86 runs after the first innings and we were just five runs on with four wickets down when I arrived at the crease. That soon became five down for the addition of just four more runs and David Holford joined me in the middle. We still had a day and three-quarters to go with Hunte, Carew, Kanhai, Butcher and Nurse back in the pavilion. It was a very sticky situation. It was a matter of getting my priorities right. I had decided even before I walked out that my policy was going to be to go on the attack.

I knew that Colin Cowdrey would move the field out against me after a couple of overs, and put the pressure on David who was playing only his second Test match, and this at Lord's of all places. Lord's can do strange things to young players. It is easy to get carried away with the aura of the ground; not to mention the situation the West Indies were in. This was a batsman largely unknown to the English players and public alike. But I knew David well, not only as a cousin but also from playing with him in Barbados. I knew he could bat and it was only a matter of seeing whether the circumstances would overcome him.

After a few overs I went down the wicket to him and told him that if he was batting at Kensington Oval in Barbados and had decided to bat on, no one would get him out. I emphasised that this was a good wicket, it was flat and there was not a lot happening for the bowlers. We had lost wickets because of rash shots and lapses of concentration. I told him to treat it exactly as he would have done an innings at home and we proceeded from there.

The beauty of my innings for me was that it was all planned and everything I wanted to do came off. I played the shots where I wanted to play them. I did not try to shield David; I let him get on with his game. Batting at five and six I rarely ran out of partners because I gave them confidence. I believe that if you have faith in your partner and do not try to farm the bowling, he will come to the conclusion that the captain trusts him, so therefore he must trust himself. If you keep refusing singles or pinching the bowling, he will know you have no faith in him and he will either fail or there will be a run out. In this instance, that was the last thing a team in our precarious position needed.

David took me at my word. He put his head down and we batted out the day with all the commentators saying that it was only a matter of time before we succumbed. But after half an hour the next morning we were still there and everyone began to realise that we were gaining the upper hand. Suddenly it was England who were trying to hold on to the game.

We were able to declare without losing another wicket. I scored 163 not out and David 105 not out, and we called a halt at 369 for 5, leaving England a nasty 50 overs or so to bat out.

We had them in a bit of trouble with Wes Hall and Charlie Griffith sending back Geoff Boycott, Ken Barrington, Colin Cowdrey and Jim Parks for 67 runs. Then Colin Milburn and Tom Graveney came together for an unbroken stand of 130 before the rain came down and finished the match.

David and I were first cousins and we were very close. We had played a lot together and captained each other. He was a brilliant boy and went away to study. He got a degree in agriculture, becoming what was known as a soil scientist, and another in computer studies, coming back to Barbados in between to play his cricket. He captained Barbados and was always a good all-round cricketer and a good student of the game.

Unfortunately, a lot of the team did not appreciate just how good he was. Some of them thought I favoured him because he was my blood relative, although it was never said to my face, but he could hold his own in every situation and he should have been captain of the West Indies. He was easily one of the best captains around at the time and he should have been given that opportunity with his knowledge and his ability to assess players and plan strategy. I think the fact that he was my cousin rebounded on him and if he had not been a relative he might have been made captain. That insularity in West Indies cricket was evident again and there were always the fellows on the sideline who would point a finger and claim favouritism. Every island hails its own, and it even existed within the team and not just on the boundary ropes.

It is a different set-up from England where you can jump in a car and drive from London to Yorkshire or Warwickshire or Somerset. In the Caribbean, it is not so easy to move around. This causes the insularity – the public and officials believe that their players are better than anyone else's because they simply do not see the others often enough.

Even in Australia, with huge distances between cities, it is easier to travel around than it is in the Caribbean; no one thinks anything of driving or flying hundreds of miles for a game or even a party. In the West Indies, people tend to remain in their own environment, and with the kind of praise you receive from your own people when you return from tour, it's easy to foster that insularity because the praise feels good.

No one could be prouder of being Barbadian than I am but I always tried to do what I thought was the best for West Indies cricket. I believe that once players are selected, they become West Indians and not Jamaicans, Barbadians or whatever else. The only time I became embroiled was when the selectors forced it on me, and I could show what was proposed was not in the interests of helping West Indies cricket.

When Frank Worrell became captain in 1960, we at last became united, played as a team and earned our results collectively. When Clive Lloyd took over in 1974, it was different because here was a team that was developing at a time when the organisation of the game was changing. Financial benefits were improving and players were earning good salaries.

We went from poverty to pay packets because of Australian television magnate Kerry Packer. It all started from Packer. The Packer series is what really brought the West Indies together under Clive because when the team went to Australia to play in his competition, they were being paid money beyond their dreams plus good bonuses, really good bonuses. So even if players did not agree off the field, they would play together on the pitch. They had to play as a team to win and winning brought the rewards.

We were back on the winning trail in Nottingham for the Third Test, recovering from a first-innings deficit after being bowled out by Snow and Higgs who took four wickets apiece. We were still behind the England first-innings total when Rohan Kanhai and Basil Butcher came together at 65 for 2. They put their heads down and fought a rearguard action. They were booed by the crowd for their slow play and slated by the media. Why? When England did the same thing, they were occupying the crease; when we did it, we were killing the game. Once we were re-established, we put England and the critics to the sword as Basil piled up 209 while I came in to score a rapid-fire 94 before declaring at 482 for 5.

Now it was England's turn to crawl but there was no happy climax for them. Charlie Griffith and Lance Gibbs took seven between them while I took four catches in that second innings.

The series was clinched at Headingley in August and but for the personal satisfaction of saving the match at Lord's, this one would have been the most memorable. Not only did we win by an innings but I contributed 174 runs in our first and only innings, scoring 100 between the lunch and tea intervals in a stand of 265 with Seymour Nurse. I followed that with five wickets in the first innings and three in the second.

I remember going to Seymour when opening bat Bob Barber came on to bowl his leg breaks. Barber was one of those unusual players who bowled right-handed and batted left-handed. He bowled a couple to Seymour who didn't look too sure against him so I went down the wicket and offered to take strike until he felt a little more comfortable. No sooner had I made the offer than he went on the charge and started hitting Barber to all points of the compass. When he came in he told the fellows, 'I don't understand the captain. He wants to make all the runs himself. He telling me he can take Bob Barber, beating him around the ground when I know I can take Barber just as well.' I should record that Barber eventually clean bowled me!

We were able to bowl out England for 240 and I enforced the follow-on. Most folk thought I was doing the wrong thing because the wicket was so good; leading England by only 260 and having to bat on the last day was going to be detrimental to West Indies cricket and our hopes of a win. On top of that, I went on myself to open the bowling and threw in the unexpected in the shape of Peter Lashley.

Peter bowled three overs, two maidens, and took 1 for 1. The wicket was a valuable one – Geoffrey Boycott's. It was all part of the captain's tricks of the trade, knowing not just your own players and their capabilities but your opponents' weaknesses as well. Sometimes a ploy came off – like this one.

That game showed that cricket at this level is a psychological game. I knew that the England players were being prepared to face Wes Hall and Charlie Griffith. That meant they were anticipating five overs at the most and they would have planned for that, but when they came out and soon saw Peter Lashley with the ball, they suddenly realised that they were going to have to face double the number of overs. Peter was an ordinary bowler who bowled off seven or eight steps while I went off 11. Compare that with Wes and Charlie who both went off about 24. That changed their entire thinking and suddenly they were playing to take as many runs as they could while Peter was bowling. I reasoned that survival would still be uppermost in their minds. Peter could swing the ball. They would not take a lot of runs off him and with the movement, he had a chance of getting a wicket – and that is what he did.

I told Wes and Charlie of my plans and they were fine. We were a team and they knew the decision I made was for the team. There were no fixtures, no guarantees. When Peter had Boycott caught behind by Alexander, everyone said that I was a genius; but if the plan had failed, I would have been an idiot. We won the game and I was the best captain around but when I did a similar thing in Trinidad and we lost, I was a fool and a bad captain.

I tried the same trick against England in Jamaica when I opened with Wes and myself and I took a couple of wickets, including bowling Geoffrey behind his back. Time is important when you have a limited amount, and a limited number of overs. I always fancied myself to get Geoffrey out early. He was suspect to left-arm inswingers because his front foot would go across instead of down the line and he used to end up right in front of all three. That's how I bowled him behind his back – his front foot went across. With the swinging ball, he was looking for protection, not to score, so I could fiddle with things and try different balls. Even if the experiment didn't work and I bowled a bad ball, he wouldn't take full advantage because priority to him at that stage was survival. It was the same with Peter Lashley; they wouldn't take risks because they would be crucified. It also gave us more overs and it worked on a number of occasions.

With Colin Cowdrey as captain you could get away with a lot because he showed top players so much respect. If he liked you and respected you as a player, he would arrange the field early on to try to take your wicket, but once he saw you were getting on top, he would quickly push everyone out, taking the tension away. Brian Close, on the other hand, would stay there, breathing down your neck and putting on the pressure with an attacking field. He did something to me in the Fifth Test at The Oval that I'm sure helped England win that match. Every time I had gone in on that tour, I had scored runs; 161 at Old Trafford; 46 and 163 not out at Lord's; 94 at Trent Bridge and 174 at Headingley. At The Oval, we scored 268 in the first innings with me contributing 81. Tom Graveney scored a lot of runs (165) but we had them struggling on 166 for 7 before wicket-keeper John Murray joined Graveney, scoring 112. Ken Higgs at number 10 chipped in 63 and John Snow made 59 not out as England piled up 527. We still fancied our chances of getting a result but as soon as I walked in, Brian came to field at bat/pad with Snow bowling.

Few fielders did that in those days, especially to me, and as he crouched there I knew what was going through his mind – 'Bouncer. Bouncer.' Sure enough, Snowy bounced one at me and I quickly moved into position to hook. But the ball suddenly dipped on me as I was making the stroke and it caught the bottom edge, hit my leg and there was Brian, eyes wide open, taking the catch. Any other fielder would have gone scampering, particularly with the sort of form I was in, but not Close. He just stood there without flinching and said, 'Thank you very much.' They went on to win and I'm sure, with the sort of confidence I had and the form I was in, if I had stayed in we could have built a total to challenge them.

That was good captaincy by Close. No one is a great player when he first walks in to bat. A batsman may have a reputation but when he walks to the crease for the first time it's a new day, he's vulnerable and that's the time to attack. It has to be early. Get them in the first 15 or 20 minutes or you are going to pay the penalty. That is something Colin Cowdrey did not do as a captain; he often let me off the hook. I would face a couple of overs, play a few shots and Colin would back the fielders off – but not Closey.

CHAPTER SEVEN

The reluctant captain

When Frank Worrell eventually took over the team in 1960–61 for the tour to Australia, there were many in the Caribbean who felt that there was some sort of ongoing riffle between Rohan Kanhai and myself. It was supposedly caused by a little jealousy on Rohan's part; it was said that he was happy only when he had made more runs than me. I never believed this fantasy but this is what people felt. The truth is that we got along famously together and shared a mutual respect for each other's talents.

Frank sorted it out in his usual perceptive and diplomatic manner. He said, with tongue-in-cheek, that if Rohan batted at number three and I batted at five or six, Rohan would never know how many runs I was going to make and, to be safe, he would have to make a big total every time he batted. He explained that I had the ability to read the game, to know whether to attack, defend, when to go for quick runs or when to stay there. If the batsmen in front accumulated a lot of runs, I would know to go out and score quickly but if the team were 60 for 4, I could go in there and bring the team together by helping the others.

He told me I was the only player in his team who could do it and that was why he wanted me at five or six, because they were very important positions. It was wise counsel and all part of my learning curve.

I never intended nor wanted to be captain but, without realising it, I started my tuition from the moment I went to England to play league cricket for Radcliffe. I learned a great deal from Frank while I was there and when we went on tour we spent a lot of time together. At the end of a day's play, Frank would call me to have a drink and talk about the match because, he said, I knew more about the game than anybody else in the side. Frank would discuss most things with me, asking what I thought and what I would do if I were in his place. More often than not we had exactly the same ideas and more often than not they worked. I would often go up to him during a game and suggest a change of bowling or an alteration in the field, or I would ask a bowler to try a particular tactic to a particular batsman and quite often it would work out to our benefit. From the time Frank took the captaincy until he retired in England at the end of the 1963 series, we continued to collaborate although Conrad Hunte was always his vice captain.

Frank was the best captain I played under. He was able to motivate people and he knew the game. He was able to do things in such a diplomatic way that if you had enough sense you would understand what he was trying to put over. He was never harsh with anybody. He was flexible and would listen. One of his characteristics was that if he disagreed, he would not say so directly; instead he would often use phrases that were the opposite of what you were saying and you would eventually realise he was taking the mickey.

But despite what many saw as an apprenticeship, I never wanted the captaincy. I was a freedom-loving, happy-go-lucky sort of person who would play under anybody and give them 100 per cent support so long as they did not try to tell me what to do with my life. When I'm on the field, they have me totally, body and soul, but when I'm off the field, I don't want them to tell me what to do. I want them to leave me alone because my life is mine. If I didn't perform on the field, they could tear me off a strip, but as long as I was playing good cricket, what I did off the field and how I lived my life was up to me and no one else. Frank picked up on that and respected it because he was a similar type of person. His attitude with me was that it was up to me if I wanted to go out all night, provided I made runs the next day; and I knew that he expected me to make those runs to justify his attitude. Things like that made him a good man to play for. We thought in much the same way but I was my own man.

When Frank retired he didn't ask me if I wanted the captaincy; he went straight to the Board and recommended to them that they should elect me as captain without asking if I wanted the job.

In our last game at The Oval he asked me to lead out the team the day before he retired. I don't know what he was thinking; maybe he was just making a point in public that I should succeed him and that he was recommending me. But when he confirmed his recommendation all hell broke loose in the Caribbean because everyone expected Conrad Hunte to take over.

I had remained in England when the tour finished and when the Board wrote and told me I was going to be captain it took me all of six or seven weeks to reply to that letter. A captain has to set examples and that had never been my role. A lot of the players in the team knew what type of person I was and how I had behaved under other captains, ploughing my individual furrow. How could I tell them what to do and expect them to do it when they knew me and what I did with my life? I had to argue it out with myself, but I mentioned it to a few other people. I was playing for Norton in the North Staffordshire League when I heard the news and I sat down with the captain Jim Flannery and a couple of friends I mixed with at night, and we talked over the ramifications.

They persuaded me what a great honour it was to captain my country and that it was something every cricketer should want to do. In turn, I told them it was not an easy thing for me to accept because, in order to set an example, I would have to change my lifestyle, something I was not sure that I wanted to do. Up until now, I hadn't had anything to worry about because I had always backed up the way I lived my life with my performances on the pitch. I was concerned whether the team would accept as a captain a player who bent the rules.

When Frank took over he said that he didn't want to see me in the hotel at 11 o'clock; he told me to go out and come in whenever I wanted to, but some of the other captains I played under set a curfew. Everyone was to be in by a certain time, but I would say, 'Who? Me?' and I would sneak out anyway. I told the other players that it was a rule for them and not for me.

I couldn't be a hypocrite and when I took the job I never imposed curfews or anything like that. I always believed that if you want to play cricket for your country, and play for a long time, you must know your own limitations. If you know that you cannot perform the day after a night out and you still go, you are not made for a career in cricket. If you know that you can do it, there should be no bother. If anyone had locked my door and sat outside my room, I would not have performed the next day on purpose. I would have been stubborn and obstinate and gone the opposite way just to prove my point. If you pick a West Indies team and they really want to play for their country, they should do what is best for them.

If I went out until five in the morning, I had to make sure that I performed because I might want to go out until five again the next day. The only thing to do was to go out there, put my head down, and make my runs, ensuring that my team was in a solid position. Once that was achieved, it didn't matter if I was out or how many runs I made. Sure I could go to bed early, come out the next morning and make 100, no problems. But equally, if I wanted to go out on the town, I would go out.

When I first went to England in 1957 I used to go to bed early. I would lie there thinking of cricket, imagining Freddie Trueman and Brian Statham and the great bowlers running up to bowl to me. I would toss and turn and by the time I went to sleep it was time to wake up again. I couldn't sleep for thinking about cricket. I said no, no, no, no, this isn't the way it's supposed to be played. It is supposed to be played on the field not off it. From then on I started going out and when I came home I would go straight to sleep and not even dream of cricket. When I woke up in the morning, I had a clear mind and that is when I could think about what lay ahead. That was very relaxing and very comforting.

To relax after a day in the field I would go to a club, have a few drinks and a few dances. That was fine as long as your mind was on the game come the next day. I could enjoy my evenings and my cricket; nothing was allowed to interfere with my cricket.

I had no problems going back to my hotel room when the milkman arrived at dawn and then playing. None of my team-mates seemed to mind or object. I never had that many problems or objections with other cricketers wherever I played. In fact, I was lucky – I never had trouble with anyone.

In the end, I picked up a pen and wrote to the Board accepting the task and telling them what a great honour it was and saying that I would do my best to maintain standards. Maybe if I had had a younger team, they would have looked up to me and listened to what I had to say, but I took over an older team. There were probably four or five players who would have liked the captaincy, or thought they should have had it instead of me. Conrad Hunte felt really let down although I didn't know it at the time. I had never pushed for the job while he had been second-in-command for so long.

I took up my responsibilities against Australia in March 1965 and we won against them for the first time ever in the Caribbean, taking the series 2–1. Frank Worrell, now Sir Frank, having been knighted the year before, was manager. This was the series viewed by many around the globe as the unofficial cricket championship of the world; certainly we were the two best sides around at the time.

My first Test as captain was at my lucky ground, Sabina Park, and it did not let me down. I won the toss against captain Bobby Simpson and, on a wicket as bright and shiny as a mirror, I reluctantly decided to bat, knowing that I had two bowlers in Wes Hall and Charlie

Griffith who were faster than anyone they had. Later in my career, I would have gone for it but in my first Test as captain it was so much more difficult to gamble. Neil Hawke, their best bowler on that tour, exclaimed, 'I'll bring my razor out and shave on that in the morning instead of using my bathroom mirror.'

Hawke and Laurie Mayne proved my theory right as they bowled us out for a paltry 239 but Wes, bowling as fast as he had done in his entire career, ripped the heart out of their first innings with five wickets. He followed up with another four in the second innings and Charlie backed him up with two in each. We went on to win by 179 runs.

During the match, one Australian wrote a newspaper column questioning Charlie Griffith's action and tried to back up his claim with photographs. By now it was water off a duck's back to Charlie and he became even quicker and more hostile.

I was hampered by a rare injury – a thigh strain – but I celebrated the captaincy with my 100th Test wicket when I had all-rounder Peter Philpott caught in the slips by Rohan Kanhai.

The Second Test, in Port-of-Spain, was a high-scoring, uneventful draw, the highlight being a brilliant 143 from Bob Cowper, the top-scoring Australian on the tour. Cowper retired far too early from the game but he went on to become a very successful businessman.

The Third Test, in Georgetown, was marred by a pre-match row over the umpires. The local association demanded that Gerry Gomez should stand, even though he had never umpired a Test match before. You have to start somewhere and he did a fine job. We did an even better job, winning by 212 runs with Lance Gibbs taking match figures of 9 for 80.

It was in this match that I made a crucial decision as captain, switching Lance to my favoured end when the Aussies were battling at 80 for 1. He went on to take 6 for 29 and I weighed in with a couple of catches at leg-slip and a couple of wickets from the other end.

The series victory was complete when we drew in Barbados, but I didn't enjoy the game. I abhor time wasting and, in a high-scoring game, Bobby Simpson did exactly that, batting on until the middle of the third day as he and Bill Lawry both scored double hundreds and put on 382 for the first wicket in a massive total of 650 for 6 declared. We responded with 573 led by another double century, this time from Seymour Nurse.

Then, surprisingly, Simpson declared his second innings at 175 for 4, setting us a very sporting 253 in 270 minutes. But when Conrad Hunte and Bryan Davis put on 145 for the first wicket he lost interest, spread his fielders around the boundary and asked his bowlers to keep the ball well outside the off stump. Even so, we finished just 11 runs short with me on 34 not out to add to my first innings half century. I wasn't going to be rash and throw away my wicket in a vain chase for glory against a field like that. It should have been Simpson going for the victory because a draw was of no use to him in the series. I have no doubt that he should have continued to attack and might well have bowled us out with the challenge thrown down. I showed my displeasure by my actions at the wicket. I was not a happy captain.

With the series won, we lost the Fifth and final Test by 10 wickets on a dreadful pitch in Trinidad where the batsman never knew whether the ball was going to creep low or jump up at his head. Charlie Griffith took 6 for 46 but this was not going to be enough. I was clean bowled in both innings, the first by the man the Aussies called 'Evil Dick', David Sincock, who bowled slow left-arm chinamen and googlies. He bowled me with a ball that pitched a long way outside my leg stump and hit off.

'What happened?' I asked keeper Wally Grout as I turned and looked at my shattered wicket. He answered with a grin, 'Evil's done it again.'

As someone who practised the art myself, I appreciated a good delivery, but with Sincock they were few and far between; hence his having played three Test matches only. I just happened to face what was probably the best ball he ever bowled in Test cricket.

We went to England in June 1966 and won that series 3–1 when the whole of England was jumping up and down because they had won the football World Cup, beating West Germany at Wembley.

I could not have wished for a better start to my career as a captain if I had written the script myself, beating Australia at home and then England away. We lost a Test to each of them but both were relatively unimportant games because the series had already been clinched.

The conversion to captaincy had been painless. All the field placings and bowling changes had come naturally because I felt that I knew my cricket better than anyone else in the side. I wasn't someone to follow tradition and do what other captains might do. That is the easy way to avoid criticism. My approach was always different. I saw the game differently from other people. I was there to win but I was also there to play cricket. I have always believed in my heart and soul that cricketers are entertainers and I could never stand a boring game of cricket. It had to have something in it for me to play, something I could fight for. I've seen other captains declare, leaving the opposition with a target of 300 to win in 110 minutes, and then go out to defend. That is something I would never do because it is such a waste of time.

This is supposed to be Test cricket, the best there is. You go out with the intention either of winning or of giving the opposition a chance to win and maybe sneaking in while they are going for it. If they win, bad luck! It is just one of those things.

I won my third series as a captain, beating India 2–0 in India – a first, I thought, for any captain of the West Indies to win the first three series in a row. Everything was going well and all the time I was captain and winning, everyone was with me, but the day I stopped winning many of those same people were against me.

I do not believe that I have yet been forgiven for my decision when I declared against England in Trinidad in March 1968, leaving them 215 to win in 165 minutes. It was no spur of the moment, cavalier decision; it was very much calculated and I asked every player and the manager, Everton Weekes, if they agreed with what I planned to do. I said to them, 'Gentlemen, this is a turning wicket. I think we should go for it. Do you agree?'

Basil Butcher, not a recognised bowler, had taken five wickets with his occasional leg-breaks in the first innings; in addition, we had Willie Rodriguez, Lance Gibbs and me in the team, on a wicket that did not favour fast bowlers. I would have declared earlier if I could. When I went to the players they said they saw nothing wrong with my ideas and told me to declare anytime. I went to Everton and told him the same thing. Some of them even suggested that I should declare 10 minutes earlier but I opted to go on to even up the equation. Everyone was happy and in agreement when I called in the not-out batsmen Joey Carew and Rohan Kanhai at 92 for 2.

When I opened the bowling, I fooled John Edrich with my second ball, an outswinger, but Derrick Murray, standing back, dropped the edge. Although Edrich scored only 29, he shared in an opening partnership of over 50 with Boycott; had he gone early, England would have had an entirely different approach.

As it was, we lost by seven wickets with two balls left of Lance Gibbs' 17th over and everyone said that I was the worst captain that the West Indies had ever had. Amazingly, people still discuss and debate the issue all of these years later. They said I was a gambler and because of that I would gamble on cricket decisions. That was a slanderous comment uttered on television but I took it very lightly – even though I kept the tape.

Everything in life can be a gamble, but this was no gamble because the entire team and the manager agreed. England weren't going to make the attempt to go for the runs until Basil D'Oliveira got together with Colin Cowdrey and said they should respond to my challenge because I was trying to make a game of it.

That series was so boring; the first three Tests had been drawn. England were bowling something like 12 or 13 overs an hour operating with two spinners for much of the time and eight men on the off side, bowling on the off stump. They would field the ball in the middle of the wicket, throw the ball to the wicket-keeper and then wait for it to be thrown back although no one was running. You won't find those statistics in *Wisden* but I got so sick of it. I was so fed up. I was there to play cricket and this wasn't what I thought of as cricket.

What hurt most was that when I was criticised for being a bad captain, none of the players said a word or backed me up and even Everton Weekes shrugged and told the media, 'You can't tell Garry Sobers anything.'

If I had my time all over again, I would do the same thing. I would still consult the manager and all my players and I would still declare. You have to know your game, read all the situations and make your calculations. If Basil Butcher could take five wickets on a spinner's wicket, surely he, Sobers and Rodriguez should be able to bowl out England, or at least keep them quiet on a turning wicket, without them being able to score runs. They had not scored at more than 35 runs an hour throughout the entire series. Whether the bowlers went out with the idea that they couldn't win, I will never know.

Clive Lloyd has always been called the West Indies' greatest-ever captain, yet Clive declared in Trinidad in 1976 leaving India over 400 to win – and lost with 15 minutes to spare. I left a target of 215 and lost in the last over, and I didn't have fast bowlers. Which is worse?

That declaration and result followed me for the remainder of my career. Everyone remembered it. It is very difficult for the world to understand how a man can do so many things on a cricket field and still be a great or good leader. A lot of people were standing by, critics such as Brian Close, waiting for something to go wrong so that they could say to the world, 'I told you so.' They could rarely fault me in what I did as a bowler, batsman or fielder and when I took on the captaincy and won the first three series, they saw the man as becoming impossible. They waited and pounced as soon as we lost because of my declaration.

But I accept that not everyone can like you. There have to be critics waiting for you to make mistakes. I have never really bothered about it; it has changed nothing in me. I will always be the same. To me, that was cricket. Many of the critics didn't know enough about it and many captains only followed tradition, doing what other captains would have done. Waiting to declare so that you gave the opposition no chance of winning was not my way; that was not how cricket should be played. I certainly wasn't going to give England 250 to get in 100 minutes. I would rather not have declared at all and then it would just have been a boring, sickening game. England would have been kept out in the field, they would have given the ball to non-bowlers and, most important of all, the spectators would not have enjoyed it.

But despite all the aggravation and the problems, I enjoyed being captain. It was never going to be easy. If you captain an ageing team, half of whom think they should be in charge instead of you, there are bound to be problems. I had no axe to grind personally against any individuals. Conrad Hunte was fine and always gave 100 per cent. It was only when he retired and said in public how upset he was to have been overlooked that I knew the truth. I never looked for resentment in the others; I always looked for the positive and tried to squeeze everything out of them, even though I had been warned to watch out for certain players. My attitude was if they couldn't or wouldn't do it for me, I would do it myself, but I could not bowl or bat at both ends and neither could I keep wicket to my own bowling. Cricket is a team game.

West Indies cricket was very important to me. I played for the West Indies and not for myself. Anyone could have captained the team and I couldn't have cared less. I was ready to do the job and pull my weight for my country because I had been asked, not because I wanted the job.

Being captain never affected my form with the bat or the ball, as the records show. I tried to read the game and assess players on both sides, what wickets would do and where the weaknesses were, and apply that to the match situation. I'd ask Lance Gibbs what he thought. In fact, I would talk to all my bowlers. I might offer up a little advice, such as the incoming batsman plays far from his pads, or ask the bowler to throw it a little bit higher or tell him that this guy is not good off his legs. I would try to work out a strategy, using certain bowlers to certain batsmen.

At times you are under real pressure, having to work out what you are going to do when a player is on top. Do you bowl tight and let him make a mistake or do you attack him and force him into an error? There are many facets to good captaincy. When people see you stop to think, they may assume you don't know what you are doing or that you are doing things on the spur of the moment. That was never the case with me; neither was it a one-man band. We always had team meetings during which the players would discuss the ongoing situations and air their views if they did not like what the other fellow was saying. I was always open to suggestions; I never thought I was above the law.

Although I had no practical experience of captaincy before taking over the West Indies, I learned a great deal from playing in the League. I was only 21 and I had to coach a lot of players who were older than I was. I went to see the chairman and the captain after a year and said, 'Gentlemen, I don't feel right having to talk to people in their thirties and forties and me being so young. I would like to be relieved of those duties. If I feel like advising I will do so, and if they ask me I will tell them, but I don't feel right telling them to do this and not do that. I don't have that sort of experience and I feel, not shy, but out of place and embarrassed.'

They were very kind and agreed to that. I carried on with my other duties, advising the captain, telling him where I thought fielders should be placed and which bowler might be useful against which batsman.

Being captain could create difficulties and unfortunately it was in my role as captain that I had a major disagreement with Frank Worrell. It created a gulf between us for a while.

As captain I had my way most of the time but there was one incident in 1966 when I thought that Robin Bynoe should have gone to England. He was far and away the best opening batsman. This was where Frank and I ran into problems.

Frank was one of the selectors. I had sat with him and watched Bynoe score four or five 100s and we had both been hugely impressed with his technique and application. Joey Carew and Easton McMorris had made a few runs but nowhere near as many as Robin and, what's

Left Me as a wide-eyed teenager in 1955 and already a Test player

Right A little older, a little wiser, relaxing in Weymouth, Barbados

The thrill of my first Test wicket. Special because it was against England in 1954 and it was the barnacle himself, Trevor Bailey

Main picture Another record – this time in the First Test of the 1959–60 series against England when I shared a stand of 399 with Frank Worrell for the fourth wicket. Here I am setting off to complete my century

Inset from top: With my later much-lamented friend Collie Smith at the start of the West Indies tour of England at Eastbourne in April 1957; Later that same summer, going in to bat with the great Frank Worrell on the first day of the Fourth Test; I always enjoyed batting at Sabina Park in Kingston, Jamaica, but never more so than when I scored my world record 365 not out against Pakistan in the 1957–58 season

DAVID FRITH

With my film star fiancée, Anju in India

WILLIE ALLEYNE

Happy in the company of ladies at the Marine Hotel in Barbados

Above The best Test I played in.
The famous tied Test at the Gabba
in Brisbane in 1960 which set up an
unforgettable tour

Right Another day, another innings,
this one in Sydney, Australia, in the
1960–61 tour

DAVID FRITH

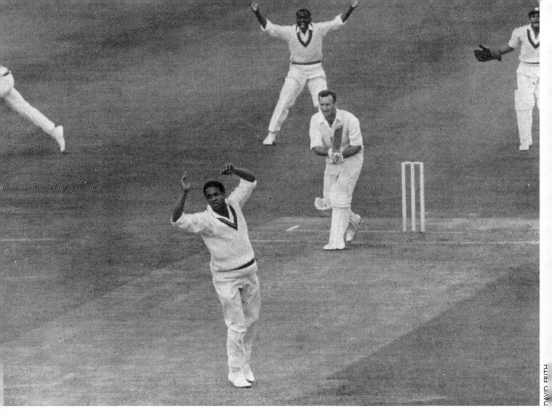

Sorry mate! I capture my friend Ted Dexter leg before in the Lord's Test in 1963

Taking a sharp one to dismiss Ken Barrington at The Oval on the same tour

DAVID FRITH

EMPICS

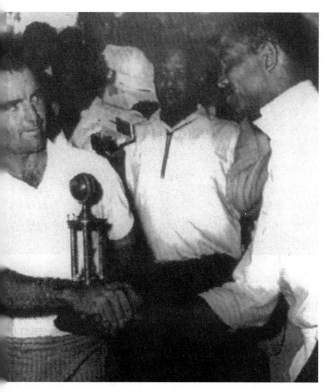

Above left Me and the Don in Australia. The late Don Bradman was a great supporter during my many visits to Australia

Above right Captaining the Rest of the World against England at Scarborough in 1965

Left Australian captain Bobby Simpson hands over the Frank Worrell Trophy for the first time at the end of the 1964–65 series

Overleaf Bowling against the Duke of Norfolk's XI at beautiful Arundel in the cold of April 1966

more, they had been to England on the previous tour in 1963 and had failed. In fact, they failed so miserably that we tried all sorts of partners with Conrad Hunte, even using Willie Rodriguez in the Fifth Test at The Oval.

Robin had been on two tours to India and had not done well on spinners' wickets; he was far more suited to the quick and moving ball. In other words, he was just right for England. I had a casual conversation with Frank and he gave me the impression that Bynoe was second only to Conrad in his personal opinion. All the other selectors I spoke to were under the firm impression that Frank would go for Robin.

When the end of the season came, we sat down in Trinidad to pick the squad. The selectors consisted of former captains John Goddard and Jeffrey Stollmeyer, who was chairman with the casting vote, Gerry Gomez, tour manager Berkeley Gaskin, Frank and me. We began the debate with the openers and I immediately volunteered Hunte, Bynoe and Carew as my three to travel. Goddard agreed with me and went to Frank who, to my great surprise, said no. He went for Hunte, Carew and McMorris. It took me aback and I couldn't believe what I was hearing. I asked Frank how both Carew and McMorris were in front of Bynoe. His reason was that they had been to England and would be experienced with the conditions. Berkeley Gaskin agreed with him, Jeffrey, being a Trinidadian, voted with him and suddenly Bynoe was out of the tour.

John Goddard and I were immediately up in arms. It was absurd to pick McMorris in front of Bynoe. I smelled a rat. There was something going down. I kept my mouth shut and waited to see what other surprise was lurking for me around that table. Sure enough, it was waiting in the shape of the promising young batsman Clive Lloyd. Gaskin voted yes for a youngster who had done well and clearly had a good future. But when it came to me, I dug in my toes and said no.

I said outright that I was not going for Clive Lloyd; I said that I preferred to go for Rawle Brancker. I backed it up by telling them to look at Brancker's record batting for Barbados. He had a better record than the young British Guyanese Lloyd who had only just begun at the top level. I told them to look at Brancker's bowling as a left-arm spinner and the wickets he had taken. An all-rounder of that quality had to take precedence over an inexperienced batsman. John Goddard agreed with me, as did Frank. Now Berkeley Gaskin was left out on a limb with no chance of getting his man in the side.

That is how political it was. It was disgraceful. But I had guessed what was going on. Frank was clever. He manoeuvred Gaskin on to his side but he knew that I was going to get one in somewhere. That's the way it was. Whether it's the same now I don't know, but it is not the way to select a squad because it means that the best players are not always picked.

It was not the only time I had a problem. I think that at the level of West Indies cricket, they probably thought I was getting too big for my boots. I would not stand a lot of nonsense and I would tell them what I thought, especially when they picked teams and left out players I knew should be going or picked others because of island politics. One of the biggest rows I had with the selectors was when we were preparing to go to Australia in 1968–69. They wanted to leave out Wes Hall. I told them straightaway that if they didn't pick Wes, I wouldn't be going either, and I meant it. They reckoned Wes was past his best but that was rubbish; he was still one of the best bowlers in the West Indies. They eventually conceded and picked him, but one of the selectors was told to tell him that they had picked him only because of pressure from the captain.

I had put them on the spot and that clearly hurt them. They probably held that in their minds and the first opportunity to have me out they used it. It wasn't as if I was always arguing about who should be in or out or threatening not to play. It was only when I felt that there was a real injustice that would harm West Indies cricket.

My commitment to the West Indies was always total whether I was captain or not. A bad stomach interrupted an innings once but I figured that my job was to be out there and it would take something special to take me away. I felt that my presence was always needed but

I would not say I was fit when I wasn't because I would not put the West Indies team in jeopardy. That was always it for me – West Indies first and Garry Sobers second. How many others, particularly those on the Board, can say that and really mean it?

CHAPTER EIGHT

Six of the best

I would have loved to go into county cricket before 1968 but I wasn't going to spend two years qualifying and not playing for my country. If that rule had not applied, I would have played county cricket much earlier. I loved cricket so much that I would have been happy to play every day instead of two or three times a week, but the rules stated that you had to stay in the country for two consecutive years. I was playing for Norton in the Staffordshire League when the rule was changed. Five or six county secretaries, including those from Lancashire, Gloucestershire, Leicestershire and Northamptonshire, had already come creeping round the back of the pavilion after games to tell me that the laws were going to alter the next season and that they would like me to play for them.

I went home to the West Indies to play in the 1968 series against England. We were playing at Kensington Oval when Bunty Ames, wife of Les Ames who was managing the MCC party, asked if I had seen the day's paper, which headlined the fact that I was going to join Nottinghamshire. After the day's play, I was sitting down at a cocktail party when I was asked what sort of position I could get Notts to in the County Championship, considering that they had run last for the past 16 seasons. I hadn't a clue but predicted that we could climb into the first four. Bunty turned to me in amazement and said, 'I know you're good but you're not that bloody good!' She bet me a couple of bottles of champagne that I couldn't get them into the top six and I answered that as I was not a big gambler I could accept that wager.

The move to county cricket came a little later in my career than I would have liked. I was 31 and had played 14 solid years of cricket around the world. The offer was a good one – £5,000 per season with accommodation, tickets home to Barbados and a car. Trent Bridge suited me nicely because whenever I had played there I had found it to be a true batting wicket, and to prove the point I had scored a couple of double centuries there for the West Indies.

I was appointed captain, taking over from Norman Hill and, it was said, much to the disappointment of Brian Bolus who apparently expected the job. If he did, he never showed it and he was a fine example to everyone at the club.

The season started extremely well and when we went to play Glamorgan at Swansea at the end of August, we were poised to finish fourth if we beat them. The Welsh side were well placed and if they beat us, they stood every chance of winning the championship. So the scene was set with everything to play for, not to mention my couple of bottles of champagne.

I went in when the score was about 300 for 5. I played a few overs, looked up at the scoreboard and realised that we needed a few quick runs to get Glamorgan in if we were to try to bowl them out for a victory. The wicket at St Helen's always aided the spinner on the last day. Bolus had propped up the innings with a big 100; with an hour to play I was on 40 and thought I should go for it. As a result, I became the first batsman in first-class cricket to hit six successive sixes in a six-ball over.

The unlucky bowler was Malcolm Nash, a 23-year-old Welshman who had opened the bowling with his medium-paced deliveries and was now bowling his left arm over the wicket spin. As he prepared to bowl, I remembered the two versions of how to go about the proposed assault. Everton Weekes used to tell me that if I kept the ball on the ground no one could catch me while Sir Learie Constantine preferred the alternative, saying if you hit it up in the air and out of the ground no one could catch it anyway. Obviously, if you want quick runs you have to make sure that you hit it over the boundary. There were no thoughts of six sixes at that stage, just runs, and I was not even bothered whether I was out or not. All I was interested in was quick runs and a declaration.

There was a fairly small boundary on the right-hand Gorse Lane side of the ground which, with Malcolm being a left-arm spinner who was not turning the ball a great deal, presented a perfect target. I tucked the first two over that short boundary without a problem. Malcolm bowled a little wider for the third one, which I put over wide mid-on. The fourth one I hit way over the bowler's head and into the stand.

It was only then that I even contemplated going for the six sixes. The crowd, although partisan Welsh, were caught up in the excitement and were chanting 'six, six, six'. I thought I should give it a go; there was nothing to lose.

The fifth ball was wide of the off stump and although I caught it well I didn't middle it and there was a fielder, Roger Davis, underneath it. He was furiously back-pedalling all the time and as he caught it everything went over the boundary. I started walking but the crowd shouted to me, 'You're not out, get back, get back.' This was the Welsh fans but they didn't want me to go; they were obviously enjoying themselves. The rules had recently been changed and I wasn't exactly sure where I stood. I stopped as umpires Eddie Phillipson and John Langridge converged and conferred. After a short while, up went both of Eddie's hands. The crowd hollered for murder and they and I began to think seriously about the possibility of being the first batsman in history to hit six sixes off an over in a first-class match.

Tony Lewis, the Glamorgan skipper, spread his fielders all round the boundary with a preponderance on the leg side. All sorts of things were going through my mind. A no-ball or a wide would spoil it and make it difficult because that would require a seventh ball while Malcolm would certainly not fancy becoming the first bowler to be on the wrong end of this particular record. I felt sure that he would try to deceive me; being a former fast bowler he would run up as if to bowl another off-break and then bowl a straight, faster ball.

Unfortunately for him, he obviously didn't realise that we were both thinking along the same lines, and he pitched his quicker ball a little short. I was seeing it as big as a football by this time and I had one eye on the ball and the other on that short boundary. Even if I had a top edge it would have gone for six but I caught it right in the middle of the bat and it not only cleared the short boundary but went over the stand as well, rolling down the hill towards Swansea town centre.

Wilf Wooller, who was called the Mayor of Glamorgan because of his great and long-lasting service to Glamorgan CCC, was commentating for the BBC. When I hit the first six he was supposed to hand back to the studio but he persuaded them to hold on and when I hit the third six he told them he wasn't going back at all whatever they said. That's how they managed to film the entire over for television. If it had not been recorded, it would not have had the same powerful effect, especially with the disputed catch that is shown quite clearly as the fielder goes over the line.

When I hit the sixth six, Wilf shouted, 'It's gone, it's gone, it's gone over the houses, over the buses, it's gone to the Guildhall, clean into Swansea.' A young boy found the ball, battered and torn, still rolling down the street and he dutifully returned it to Wilf the next day. It was mounted and sent to the Nottinghamshire County Cricket Museum.

I might have gone on for the quickest 100 but that wasn't in the script and I quickly declared at the end of the over. We bowled them out and went on to claim our fourth place and I duly collected my champagne from a delighted Bunty at a John Player League game at Kent on the following Sunday. I had played in all but two matches, bowled 773 overs, taken 83 wickets and scored a few runs.

The television waited for our comments until the end of the day's play and as Malcolm and I walked across the field from the dressing rooms towards the interview room together, out of the corner of my eye, I caught Malcolm smiling to himself. I asked him what he was smiling about.

'I want you to understand that I'm with you,' he replied. 'I don't mind that I'm at the wrong end, I'm in the record books with you.'

Malcolm has been regularly invited to sportsmen's nights to talk about the six sixes from his perspective. Unfortunately, we had no nights or dinners like that in the West Indies so Malcolm probably had the last laugh on me by making more money out of my record than I did! But when I see him now and tell him that he owes me some of that money, he just laughs.

I see him quite often when I go around North America talking about Barbados and tourism. He has done a wonderful job in California. Last time I saw him, he had just helped to stage the first international cricket match between the Under 13s of Canada and the United States. I went to watch in my capacity as one of the ICC's 26 international ambassadors. I was very impressed with what I saw. If they can introduce cricket into the schools in North America, it could take a toehold and begin to develop. Cricket is bigger than people think in the States although most of the teams have their origins in the ethnic communities – Indians, Pakistanis, West Indians, Australians and, of course, the British.

Ravi Shastri, the Indian all-rounder, equalled my record in Bombay in 1984 when he struck Tilak Raj for six successive sixes and went on to score a rapid fire 200.

I don't think I would enjoy it as much if I played these days in England because the wickets are now very much the same as they are in the rest of the world. There is little difference. I looked forward to going to play in England because it was going to be something unusual, a new challenge where I could tighten up and develop my technique. You had to watch the ball closely before you could play your shots. Today it is not the same.

I remember at Notts when we played against the Buss boys of

Sussex, and Thompson and John Snow and those fellows. It didn't matter who bowled, they were all good because they knew how to use the conditions and if you were going to make runs you had to bat well. With the wickets so green it helped the bowlers much more. Even an ordinary bowler could be hard to play; that showed when they travelled away to wickets that weren't so helpful.

I went back to Hove as manager with Barbados village side Holders Hill seven or eight years ago and the same groundsman was still working for Sussex. I asked him what was wrong with the wickets. They were not the same as those I remembered so well. He replied that if the ball moved sideways he was reported and the county could even be fined points. It was such a big change.

When you made runs on those wickets you could come off at the end of a day's play and say to yourself that you had batted well. Back home in the West Indies, the ball came through and if you concentrated, run making was so much easier. There was occasionally a bit of swing, and maybe a little spin, but you didn't get the real seamer's wicket.

During the tours in 1957, 1963 and 1966 bowlers such as Bob Woolmer, John Shepherd and Ken Higgs were a joy to play against; the wickets began to change by 1973. They were bowlers who tested your mind, made you play cricket, made you bat, because you knew something was always going to happen. It wasn't just a straightforward matter of playing your shots. But, as good as they were in England, to select that type of bowler for the West Indies would be a disaster, someone like Bob Woolmer would have been a waste of time, or even Higgs. That's why Alec Bedser never came to the West Indies, so I was told. The wickets were too good. The Australian wickets were similar to ours but gave a bowler like him a bit more assistance.

Trevor Bailey bowled well in Jamaica because he could bowl seam up and the Jamaica wicket always offered the bowler something. Trevor was a good bowler. Whenever we went to Essex, Trevor and Barry Knight were always tough to play against but I enjoyed it because if you could play against those fellows and make runs on their wickets you knew you were an accomplished player.

It was said in those days that you wouldn't be recognised as a truly great batsman until you scored runs in England. I always wondered why until I played there. Rohan Kanhai was a great player who played a lot of his career in England but in Test matches there he scored just one century and that was in his last Test match at Lord's in 1977 – and he was rated one of the tops.

He was often described as unorthodox. It is a word that I feel is often abused in cricket. There is a big difference between good players and great players. Great players may look unorthodox to the good player because they are able to improvise, therefore the great player can do what the good player cannot do.

The good player relies on bad balls while the great player takes good balls and turns them into bad balls. He looks for gaps in the field and gets the ball through there without any trouble. To lesser mortals it looks unorthodox but to the great player it is normal. You can only direct the terms orthodox and unorthodox at certain levels of players.

CHAPTER NINE

Troubled waters

All of my five series in England were significant in one way or another. The first was important because it fulfilled a dream; the second because it was under the captaincy of Sir Frank Worrell; in 1966, it was my first overseas tour as captain. It was such a magnificent tour for me both as a player and a captain. It was a job well done although we lost that last Test, but I knew the time had come for the introduction of some new blood before we started to get stale.

The 1969 tour had its problems for us. I would have liked some of the players I recommended to have been selected but I am not saying that was the reason we lost. We tried our best and were beaten fair and square. Ray Illingworth was a good captain for England and their team played well.

We were badly beaten in the First Test at Old Trafford. Geoff Boycott gave England the foundation they needed with a patient 128 in a total of 413; then John Snow and David Brown bowled us out for 147 and we were forced to follow on. We all had starts at the top of the order but were bowled out, leaving England needing just a handful of runs in the second innings.

It was a much tighter match at Lord's with England seven wickets down and still needing 37 runs to win and in that last session the result could have gone either way. I was forced off the field with a thigh strain when England were 241 for 6 but I managed to score 50 in the second innings with Steve Camacho acting as a runner – only the second time in my career I required a substitute. In England's second innings I limped through 29 overs.

But England clinched the series at Leeds in the Third and final Test, winning by just 30 runs. I took seven wickets in the match but was bowled by Barry Knight for a duck in the second innings when any sort of knock from me would have won us the match.

It was that sort of tour. I averaged 30 and took just 11 wickets. I was tired. We were without Rohan Kanhai, Seymour Nurse, Conrad Hunte, Wes Hall and Charlie Griffith and, all told, there were 11 newcomers to English conditions in a party of 16.

Between the 1969 and 1973 tours of England, I gave up the captaincy. They had to find a new captain for the Aussies' 1972–73 trip to the Caribbean and Cecil Marley, who was president of the West Indies Cricket Board, came over to England where I was playing county cricket for Nottinghamshire to ask me whom I would recommend as my successor. I opted initially for David Holford. I thought he was a superior captain, better than I was. He was a good leader, very intelligent and he captained Barbados for many years when they were champions of the Shell Shield more often than any other island. One of the difficulties was that he was not in the West Indies side at the time but it was clear to me that he was still worth his place. I told Cecil that I thought he had been the best captain in the West Indies for a long time, but I didn't think he would be accepted as my nomination because he was my relative.

I offered Clive Lloyd as an alternative choice, but Clive had not even been invited to join the squad for preparation for the series. So if they weren't prepared to pick him, my third choice would be Rohan

Kanhai. Rohan had done a lot for West Indies cricket, he was a senior player and it would be a wise idea to give him the opportunity. He had the knowledge and I thought he could do a good job.

Cecil asked me about my own availability but I had just had a serious operation on my knee and I had to wait to see how it recovered. I told him I couldn't accept the offer from the Board to pay for my air ticket home because of the doubts over my fitness. I said that I would pay the airfare myself and if, during the series, I felt fit enough, if I wanted to play and if the Board were willing to pick me, then they could reimburse me my fare. Cecil said that was a nice and honest gesture; others might have taken advantage of the situation for a free ride home. He went away happy with the situation, he and the Board accepting my recommendation to appoint Rohan Kanhai as captain.

While I did not feel that I was any better than anyone else, I had just come from Australia where I had played against their main strike bowler, Dennis Lillee. I knew what type of bowler he was and I also knew that on our quick wickets in the West Indies, Dennis would wreak havoc and we needed someone who would stand up to him. He had run into me and he had some idea of what I could do. It was a great incentive for me to regain my fitness, and I worked desperately hard to be in shape in time for the series.

I went to the Board after the First Test, in which Dennis broke down with a back injury, and told them how I was coming along. I was much better but still not fit enough for a five-day Test match. I told them I would play for Barbados against Trinidad in the Shell Shield.

I opened the bowling, took a couple of wickets and scored 20 or 30 runs. I felt I had done enough to satisfy myself of my fitness and chose not to open the bowling in the second innings. Keith Boyce was playing and I suggested to David Holford that he should open with him and give the selectors a chance to look at him. I didn't think for a moment that I was playing for my place in the West Indies team. David was all for the idea. I eventually came on and bowled a few overs and the game came to its conclusion. I was quite happy. I had taken some wickets and scored some runs and while the knee was a little bit swollen, that was not unexpected and I felt fairly fit.

In the dressing room, former captain and now selector Jeffrey Stollmeyer approached me and asked if I was going to play for Barbados against Australia. I told him I thought it was better for the youngsters to play for the experience and to see what potential they had for the future. Who needed to look at Garry Sobers? Everyone knew what I did. The only question was my fitness and I felt good. Then Jeffrey shocked me by telling me that if I didn't play against the Aussies in Bridgetown, I would not be picked for the next Test match. I couldn't believe it.

'If that's the way it is, then that's the way it is,' I said, disdainfully. 'You can say whatever the hell you like, do what you like because I won't be playing.'

I was having a drink in the pavilion at the Kensington Oval when Clyde Walcott came over to me and inquired if I was going to play in a two-day game in St Vincent. I looked at him in amazement and asked him what for. He answered that they wanted to check my fitness. I was furious then, and told him that he and Stollmeyer could go and jump in the Caribbean. There was no way I was going to play in a two-day game.

'If this is what it comes to, I'm staggered,' I told Clyde. 'I remember when you persuaded me to play with a broken finger because you told me that I was a better player on one leg than the rest were on two. And now all of a sudden, I'm telling you I'm fit and you're telling me you don't believe me. Just remember all the times when it was insisted that I played whatever my injuries were and however I felt.'

I told them exactly what they could do in my own broad, Caribbean language. Roughly translated it was, 'I won't be going.'

The upshot was that they didn't pick me and they lost the series. When the Australians were leaving, their captain Ian Chappell rubbed salt in the wound when he said to the media, 'We may have beaten the West Indies but I don't believe we have achieved much because we came to play against Garry Sobers.' The West Indian people were already unhappy at the result and this was a remark to ignite the powder keg of emotion.

When the team to go to England for the three-match series was being selected shortly after that, I was asked if I was available to travel with the party. I told them no, but I added that if they thought I was fit enough and I thought I was playing well enough for Nottinghamshire, I would be available for the Test matches only. My other consideration in this instance was that Notts had given me a reasonably good contract and I had played just one full season. In 1969, I played half a season because West Indies were in England, and in 1970 I was made to play against England for the Rest of the World. I had told them I wanted to honour my contract with the English county but they told me if I didn't travel with the Rest of the World team, I would not be allowed to play for Notts during any of the Test matches. They completely ignored the fact that I was a professional under contract. When I told Notts what had been said, they suggested that I might just as well go and play as sit watching cricket at Trent Bridge. I went and missed much of the season because I was asked to captain the Rest of the World. So in 1973, I thought it wouldn't be fair to let Notts down again.

For some reason I didn't have a very good season and I really didn't expect the West Indies to pick me. I was pleased in that respect but disappointed that I wasn't doing as well for Notts as I wanted. It was a Catch 22 situation.

Esmond Kentish, manager of the West Indies team, eventually telephoned to ask me if I wanted to play in the Test matches. I replied, 'I might not in your eyes be a brilliant man but what kind of question is that? I told the Board that I would be available if the selectors wanted me. If they think I'm good enough and they want me to play and they pick me, then I will play. But don't ask me if I want to play.'

This was pure politics. A lot of things happened after they lost the series to Australia. The West Indian public were mad at them and they were blaming it on the selectors, and particularly Clyde Walcott, for not selecting me. Clyde was taking the brunt of the criticism in the media and from the public.

I was picked and I did well. We were not fancied at all but we got off to a flyer at The Oval thanks to an excellent century from Clive Lloyd, 80 from Alvin Kallicharran and a hard-struck 72 from all-rounder Keith Boyce batting at number nine. I was run out for 10 but I felt good, fit and rested and took 3 for 27 in 22.1 overs. Boyce, the Essex man, followed up his big hitting with five wickets. I scored a fifty in the second innings and Boyce took us to victory with 6 for 77 as England fell 158 runs short of their target. We had surprised everybody.

We held on to our lead with a draw in Birmingham where I bowled 30 overs and took 3 for 62 in England's first innings and scored 74 in our second innings.

Lord's, as ever, provided a fitting climax as we won the Test and the series and, at 37, I played my part in my last international at headquarters. Boyce took eight wickets to cap a fine tour for him. My 150 not out was part of a massive 652 for 8 after which we proceeded to sweep England aside for 233 and 193. I didn't take a wicket but I played my part with six catches and I finished the tour with a very respectable batting average of 76.5.

I was glad I played. We won the series and I was as fit as ever, going back to play county cricket for Notts between the Test matches. It was not so good for Clyde Walcott when he returned home. The question on everyone's lips was that if I was this fit and able now, how was it I was unfit to play a few months earlier against Australia? The team doctor came out and said that I would have been fit enough. It all backfired and Clyde found himself in even hotter water than before with the people in Barbados. It was so bad that his son had problems at school. Clyde could not even go into hotels without being abused, and social life in the Caribbean revolves very much around the hotel scene. After a while, his brother Keith called me.

'I know you don't hold grudges or bear anyone any malice . . .' he began, but I stopped him.

'Keith, who you talking about, man? I don't hold anyone in mind. I tell them what I have to tell them and then I'm done with that.'

'Well, there have been a lot of problems since you left. Clyde cannot even go into hotels because people are telling him they're going to do this and do that to him, his children are being booed at school and everything is very unpleasant.

'We are playing a match at Kensington and Clyde is due to make the presentation and I would appreciate it if you could be there with him and mix with him. Show the people that you have no malice, because I know you.'

'Keith,' I said, 'that's something I don't have to pretend to do or put on, you don't have to tell me that. I have never held Clyde in mind for anything. I just speak my mind like everyone else and then it's forgotten. I didn't know that these things were going to happen to him and his family. Of course I'll do it.'

I had a prize to come and Clyde presented it to me. I said a few words, telling the crowd that I had no grudge against him, that he had done what he did because he thought that it was right and that we were as good friends as ever. I had nothing against him. I was speaking the truth, not just trying to pour oil on troubled waters. I really and truly had nothing against him. Happily, the storm blew over and things settled down for us both.

CHAPTER TEN

Boring England

The arrival of the England cricket team was always eagerly anticipated in the West Indies but the tours were often boring because the wickets were so good that it was difficult to get a result. If you look at the early tours you will find that, apart from 1954, most of the series were drawn or decided by one Test.

In that 1954 series against Len Hutton's men, we won the First Test in Kingston by 140 runs, and the Second in Bridgetown by 181 runs. England fought back to win in Georgetown by nine wickets, we drew comfortably in Trinidad and England pulled back to 2–2 in the final Test in Jamaica which they won by nine wickets. That was my first match for the West Indies.

Once you are two up in the West Indies it's not easy for the opposition to recover, especially when the third game is in Guyana where the wickets are so good that it's always difficult to reach a conclusion. But England had a strong side and brought through a number of youngsters in that series including Peter May and Ted Dexter. Freddie Trueman, Brian Statham, Jim Laker, Tony Lock,

Trevor Bailey, Godfrey Evans, Johnny Wardle, Tom Graveney and Denis Compton were there too. It was a very well-balanced side, a better one than toured in 1948 under first Ken Cranston and then Gubby Allen when the first two Tests were drawn and the West Indies won the last two. I was a good listener in those days. I spent my time either clamped to the radio or running around the Bay Pasture in short pants. I didn't go to the Kensington Oval to watch because I would always rather play than watch.

In 1960 there were four draws and England won the series by virtue of one victory at the Queen's Park Oval in Port-of-Spain. England arrived in the Caribbean on the back of a 4–0 Ashes defeat by Australia. They reacted by dropping Jim Laker and Tony Lock, replacing them with David Allen and Ray Illingworth, both off-spinners, supplemented by the leg spin of Tommy Greenhough. Peter May remained as captain but Tom Graveney was strangely dropped.

As for the West Indies, Gerry Alexander had told the selectors that it was time for Frank Worrell to take over the captaincy but the Board disagreed and pressed him to remain in charge. Jamaican opener Easton McMorris was to partner Conrad Hunte while another Jamaican, Chester Watson, was to open the bowling with Wes Hall.

Barbados, under Everton Weekes' captaincy, beat England in the opening match of the tour. Seymour Nurse announced his arrival with a double hundred, I added 154, and with Charlie Griffith bowling at whirlwind pace we beat the tourists by 10 wickets. However, for the First Test at the Oval it was different; Ken Barrington and Ted Dexter both made good centuries in a total of 482. Our start could not have been worse when we lost three relatively early wickets. Easton McMorris was run out off a no-ball for a duck, followed by Conrad Hunte and Rohan Kanhai with the score at 102. That brought me in at 4.50 on the Friday, soon to be joined by Frank Worrell. When Fred Trueman bowled me for 226 ten and a half hours later, at 11.40 on the Tuesday, we had added 399, a record against England. Worrell closed the door on England by scoring 197 not out and we declared when 81 runs in front with only a couple of hours remaining.

What goes into making an innings like that? We were officially staying in the Marine Hotel but we were living at home. At close of play Frank would go home, have dinner and then come back to the hotel. We would go to friends' homes with Frank and his family. If Frank and I had gone out separately, we would wait for each other to come in, even if it was three o'clock in the morning, and then we would have a drink if the bar was still open. Often it would be half past four or five before we would go and rest rather than sleep.

When Frank joined me in the middle, he said that the two of us had to score a lot of runs. He told me to put my head down and not do anything silly. We batted until stumps and then for all of the next day. I was eventually out but Frank batted a little bit longer. Gerry Alexander let him bat on for his 200 but for 20 minutes Frank couldn't score his final three runs and eventually the innings was declared closed.

There were those in the West Indies who said that Frank didn't want Alexander to win and so he batted on and on, using up time and not giving him the chance to declare. It was thought that Frank wanted the captaincy and if we had won that match and the series, Alexander would have stayed on. It simply wasn't true. I spoke to Frank about that match many times and he told me he was so tired that if Gerry had let him bat for another hour he wouldn't have scored the three he needed.

Inevitably, that Test was drawn but there was disaster for us in the next one in Port-of-Spain. Trueman and Brian Statham tore the heart out of us in our first innings, a day marred by a near riot when local man Charran Singh was controversially run out to make the score 98 for 8. The crowd went mad and the English team had to be escorted off the pitch when the police replied to the rioting supporters with tear gas. We were all out for 112 but May batted instead of forcing us to follow on, and left us an impossible target – 501 to win in 10 hours. Rohan Kanhai batted for six of those hours, scoring 110, but we were all out for 244, losing comfortably, with Ken Barrington and Ted Dexter, of all people, taking a couple of wickets each.

We should have pulled the deficit back in Jamaica. This was my return to Sabina Park after the death of my friend Collie Smith and I scored an emotional 147, helping West Indies to a first innings lead of 76. England were bowled out for 305, leaving us 230 to win; we fancied our chances strongly. Then I was run out for 19 while batting with Kanhai and the innings threatened to collapse against the bowling of Trueman. We stopped the chase 15 minutes from the close of play with 55 runs still required and four wickets remaining.

There was no way England were going to throw away their lead and the Fourth Test in Georgetown was a tedious affair. Peter May had returned home injured and Colin Cowdrey assumed control in his absence. England won the toss for the fourth time and, in the face of some hostile bowling from Wes Hall, who took six wickets, crawled to 295 all out and then bowled and fielded defensively as we scored 402 for 8 declared with 145 coming from my bat. We never had a second innings as England batted out the match with 334 for 8.

It was all down to Port-of-Spain for the Fifth and final Test and, incredibly, Cowdrey won the toss again. I missed out on my fourth century of the series by just eight runs when we replied to England's slow 393. They left us a final target of 406 to level the series and we finished frustratingly short.

It was a slow and boring series brightened from England's point of view by the batting of Dexter and the bowling of Trueman while for us Gerry Alexander equalled a world record by taking five catches in an innings. The only satisfaction I derived from it was that my 709 runs broke George Headley's record against a visiting English team at an average of 101.28. I would have swapped the records for a series victory.

England were still smarting from our comprehensive victory against them the previous year when they arrived in the Caribbean in December 1967. But for the controversial defeat in Trinidad when my declaration was blamed, it would have been another boring series. All the other four Tests were drawn.

If the cricket had been organised then as it is today, and the rules were similar, I am sure there would have been different results. Nowadays you cannot laze around and indulge in slow tactics because you know you have to bowl 90 overs in a day. I wish it had always been like that.

In the 1967–68 series it was rare for more than 60 or 70 overs to be bowled in a day and there was a lot of time wasting. It was not conducive to good cricket or to the entertainment of the paying public. I believe that the spectators always have to be considered. Without those people paying to come through the turnstiles there is no professional game. That can be forgotten if players are afraid to lose and are not prepared to give the opposition a chance. Somewhere along the line you have to recognise that defeat might be a possibility. I have always played the game with that in mind and although you want to win, you must keep the game interesting so that the public will come to watch. Who wants to watch a dying game when the only result is a draw? In the modern game there is more often than not a result and that can only be good for the game and its future.

That series was not played in the spirit in which I expected it to be played. I always thought cricket should be a game with people challenging each other, not looking to see how you can draw. I always tried to win and only if that option failed would I try not to lose. It seemed to me that England captain Colin Cowdrey looked for a draw first and a win second. That attitude makes the game boring and the series was very, very dull. It probably forced me as a captain to try to inject something into the cricket, to see what I could do to resurrect the way it was going. By the time we reached Trinidad there had been three insipid Test matches and I saw an opportunity to open up the series, to bring some interest into it and try to break the stalemate. Taking into account the wickets, the bowlers we had and the way England had played throughout, the ingredients were all there. There did not seem to be any likelihood of them coming out and playing in the way they would need to win. For me, it was worth taking the risk; it was calculated.

England had shown little or no ambition in the first three Tests, although they might have won the First when Wes Hall and I had to put up the shutters for the last 90 minutes after being made to follow on. It gave England the psychological edge for the Second Test in Jamaica and again they had the good fortune of winning the toss and batting first with a Cowdrey century easing them to a total of 376 on a cracked wicket which was very unpredictable. John Snow took full advantage, including bowling me with one which never left the ground, and once again we found ourselves following on. We were still trailing when Basil Butcher was given out by West Indian umpire Sang Hue. It was to a diving catch by wicket-keeper Jim Parks down the leg side off Basil D'Oliveira and it provoked a riot that spluttered on for 75 minutes.

I was on a king pair after my first-innings duck and almost achieved it when the first ball reared nastily. I was also dropped by D'Oliveira when on seven but then I put my head down and on that difficult track scored 113 not out before declaring with a lead of 158 with half an hour plus the lost 75 minutes remaining. I took the new ball and sent back Geoff Boycott and Cowdrey before there was a run on the board. Hall had John Edrich bowled and Charlie Griffith removed Ken Barrington, so when play closed, England were gasping at 19 for 4 with the 75 minutes to be played on the sixth day.

Impossible? We didn't think so. Lance Gibbs stepped in with the wickets of Tom Graveney, Jim Parks and Fred Titmus. I bowled David Brown but we just ran out of time, having put down the not-out d'Oliveira twice. No one complained about my declaration then or about how it had almost brought an unexpected result to an otherwise dead match.

After the defeat in Port-of-Spain, we went to Guyana and almost pulled it back. There was one crucial decision that went against us. I won the toss and we ran up a total of 414, giving us a chance of victory. I scored 152 and Rohan Kanhai scored 150. I took the new ball myself and bowled 37 overs, 15 of them maidens, taking three wickets at under two an over. England were slow in reaching a score 43 short of ours and we had to hurry the scoring along in the second innings. It meant taking chances and we were out for 264 with me five short of another century when, for a change, I ran out of partners. That left England 308 to win. Lance Gibbs bowled brilliantly to take six wickets, I took three and England were struggling desperately at 206 for 9 with wicket-keeper Alan Knott on 73 not out when time ran out.

I was blamed for losing that series yet I made two centuries, scored a total of 545 runs for an average of over 90 and took 13 wickets. In that last match alone I scored 247 for once out and bowled 68 overs, 31 maidens, and took six wickets for 125.

If we had won that last match I suppose I would still have been considered a great captain, and we would have won it but for the time wasting. I remember Cowdrey saying that something was wrong with his pads, going off, bringing his new pads on to the ground and putting them on. That wasted many minutes. I asked myself why this should happen when you are playing a game. It is not our lives at stake and it should be played in the right spirit, winning if you are good enough and losing if not. I said nothing because I did not like to get involved in that type of controversy. It was surprising that Colin of all people should do something like that but it showed how important it was for the English sides not to lose, so important that they were prepared to sacrifice their principles.

It was never built in me to go out there and do something that is contrary to the game like wasting time. I found that very difficult. The spinners were bowling 12 overs an hour and yet over the years others have complained about our fast bowlers bowling 12 or 13 an hour. The difference was that we were beating teams in three and three and a half days, not looking for draws.

Tony Lock and the other slow bowlers were taking up to five minutes to bowl a single over and nothing was said to them. Today that couldn't happen because regardless of how long it took them they would still have to bowl their 90 overs. It is a wonderful rule.

Another rule that has helped is the danger of being given out leg before wicket when playing with the pads and not offering a stroke. It should have come in a long time ago. It happened a lot at Edgbaston in 1957 when the English batsmen put the bat behind the pad, pushing the pad out as though it was the first line of defence instead of the bat. That was spoiling the game, particularly if you were an inswing bowler. The umpires could do nothing about it. These are things that have changed the game for the good in modern cricket.

Despite being more than a little upset at my treatment by the West Indies Board in 1972 when the team to face the Australians was being selected, I was keen to play in the 1973–74 series under Rohan Kanhai in his final series as skipper. I had recommended him and played under him in England, and I wanted to show him my continuing support. Also, I was coming to the end of my international career and I wanted to play and say my farewell to Test cricket in Jamaica and, of course, Barbados. Had the tour been anywhere else but the West Indies, I doubt very much whether I would have played at all.

It wasn't a very pleasant series as far as I was concerned because of my own performances with just one 50 and 13 wickets in the four Tests in which I played. Five of those wickets came in the First Test at Port-of-Spain where we bowled England out for just 131 in their first innings. Despite an opening stand of 209 in the second by Dennis Amiss (174) and Geoff Boycott (93), we won with something to spare.

It was a Test that had its own problems. Alvin Kallicharran was 142 not out in the evening of the second day when he played the last ball to mid-off Tony Greig who was fielding very short. The tall South African-born all-rounder ran after the ball with his back to the wicket and when he turned and saw Alvin out of his wicket he threw down the stumps. Greig appealed and the umpire gave Alvin out. It was all very controversial because Alvin was taking off his gloves and heading for the pavilion, convinced in his own mind that play was over for the day. Tony didn't know what was going on behind his back and the umpire had to give the decision of out because the ball was not dead. Alvin had only himself to blame for this unusual dismissal because he should have waited until the ball was dead.

The local Trinidadians were very angry and there were threats against Tony because they thought he was being dirty and unfair. A crowd gathered outside the dressing rooms; calypso singer Mighty Sparrow was there, telling everyone what he was going to do to Tony when he came out, and it had nothing to do with singing. Tony, a brave man on the field, was very frightened but I knew the Mighty Sparrow well – he was one of my best friends – so I told Tony to come out with me and he wouldn't be hurt. I steered him through the crowd, we talked to Sparrow and all was fine. Tony was very grateful and we have remained friends ever since.

Tony allowed Alvin to come out and bat the next day and he went on to complete his 150. In fact, he scored 158 out of a total of 392 and set up our victory. Alvin was a good player but I still do not think he should have batted again. It was his own fault and the decision should not have been reversed. I wasn't captain so there was nothing I could do about it.

Another big innings by the Warwickshire opener Amiss, this time 262 not out, in the Second Test at Sabina Park ensured a high-scoring if dull draw. My contribution was 57, caught by Bob Willis off Tony Greig.

England held us off again in Barbados thanks mainly to a gritty innings of 148 from Tony Greig while Lawrence Rowe celebrated his first Test century by going on to score a glorious 302. I bowled a lot but scored a duck, this time caught by Greig, bowled by Willis. You would have thought that having saved his hide in the previous Test, Tony might have been a little more grateful than to have a hand in both my dismissals!

I missed the rain-affected Fourth Test draw at Bourda in Guyana but returned for the final Test back at Port-of-Spain where England levelled the series with a narrow victory. I was disappointed to throw away my wicket. I went to play a full toss from Derek Underwood through midwicket, played all around it and was bowled for 20 when I was feeling good. Alvin was out for nought in both innings and we lost by a meagre 26 runs.

One of the key factors in the English victory was, again, the performance of Greig. Set a target of only 226, Greig bowled like a tiger to take five wickets. In Barbados, he scored 148 and took six wickets in our one innings; he scored 121 in the rained-out Fourth Test in Georgetown; and he took a total of 13 wickets in that final match in Trinidad.

Tony Greig was to become a very hard captain. He gave away nothing and expected nothing in return and he was the same way as a player. I captained him in the Rest of the World matches in Australia in 1972 and found that he was a man you liked to have in your team. When the chips were down, you could give him the ball and more often than not he would pull something out. He was always there and always believed that he could win. He was a great inspiration in that Rest of the World team so I can imagine what a powerful influence he was on England.

If ever you made mistakes in opposition, you could be sure that he would capitalise on it. If he saw a way, he would be in there. He was a very good cricketer and, as far as I was concerned, a bit underrated. He wasn't a top-class bowler but he could bowl off-spinners and he could bowl medium-paced stuff. His attitude helped him along because he was always at you and never gave you a break. When he was captain, he handled his team well and got the best out of the players, and even though Mike Denness was leading the MCC on this tour, Greig was a towering influence and established himself as favourite to take over from the Scot. It was a good series, a fighting series.

Greig had a strong personality and a lot of people didn't like him, especially after his involvement with Kerry Packer. I know that a lot of our players didn't like his attitude, including Rohan Kanhai. Every time Rohan led out the side, they reckoned Tony couldn't bowl a hoop downhill. That was part of our problem because some of our team refused to rate him even when he kept taking wickets. Everyone was trying to hit him over the top or blast him out of the field and he just kept getting them out.

It was a disappointing way for me to finish my Test career but I was almost 38 years of age and all that bowling and batting was beginning to take a toll on my body. It was fitting that my last game should be against England, a country that dominated my cricket career home and away.

CHAPTER ELEVEN

The Don down under

Australia matured me. It turned me into a hardened competitor because the cricket was tough at whatever level you played. In Australia, the players have always had to be strong mentally as well as physically. The competition in the Sheffield Shield was the best in the world at that level, with four or five Test players in every state side. It was different in England where the county game was not that fierce or competitive because they did not have the same sort of club system from which to select their teams.

In my time, Yorkshire in England, New South Wales in Australia and my native Barbados in the Caribbean were the three strongest teams outside the Test arena, bristling with world-class players. What a shame those three sides could never come together to play out a tournament; it would have provided true top-class cricket.

I believe I am in a good position to compare the two countries because I played a lot of my cricket and also lived a large portion of my life down under. Apart from the Test matches, I played for South Australia and captained the Rest of the World in the series against

Australia in 1971–72. I also played at grade level. To cap it all, I married an Australian girl, Pru, and for a while after my retirement made my home there. I was always made very welcome.

I was hugely influenced by my first-ever trip to Australia in 1960–61. Five years after playing against the Aussies in the Caribbean, I at last took the long boat trip from London for what is still my most memorable ever tour, starting with that incredible tied Test at Brisbane.

All the team members who were earning their living playing in the various English leagues, including me, embarked in Southampton, joining those who came direct from the Caribbean. The boat was very nice, well equipped, and it took almost two weeks to make the journey. It was a pleasant trip but no holiday cruise. Manny Alves, our physiotherapist and trainer, and our captain Frank Worrell were keen for us to arrive fit and did not want us to laze around doing nothing. We would be up early every morning, run around the decks, play a bit of deck cricket . . . and then go back to bed! We would get up for the second time in time to enjoy the food, the entertainment and the drink. Ernest Eytle, who worked for the BBC and was an accomplished pianist, would play for us and we would dance and sing. Sometimes we never quite managed to get back to bed before the training started the next morning.

We were fit and in a good frame of mind when we arrived, but there was no doubt that we were rusty. We started off poorly, being beaten by a couple of state teams and an Australian XI, and there was some disquiet in Australia that it was going to be a one-sided series. But we were planning for the Test matches and getting used to the wickets, which were quicker and bouncier than in the Caribbean. We also had to get used to the tough cricket; even the smaller sides played to win. In Western Australia in the opening game, Tony Mann, who was only 14 years of age at the time, bowled leg-breaks at us. From that match alone you could see how the tour was going to go. That Western Australia team was rated third class but they put up a good show and gave us an insight into what we could expect against the higher graded teams. Bobby Simpson took 221 off us and although I managed a century in our second innings, it was not enough to save us from defeat.

In the next tour match, Rohan Kanhai scored a chanceless 252 to help us beat Victoria by an innings but we were quickly brought back down to earth by New South Wales who won by a similar margin. Richie Benaud bowled us out and I bagged a duck and a low score in the second innings. That started rumours that I couldn't pick Richie. The West Indies were looking to Worrell, Rohan Kanhai, Conrad Hunte and me as the backbone of the batting but in the end it was wicket-keeper Gerry Alexander, who had never shown that sort of form before, who played magnificently and top scored. He made 50 or 100 in almost every innings.

Everyone was disappointed that we weren't doing well. I was sitting in the dressing room watching the game against New South Wales, looking a little gloomy and sad, when Sir Donald came up with Frank who introduced him to me. The Don put his hand on my shoulder and said, 'Don't worry, sonny. You'll get them at the right time.'

'I'm not really worried,' I replied. 'I'm just concentrating on the game.'

That was the sum total of our conversation. He moved on to meet someone else.

I am told that before the tour, Sir Donald gathered Richie and others together for a meeting and they decided that they wanted a good series without draws and without boring cricket. Frank told our players the same thing. If we received a half-volley, he expected to see us hit it and not push it back down the pitch, whatever the state of the game. From that point of view, the series was made.

Nevertheless, we looked more than a little fragile as we approached the First Test at the Gabba, and although Frank won the toss and batted on what looked like a good track, we were soon three wickets down. Alan Davidson took out Conrad Hunte, Cammie Smith and Rohan Kanhai. My form had not been particularly good since that early century in Perth but now our backs were to the wall as Frank joined me in the middle.

Everything went beautifully and we put on 174. I went on to score 132. Richie came on to bowl to me early, having taken my wicket twice in the state game, and I watched him carefully. When he bowled me a googly and I started to go forward, Richie put his hands in the air thinking he had me, but I changed my mind at the last moment and hit it back past him like a bullet. Before he could get his hand down, the ball had hit the fence. He stood up and applauded.

Alan Davidson always talks about that innings, claiming that he had never seen anyone hit the ball so hard. He said that he remembered bowling at me with Colin McDonald at deepish mid-off. When I hit the ball it hit his hand and by the time he looked round, the ball was back by his feet off the boundary boards.

Many people who saw it describe it as one of the better innings of my career. Frank went one better and thought it was the best he had ever seen, as did Sir Donald Bradman. He came straight up to me afterwards and said, 'You know, I told you you would get them at the right time and you didn't disappoint me. It was a pity you couldn't read Richie. If you had, I don't know what you would have done to us.'

We scored quickly, too, and by the end of the first day we had amassed 359 for 7, which compared more than favourably with the 106 England had scored on the same ground exactly two years earlier in their fourth day's play.

Apart from putting us in a strong position, our aggressive, attacking attitude immediately endeared us to the Australian public, something that was to stay with us for the remainder of the tour and help make the trip what it was.

We eventually reached 453 with Wes Hall contributing a well-struck 50 but Australia turned not a hair. Led by Norman O'Neill's 181, during which he took advantage of four dropped catches, Australia totalled 505 and already the game looked as though it was shaping up for a draw. But what a draw! None of us imagined the dramas that were about to unfold.

The spirit was growing in our dressing room and when the second innings began with us trailing by 52, there was a light moment that relieved the pressure when it could quite easily have been demoralising. Alan Davidson was bowling to Cammie Smith with just one outfielder, Norman O'Neill, who stood in glorious isolation. Alan bowled Cammie a juicy half-volley outside the off stump and Cammie drove the ball straight down Norm's throat. The situation looked bad – we were 13 for 1. But Cammie came in laughing as he walked through the dressing-room door. He always laughed in the most difficult situations and could always see the funny side but this hardly seemed the moment and someone said sharply to him, 'What have you got to laugh about, Cammie? You out and you come in laughing.'

'That's exactly why I'm laughing, man,' Cammie replied. 'I get a half-volley and hit it straight to the only man in the covers.'

Davidson bowled me for 14 and it took Rohan Kanhai's half century and another fine knock from Frank Worrell, matching his 65 from his first innings, plus Wes Hall's 18 to add to his first innings 50, to leave Australia 233 to win. It was not a huge task but at least it gave us something to bowl at, although there weren't many outside our dressing room who gave us a chance.

But there were more twists and turns to come as the game developed into a wonderful, exciting Test match. At one stage, we had it in our grasp. Wes Hall bowled a sustained, hostile spell that ripped apart the Australian top order. Bobby Simpson was caught by our substitute Lance Gibbs and I dived full length to catch a low one from Neil Harvey, stubbing my finger as I did so. It was immediately evident that the finger was dislocated but this was no time to fret. Gerry Alexander, a veterinary surgeon, gave it a sharp yank to put it back in place.

When Richie Benaud and Alan Davidson came together at 92 for 6 we were in the driving seat and firm favourites with the bookmakers. Davo was a fine batsman, an accomplished all-rounder, and Richie, too, was a quality bat. Never had we been more aware of the fact that Australians were never finished until the last man was out as these two set about us. The pair pulled Australia out of the mire and to the brink of victory, taking the score to 226 before the next wicket fell, just seven runs away from inflicting defeat on us. The partnership was finally broken when Davo tried to take on Joe Solomon at midwicket for a quick single and was run out for 80 by a direct hit. That was critical. As it transpired, it was a match-saving piece of fielding brilliance.

Wicket-keeper Wally Grout joined Richie and they added a single, leaving them needing just one big hit on the small Woolloongabba ground to win this First Test.

But Frank Worrell had also learned his cricket the hard way and was every bit as tough as Richie. He called us together and told us to get stuck in, bowl tight and field tight in what was the last over. He believed we could still win, especially if we could take Richie's wicket. He went to Wes Hall and told him to keep the ball up and not to risk bowling any bouncers.

The first ball went for a leg bye, bringing Benaud on strike. Wes immediately let rip one of the fastest bouncers I have ever seen and Richie went for the hook, took a thin edge and was caught behind by Alexander. Getting Richie was key and Wes was so pleased that he collapsed on to his knees on the wicket and raised his arms to the sky. Wes looked up at Frank and shouted, 'Skipper, skipper, I got him, I got him,' only to be met by a stony silence.

Frank walked over to him and admonished, 'What did I tell you about bowling bouncers?'

'But I got him,' Wes spluttered.

'That's not the point,' said Frank. 'I told you not to bowl a bouncer. What would have happened if it had taken a top edge and gone for six? We would have lost.'

A chastened Wes walked back to his mark, realising now what could have happened, moments after feeling the adrenalin rush of a crucial wicket and expecting Frank to be as excited as him.

Australia were still favourites as in came Ian Meckiff, the Aussie fast bowler who was no great shakes as a batsman, to face the third ball. By this time, Wes was hopping up and down in his anxiety to get at him but again Frank walked over and calmed him down.

A dot ball was followed by another extra off the fourth ball and then calamity off the fifth. Grout mistimed his shot, pulling it towards

Rohan Kanhai who stood waiting for the simple catch. But a giant figure came bounding up, brushing Rohan aside. It was Wes, shouting 'mine'; he got a big hand to the ball . . . and dropped it. In his enthusiasm, the big man had followed through almost to square leg, nearly knocking Rohan down in the process. Not only did he drop the catch, he then picked up the ball and compounded his error by flinging it wildly at the stumps. It was a good job Alf Valentine was backing up otherwise the game would have been lost there and then with overthrows.

The Aussies had moved on to 230 for 8 and there were still three balls left – they were eight-ball overs in those days. The atmosphere was heavy with tension; it was so exciting it was tangible and this led to both the batsmen and the fielding side doing things they might not have done normally.

Meckiff was now on strike and he tentatively played the ball behind square on the leg side. The batsmen ran two to tie the scores and were setting off for the third match-winning run when the chasing Conrad Hunte, who had a good arm, whipped the ball over the stumps from deep midwicket to run out Grout. The Aussies had the cheek to blame their groundsman for not having cut that part of the field low enough, claiming that had he done so, the ball would have run that much further and that much quicker, allowing them to complete the three runs they needed. They were so serious about their complaint that they were still going on about it when I went to a reunion many years later, still blaming the groundsman, claiming that they had been robbed. We knew it was Conrad's refusal to give up that saved the ball going for a boundary.

Now the scores were tied with the Aussies on 232 for 9. They needed one run from the last two balls to win as their last man, Lindsay Kline, joined Meckiff in the middle.

Frank again went over to the excited Wes Hall and this time said to him, 'If I move Solomon two steps to his right and then two back to his left, the field will remain the same but the batsman will not know what I have done.' It may have looked meaningless to the spectators but he was cleverly sowing the seeds of doubt in the minds of the batsmen. He also reminded Wes that he would never be able to go home to the West Indies, never mind Barbados, if he bowled a no-ball. When Wes let it go, in that heady atmosphere I prayed that if the ball came to me at leg slip it would be in the air and not on the ground, but Lindsay Kline played it off his legs towards square leg and set off for the winning run. Meckiff hesitated just a fraction and that was enough for the deadly Solomon to run him out.

I don't think I would have hit the stumps under those circumstances. They picked the wrong man – there was no one better than Joe and even though he could see just one stump, he threw the wicket down with Meckiff diving full length and only just failing to make his ground. The match was tied, the first in the long history of Test cricket.

It was chaos. Everyone in the ground was going berserk. Rohan Kanhai and several other players were jumping up and down thinking we had won while others were not exactly sure what was going on. We all realised the magnitude of the moment when the Australians came out to meet us on the way in to the pavilion to congratulate us on the first tie in 498 Tests.

I never had any doubt about the result. I knew it was a tie because I always kept the score in my head. I did not even have to look at the scoreboard to confirm it.

We danced into the dressing room, jumping for joy. Only Frank flopped down; he was so tired and mentally worn out that he couldn't even take off his boots. He was exhausted from the responsibility of captaining the side and plotting every over and every ball. He always hid the pressure he was under, concealing it so well. Now it washed over him in waves.

The Australians were as confused as we were and they came into our room to join the celebrations. We asked the room attendant to find us some beers, not a difficult thing to do in Brisbane, and we sat there together, drinking and talking about it. Some of us did not leave the dressing rooms until after 10 o'clock that night. We just sat there and let it digest. This was history.

It seems about 50,000 people witnessed that last dramatic day, 14 December, judging by those who claim to have been there when I go to Australia now. In fact, about 4,000 were present.

That tie set the stage for the series and, far from being the anti-climax it could have been, the rest of the tour went like a dream with brilliant matches, responsive and appreciative crowds and two teams who meshed well.

We lost the Second Test by seven wickets in Melbourne; I scored 9 and 0. Joe Solomon, who scored a duck in the first innings, was given out hit wicket when, in pulling Benaud, his cap fell off and broke the wicket. The crowd liked us so much that they booed Benaud! That was the kind of support we received from the home crowd throughout that tour.

We levelled the series in Sydney, winning by 222 runs. I scored 168 with Alan Davidson taking my wicket in both innings. Lance Gibbs bowled beautifully for 5 for 66, backed up by his fellow spinner Alf Valentine who took 4 for 86.

The only drawn game was in Adelaide but even that was a cliffhanger with Ken Mackay and Lindsay Kline hanging on with Australia nine wickets down and a long way behind. They shared an unbroken stand of 66 to save the match. I didn't score many runs that time round but contributed five wickets.

We thought the game was all over and won when, with Frank Worrell bowling to Kline, I stole in and took a catch almost off the bat face. Many watchers thought we had won the game and some who saw it on television switched off thinking the game was over. They could not believe it when they switched back on and saw that the match was still going on. We ignored it and got on with what we had to do. We did not know that Kline and Mackay would bat for more than 90 minutes.

To this day I do not know why the catch was not given. I can only assume the umpire thought that it came off the pad. Unlike today, there was no great debate sparked by television, slow-motion replays and panels of experts. Also unlike today, there was no great fuss in the middle. We accepted the decision and carried on with the game, confident that we had enough time left to take the wicket. It may seem strange now but it was no big thing for us and, as far as I know, nobody asked the umpires about it afterwards.

There was never any arguing or disputing with umpires; that did not happen with West Indian cricketers. It would come up in the captain's or manager's meetings, not as a specific point, just a reminder of how we were expected to behave. How that has changed. Nowadays they have to have referees, third and fourth umpires and a system of fines and punishments for those stepping out of line. I find that all very sad.

It was almost inevitable after all that had gone on that there would be a terrific climax and it all came down to the final Test back at Melbourne. The game was full of excitement, watched by a total of 274,404 people. The second day attracted a then world record crowd of 90,800. I was top scorer with 64 out of a total of 292 in the first innings and then took 5 for 120 from 44 overs as Australia eased into the lead with 356. Colin McDonald top scored for them with 91.

It was still nip and tuck in the second innings as we scored 321, leaving Australia needing 258 to win. Bobby Simpson, Norm O'Neill and Peter Burge chipped away at the total while wickets fell at regular intervals to Worrell, Gibbs and Valentine. Australia needed four runs to win with three wickets in hand when a ball from Alf Valentine beat Wally Grout and clipped the stumps. The ball diverted past our wicket-keeper Gerry Alexander and the batsmen ran two. We appealed but the umpires Col Egar, a good friend of mine, and Clive Hoy came to the conclusion that it was Alexander who had broken the stumps, not the ball, and gave Grout not out. There were no arguments from us. Frank had decided at the start of the tour that we would play like sportsmen at all times, win, lose or draw and that is what we had done throughout. Now was not the time to change. Wally Grout, also realising how the series had gone, showed remarkable understanding and promptly and deliberately skied the next ball to Cammie Smith off Alf Valentine to give away his wicket. It was a tremendous sporting gesture with the game in the state it was in.

It was so tight that it could easily have been another tie. But it was a step too far at the end of a long tour and Ken Mackay, batting down the order at number eight, scored the winning runs off Alf Valentine. It was over; Australia had won the game by two wickets and the series 2–1 with one tied and the other drawn.

The entire series was magnificent. It would have been nice if it had finished level. There was so much more than just the cricket. Off the field the two teams just meshed. We all got on so well together; even the umpires were part of the family. Davo, Simpson, Miller, O'Neill, Harvey, in fact every one of them, were great company and good mixers; you couldn't pick out one of them and say they weren't friendly or that they didn't attend the many parties. Whenever there were parties, everyone from both sides went, and if there were two parties clashing, we all went to both. Every Test was akin to a club match or a festival game where everyone drank and socialised together. As a youngster on my first tour of Australia, I had no particular friends among the Aussies. I had played against Alan Davidson, Richie Benaud, Keith Miller and Neil Harvey in 1955 under Ian Johnson, but I didn't mix with them other than when Miller and Lindwall used to come to our hotel room to keep an eye on Collie Smith and me.

Frank Worrell was not a man for curfews but what he did insist on was that players were not seen falling about in public. He was quite happy if you sat in your rooms and had a drink and stayed up chatting until the early hours of the morning. What he didn't want was for people to point the finger and say they had seen us in the bar or out on the streets at three o'clock in the morning. The players respected the fact that they were treated as men and not as boys; if they wanted a drink, they could have a drink. When you have a leader like that, you go out and perform because you know that if you don't, those privileges will be withdrawn. It was important for the players to show their appreciation.

In my experience, if you treat big men like little boys they will behave like little boys. You certainly won't get the best out of them because they will feel mistreated and not trusted. Trust them and most will repay it. Of course, there are some who need the law laying down but you have to know who they are, and not lay it on everyone. After a while on tour, as either captain or manager, you come to know who can and who cannot mix the social side with the cricket. Those who can't should be pulled to one side and have it explained that if they want to stay, they must do what is best for the team. If they feel they must go out and then don't perform, they should be in no doubt what the consequences will be. With Frank, it was a case of, 'If you don't perform, you don't make the team. It's your decision.'

Even the public joined in the spirit of the cricket and when we left Melbourne, thousands upon thousands of people poured on to the streets to give us a ticker-tape farewell, something that had never happened before and has not happened since. People had tears in their eyes as we left and that, in turn, brought tears to our eyes. They were begging us to stay and not go – and we had lost the series.

I felt that I had had a good series, starting badly but then coming on, and I'd had a good run in the Test matches. Sir Donald Bradman was so excited by my form that he recommended South Australia to bring me back to play for them. He said that I was the right sort of player for the team. At the same time, Wes Hall went to Queensland and Rohan Kanhai to Western Australia.

The year before I joined them, South Australia had finished last in the Sheffield Shield but in my first season we moved to second place. I started poorly but, in the end, had a good season despite having a bad knee, becoming the first player to do the double, that is score 1,000 runs and take 50 wickets in their short season.

They sent me to see a top specialist in London to fix the knee and when I went back the next season I broke my own record with the bat and ball. I scored over 1,000 runs, including five Shield centuries, and took 51 wickets, helping them to win the Sheffield Shield. My average was over 70 and I was delighted because, at the time, cricket in Australia was undoubtedly the best in the world. The strongest players were there and the Shield was the toughest domestic competition. In fact, it was the hardest and best cricket I have ever played. I enjoyed it.

Even the club cricket was very good because there were so many quality cricketers. Australia is such a proud sporting country and they believe in doing whatever they do well. You can see that at every level from childhood upwards.

Club cricket is strong. The players turn up on time, they are keen and bat and bowl hard without giving an inch. After playing in English conditions and learning the technique, I went to Australia to be toughened up, to work and to play until the last ball was bowled. That's why the Australians always have a good team – because they are fighters.

Their state sides were awesome; every one of them boasted a roster of top Test players. Queensland had some of the best with Wally Grout, Ken Mackay, Peter Burge, Wes Hall, Sam Trimble and Tommy Veivers while New South Wales boasted Richie Benaud, Norman O'Neill, Neil Harvey, Brian Booth, Graham Thomas, Bobby Simpson, Frank Misson and Johnny Martin. Perth had Tony Lock, Barry Shepherd, Ray Inverarity, Des Hoare and Hugh Bevan. Victoria had Bill Lawry, Ian Meckiff, Ian Redpath, Alan Connolly, Froggy Thompson, Bob Cowper, Jack Potter and Ian Stackpole while South Australia had Barry Jarman, John Lille, Ian McLaughlan, Neil Hawke, Neal Dansey and Les Favell, all class players. Ian Chappell came in later.

The wickets were good. Sometimes in Brisbane or Melbourne you could be playing in temperatures of over 100 degrees in a four-day match, but there was no let up. You were made to fight for every run and every point in the Shield and if you needed 10 runs to win with eight wickets standing, they still didn't give you an inch. They still believed they could win. That was something you learned in Australia. In the West Indies if you wanted four to win with three wickets left, the bowler would bowl a full toss to get it over. English cricket was altogether more sedate.

Playing against New South Wales, I would find myself bowling at openers Graham Thomas and Bobby Simpson followed by Norman O'Neill at three, Neil Harvey at four, Brian Booth at five, Richie Benaud at six – and Alan Davidson was in there somewhere! Then you had to make runs against Davidson, Benaud, Simpson, Johnny

Martin and Frank Misson. There was no escape. It was like playing against Australia.

Norman O'Neill carried a burden throughout his entire career by being labelled 'the new Don Bradman'. That was heavy baggage to carry. The same thing happened to Ian Craig. Norman was good but he wasn't near Sir Donald, very few were.

Australia produced so many good cricketers. They talk with reverence about Jack Iverson, whom I never saw, because he could move the ball both ways and you couldn't tell which way he was going. Johnny Gleeson was similar. When you saw him for the first time you wondered what he would do next. He might bowl a leg-break, followed by an off-break with a googly thrown in for good measure. It was a mystery and difficult to confront.

I well remember my first game against Gleeson. I was playing for the West Indies and he was representing New South Wales. Going into a Test series, he had the capability to demoralise a batsman in a state match if you weren't careful, and clearly they were hoping he would upset me. I scored 100 and never tried to pick one ball; I just played him off the track and used a bit of cross bat. My whole idea was that if I went out there and tried to pick him and suddenly found I couldn't, then right away I would be defeated and when I went into the Test match I would have been undone. There were some critics watching that innings who assumed I had read every ball he bowled. I picked one or two but I wasn't that interested because I scored runs against him then and in the Test matches.

I heard that England had been worried about his spin and when Basil d'Oliveira and Geoffrey Boycott were batting, Basil took Gleeson all the time so that he could go back into the pavilion and tell the boys how to do it. He eventually looked pretty comfortable and finally went up to Geoffrey and said, 'I think I have him worked out. I know which way he's going.'

Apparently, Geoffrey replied, 'So have I since the first ball he bowled but I'm not going to tell those buggers in there anything. Let them work it out for themselves.'

Sometimes when you are facing a good or difficult bowler and you try too hard to read him or pick him, it can become a big worry. If you go out and play him with confidence, he is on the back foot and the captain will wonder whether to bring him on. If you take him too seriously and look for too many hidden traps, the bowler will know and so will his captain.

I didn't have that many problems in that respect but Gleeson was certainly one of the most dangerous bowlers I faced. I even went to have a look at him in the nets when the Australians were practising but it was difficult because of the way the hand moved.

Sonny Ramadhin was like that. He never bowled a googly in his life, just off-breaks and leg-breaks, but his wrist and his hand moved so quickly it was hard to spot which one he was going to bowl. He ran up with his hand flat and changed it at the very last second. He always had his shirt sleeves rolled down to help disguise his delivery. He admitted later in his life in a newspaper article that he chucked but I don't know about that. I never noticed him throwing and no one else ever mentioned it.

Whenever I played against these difficult bowlers in a state match or a county match, I never let them concern me overmuch. I just went out there and played. It was in Test matches that it was time to have a closer look.

My last state match in my second season was against Victoria where I faced Wayne 'Slug' Jordan. For some reason, I rarely made runs against Victoria and Slug always used to tell Les Favell and anyone who wanted to listen, 'They say that Sobey can bat – but I have never seen him make a run.'

In this particular match, we had to beat Victoria to win the Shield. Before the game, Les Favell gathered a few of the boys together and brought them round to my apartment where they sat down, had a few drinks and talked about the game. They told me how this Slug Jordan said I couldn't bat and how they needed to fix me up. We won the toss and batted, as far as I can remember, and I made 160 in a hurry and we topped over 300. Then I bowled them out, we put them back in and bowled them out again to win by an innings with half a day to spare.

After the match, Les went up to Slug and in typical Aussie fashion asked him, 'What the f*** do you think about Sobey now? Do you think he can f****** bat?'

I think he might have changed his mind after that match.

Another state game that remains fixed in the memory was when I was playing against New South Wales in my first year. I was batting really well and had topped 150 when Alan Davidson bowled me a good bouncer just outside off stump. I stood up and slapped it right over mid-on. It landed on the farthest part of the boundary and went first bounce into the Adelaide scoreboard. It went so far that they still talk about it now.

Everyone went crazy – except for Davo who gave me a hard look. The next ball was a beamer straight at my eyes. I managed to get the bat up, turned it and it flew off the back of the bat to the boundary. Davo apologised and said that it slipped out of his hand. I wasn't so sure but went on to score 250.

The following year I was talking to the Australian umpire Colin Egar who was from South Australia, and the conversation came around to Davo and the beamer he bowled at me. Colin had been standing at the bowler's end and he heard Davo mutter as he went past after the big hit, 'That little bastard . . . I'll show him!'

During the 1960–61 tour, Egar was a good friend to the West Indies team. He would come and talk to us and join us for a beer at the end of the day's play. We often sat chatting in my hotel room until dawn came creeping in. But when you went out there on to the square, he showed no favours. If you were out, then out you went. He was a very good umpire, one of the best.

Don Bradman also remembered that shot against Davidson because he claimed that it was the longest boundary in Australia, a boundary so distant that frequently batsmen ran five – and the scoreboard is another 20 yards back beyond the rope.

I hear a lot these days about the chatter that goes on around the wicket, especially in Australia. I never had any problems with sledging but I'm sure it went on because I heard others complain about it. Perhaps there was no reason to have a go at me. I walked if I touched the ball, I never stuck my pad at the ball and if anyone did or said anything directed at me, I never used to let it bother me. I just used to play my innings and it was always the sort of cricket that the fielding team admired because I put bat to ball. Maybe it was just that the word went round that the more I was abused the more runs I tended to score!

I remember on one occasion someone making a racist remark to me. I ignored it, went on to score a big century and walked off. I thought that was the best argument. If someone is going to get angry with me, whatever the reason may be, I am not going to get involved in a fight. I would answer with my bat.

I had a bit of a problem when I was playing for the Rest of the World in Australia. When I arrived at the ground I took a call from Pru saying she was going to leave me and take our son Matthew with her because of a letter she had received from a girl I knew. I had to go in to bat soon afterwards and went on to score 254. I told Ian Chappell about it a few years later and he said, 'Bloody hell! Now you tell me. You didn't have to take it out on us. Next time anything like that happens I'm going to ask your wife to let me know first so that I can take cover.' Out there at the crease you can forget about pretty well everything when you are seeing the ball well.

Sir Donald Bradman was a major influence on me while I was in Australia, having been instrumental in me playing state cricket for South Australia and maintaining an interest in my career after that. He would come into the dressing room when South Australia were struggling and ask where I was. Invariably I would be sleeping. I would watch the cricket for 10 or 15 minutes and then go to sleep on the massage table. He would come in and wake me up, saying, 'South Australia are in trouble today, son. You will have to go out there and make a hundred.' Amazingly, every time he said that to me, I did; I went out and scored 100. Every time I would come back and he would say, 'I know, I know, you weren't going to disappoint me.'

I didn't see a lot of him. He kept himself increasingly to himself and we did not socialise together much. He was a quiet man and we did not mix in the same circles or with the same people. When I first went there, he invited Pru, Matthew and me round to his house. He did that for every visitor who went to play for South Australia. We had a long talk and I felt comfortable with him. He was very knowledgeable about the game and talked without trying to shove it down your throat. We would meet at the Sheffield Shield games and chat then but not always about cricket. He liked his golf and I occasionally shared a round with him.

I was supposed to go back to play for South Australia for a third year but, by that time, I had been made captain of the West Indies and the West Indies Board thought it would not be prudent for me to go. Australia were coming to play a series against us. I was delighted when South Australia invited me back for one last season in 1971–72. I had enjoyed such a good time with them that I had no hesitation in accepting and was looking forward to it. In the end, I played a couple of one-day matches because Sir Donald hijacked my season when he asked me to captain the Rest of the World team against Australia.

However, we were back down under in 1968–69. Australia had just managed to retain the Ashes in England after being outplayed in three of the games. I was 32 and had been playing all year, captaining Notts for the first time back in England. All the cricket was beginning to take its toll. My knee trouble had flared up again and I had a floating bone in my left shoulder, which had caused me to abandon my back of the hand style of bowling. We were a little short of bowling, too, with Wes Hall playing in just two of the Tests while Charlie Griffith played in three.

We had a mixed start to the tour but I felt in good form with a couple of hundreds and another innings in the 90s. I won the toss for the First Test in Brisbane and, thanks to Joey Carew and Rohan Kanhai, we scored 296. The Australian innings started well for us when I removed Ian Redpath for a duck, but it was a long time until our next wicket as Bill Lawry and Ian Chappell carried the score to 217.

Desperate times call for desperate measures and I brought on Clive Lloyd to bowl his medium pace. It was a calculated choice. Clive was a useful bowler and if the established bowlers could not make the breakthrough, why not give him a try and the batsmen something new to think about? Other 'second string' bowlers, such as Norm O'Neill and later Allan Border, Mark Waugh and even Sachin Tendulkar nowadays, have been well known for breaking difficult partnerships.

In the blink of an eye Clive had taken both centurions, both of them caught by me. From then on, Lance Gibbs took over and what looked like being a big first-innings lead for the Australians finished up as a 12-run deficit.

It was just the spur we needed. Joey Carew, despite an injured hand, and Clive Lloyd held the innings together, Clive providing the fire power with a quick century. The home team were set 366 to win and we bowled them out for 240. My 33.6 eight-ball overs included a dozen maidens and six wickets for 73.

There was another long spell waiting for me in Melbourne where I bowled 33.3 overs in Australia's one and only innings, taking four wickets. Lance Gibbs, who bowled 10 overs more than me, also took four – but it was in a total of 510 with Lawry scoring a double century and Chappell not far behind with 165. This was in answer to our meagre 200. We had collapsed against the pace of Graham McKenzie who took eight wickets. Only Roy Fredericks held them up with a gallant 76 scored in almost five hours. In the second innings, Seymour Nurse scored 74 and I gathered 67 but we were bowled out for 280 to lose by an innings.

It was a severe blow and our morale suffered as a result. It showed in the Third Test, which followed straightaway in Sydney. The Australians' 547, with Doug Walters scoring the sole century, over-shadowed our first innings of 264. With Basil Butcher scoring 101 and Rohan Kanhai 69, we managed to add 324 in the second innings, setting Australia a total of 42. Ian Stackpole and Paul Sheahan knocked that off in quick time.

The pattern continued in Adelaide where, despite my run-a-minute century, we still managed just 276; the Australians, led by yet another Walters 100, again topped 500. Stung by criticism of the team and myself in the media, we hit back in the second innings with 616; almost everyone scored runs, right down to Hendriks' 37 not out at number 10. I followed my 28 overs in the Australian first innings with another 50.

We did not believe that the criticism was justified but the press had their job to do and we had ours and we all got on with it. Australia, however, looked as though they would knock off the 360 runs needed when they reached 298 for 3, leaving them to get 62 runs off 120 balls.

Then came the most bizarre of twists as Ian Redpath, Doug Walters, Eric Freeman and Barry Jarman were all run out, Redpath somewhat controversially when Charlie Griffith took off the bails at the non-strike end as the batsman persisted in backing up too far down the wicket. I was disgusted with Charlie for not issuing a warning first but, by then, there was little I could do about it; Redpath was on his way back to the pavilion. That left them on 322 for 7. Then McKenzie skied a catch to substitute fielder Camacho and Griffith cleaned up Gleeson leaving the Australians teetering on the brink of defeat at 333 for 9.

This was eight years after the last pair of Kline and Mackay had defied us; now it was Sheahan and Connolly left to survive ten balls with the old ball and 16 with the new. I had to decide whether or not to give Charlie the new ball after the run-out episode, and shared it with him, but we could not shift the last pair. So we had to settle for a draw in the most exciting Test match I have played in other than the tied Test.

Any hopes of a comeback in the final Test back in Sydney evaporated with the Australians' first innings score of 619. Hopes were high when Wes Hall bowled Stackpole and I removed Ian Chappell and Ian Redpath for 1 and 0 respectively. Lawry went on to make 151 and Walters 242 after the usually safe Hendriks dropped Walters off Hall when he was 75.

We scored 279 and, with the series won, Lawry declined to enforce the follow-on, eventually declaring at 394 for 8, leaving us needing over 700 runs to win. Redpath scored 132 and Walters followed up his double hundred with another century, the first batsman to achieve the feat in Test cricket. It meant long, hot days in the field for me with 54 eight-ball overs in all and five wickets. We refused to roll over despite the impossible target, and Seymour Nurse scored 137 and I scored 113. We managed to total 352 but it still left us short by 382.

We took a lot of stick for the series defeat but how different it would have been had we held our catches. I am told that we dropped 35 in all.

We went on to New Zealand for a three-Test series after that but I would have much preferred to go home. Apart from anything else, New Zealand was my personal jinx. The first time I played there in 1955 the journey took 21 days by boat from Trinidad. That was a lot of boredom, a total contrast to the trip to Australia in 1960. Then, despite my fears about the wickets, they played perfectly well and I was getting out to what were probably good balls. Being young, I just couldn't adjust. When I returned in 1969, I still didn't score any runs. We finished the series 1–1 with one drawn.

Seymour Nurse, who had sent in his resignation to the West Indies Board, made runs in style – 558, including a double hundred – to show just how good the wickets were; but I couldn't score anything. Seymour scored 95, 168, 21, 16 and 258, while my contribution was 11, 0, 20, 39 and 0!

Seymour was a very good bat and a very proud person. He retired too soon. He didn't score many runs in Australia and got annoyed at things that happened there. He always said that the West Indies would never throw him away, he would get rid of them first, and I suspect that he thought he might be dropped for the next series against England.

I asked him why he didn't ask me before he sent in his resignation. I would have stopped him. He was only in his early 30s and could have carried on. I am sure he was sorry afterwards although he never said so. He would have scored a lot of runs in England because, having played league cricket, he was used to the wickets.

I told him I would love him to go to England but he felt that he couldn't change his mind because of the adverse publicity it would bring. He played cricket in Barbados afterwards, and I cannot ever remember him getting out in the Over-50s matches; he was regularly scoring 50s and 60s. What a waste. Not only did he make all those runs in New Zealand before he retired, but his last innings in Australia was 137 and we had put on a century stand together.

I don't know what it was about New Zealand but even when they came to the West Indies in 1972 I didn't do well. I did collect 100 against them in Barbados when Charlie Davis and I managed to stem the tide with a sixth-wicket stand of 254. He scored 183 before being run out while I scored 142, but even then I was lucky and was dropped in the slips early on. We managed to save the Test match, which was going heavily against us at the time.

That was another boring series with the Kiwis just trying to score as many runs as they could on good wickets, and all five Tests were drawn. Again, I didn't make many runs, and that was the only 100 I ever scored against them. I was lucky because that meant I had scored a century against every country I had played against.

It was amazing. I could never get going against them. They had a very good bowler in Bruce Taylor – but he wasn't that good! Seymour Nurse, however, kept hammering them.

In total, I played a dozen Tests against New Zealand and scored just 404 runs, including that 142, for an average of 23.76. My average over there was a miserly 15.10. To put that into perspective, I averaged almost 90 against Pakistan and India, over 60 against England in 36 Tests and 43.14 against Australia.

I played against the Aussies twice in the West Indies, the first time in 1955 and the second 10 years later, when I had just taken over the captaincy.

I was batting with Jackie Hendriks in Barbados when Graham McKenzie hit our wicket-keeper on the head with a vicious bouncer. It reminded me of the time when Nari Contractor was hit while playing for India against Barbados when he ducked into a ball that didn't get up from Charlie Griffith. Charlie was going to appeal for leg before wicket but I stopped him as I could see that Contractor was in serious trouble and, in fact, almost died.

Hendriks jumped into the bouncer and when he saw he couldn't get on top of it he tried to duck at the last moment. When the ball hit him, he fell to the ground and lay there twitching. He was rushed off to the hospital with everyone fearing the worst but after a two-day stay he was out again, showing little or no ill effects.

When Hendriks fell, he knocked the stumps over but Aussie captain Bobby Simpson declined to appeal so Hendriks appeared on the scorecard as retired hurt instead of hit wicket bowled McKenzie.

Australia lost that series, winning the final Test in Port-of-Spain after the series had gone. There was a lot of unrest with Norman O'Neill and others complaining about Charlie Griffith chucking, although he was never called in that series. As far as I was concerned, both he and Wes Hall bowled really well to help us to that 2–1 series win.

There was a story that Norm O'Neill went down the wicket in one match to Neil Harvey and told him that he wanted a single because he was uncomfortable playing against Charlie. Neil, apparently, looked him in the eye and said, 'The best way of playing fast bowling is to face it!'

I was glad and relieved to become the first West Indies captain to win a series against Australia. That helped erase some of the doubts and when we went on to beat England in the next series and India after that, I had managed to change a few opinions – for a while.

CHAPTER TWELVE

The best of the Rest

I had the privilege of captaining the Rest of the World for two series, one in England in 1970 and the other in Australia in 1971–72, both arranged in place of cancelled tours by the banned South African side. The irony is that I did not want to go on either of them.

The first time, I was more than a little uncertain because I did not think it was right to let down my county side Nottinghamshire for more than half of the summer. Ultimately, I was left with little choice because the Test and County Cricket Board warned that if I did not accept their invitation, I would not be allowed to play for my county anyway. Notts were to have a share of the takings from the five-Test series, so that made the decision a little easier. Also, when I specifically asked whether the series would be granted full Test status and if the averages would count, I was assured that they would. They explained that otherwise they would not have been able to find sponsors to underwrite the tour. It was not until the end of the series that I was casually informed that the averages would not count as the series was not country versus country. That was annoying because I scored 588 runs at an average of 73 plus 21 wickets at 21 each.

I should have learned my lesson but it happened again in Australia. I was keen to return to play a little state cricket with South Australia, renew a few friendships and rest my weary body. It was only because Sir Donald Bradman persuaded me that I eventually accepted.

The first series in England came about because of the Basil d'Oliveira affair. England picked a touring side for South Africa that included the South African born Worcestershire all-rounder d'Oliveira. The South African government refused to grant him a visa because he had mixed blood and was categorised as coloured by the apartheid regime. The British government immediately ordered the MCC to cancel the tour and South Africa were subsequently excluded from the game at international level.

To fill the void, the Rest of the World team was conceived and what a strong side it was – at least on paper. From the West Indies, wicket-keeper Deryck Murray, Rohan Kanhai, Clive Lloyd and Lance Gibbs, joined me. Pakistan provided Intikhab Alam and Mushtaq Mohammad. From India there was Faroukh Engineer, from Australia Graham McKenzie plus South Africans Barry Richards, Graeme Pollock, Mike Procter and Eddie Barlow. That must have been the strongest cricket side ever to be brought together and yet we did not sparkle in beating a fairly moderate England side 4–1. Why is beyond me.

It was nothing to do with the financial arrangements. Thanks to sponsors Guinness, who provided an overall pot of £13,000, there was good money to be won with £2,000 per team for each victory and £3,000 for the overall winning team. We won £11,000 – paltry now but excellent reward in those days. The games were extremely competitive.

I wondered whether the presence of so many top players led to some complacency. If that was the case, it was not at all professional. Certainly the squad mixed and blended well together, and that side of things compared favourably with tours I had been on with the West Indies. Every player took it seriously; a number were using the series to regain or cement their places in their countries' Test teams.

At number six, I did not expect to bat very often, if at all, in that line-up, but I batted twice in every Test except the opening one at Lord's where I scored 183 out of the 546 we scored in our one innings. I also took 6 for 21 in England's first innings at headquarters. It was one of my best returns in Test cricket but, oddly, it was not as satisfying as my form at Headingley where I bowled as well as I had done anywhere that summer, yet did not take a single wicket. I bowled 20 overs, conceded 24 runs and beat the bat several times per over. After watching me beat his opening partner Brian Luckhurst four times out of six, Geoffrey Boycott turned to me and said, 'You're doing too much with the ball.' I couldn't argue with that observation. At least I went on to score 114 in that match.

At Lord's we hammered an England side that, ironically, had two South African players of their own; apart from d'Oliveira they also had future captain Tony Greig. We won by an innings and 80 runs but instead of that runaway result inspiring us, we then lost by eight wickets at Nottingham, despite 114 not out by Clive Lloyd in the first innings and 142 by Eddie Barlow in the second.

At Edgbaston, I took 3 for 38 in 20 overs in England's first innings. We bowled them out for 294 and went on to score 569 for 9 through Lloyd (101), me (80) and Kanhai (71). England made us fight but we won by five wickets to regain our lead.

The Fourth Test in Leeds, played in humid conditions, was probably the best in terms of spectator interest. England were bowled out for 222 while my century helped us to 376 for 9, exactly the same score achieved by England in their second innings. We clinched the series with just two wickets in hand and with me top scoring with 59.

In the final Test at The Oval, McKenzie was the top bowler in England's first innings with four wickets, and when we replied Graeme Pollock at last showed why he was so highly rated with his first century of the series. I weighed in with 79 as we built a lead of

61. Boycott's 157 helped England to 365 in their second innings with Clive Lloyd and myself sharing five wickets between us. The West Indian contingent again came good in our second innings with a ton from Kanhai and 40 not out from me. I was at the crease to see us home.

It would undoubtedly have been easier but for the England captain Ray Illingworth who challenged us to take his wicket in every game. In eight innings, he scored 63, 94, 15, 43, 58, 54, 52 before finally succumbing with a duck.

Our most successful bowler was Eddie Barlow, maybe not the best bowler in the side but certainly the most enthusiastic. Mike Procter, an all-rounder of world class, was the quickest of our bowlers, difficult to face coming in as he did off the wrong foot, but Richards and Pollock, until the last Test, disappointed.

Sir Donald Bradman could be very persuasive when he wanted anything from me. I was pleased to accept the invitation to play for South Australia but when he asked me to captain the Rest of the World side again, I was not sure about it. I didn't really feel up to it at that stage of my career. I had had my share of the captaincy with West Indies, Barbados, Notts and the Rest of the World in 1970 in England. All I wanted to do was see some friends and play a few Sheffield Shield matches. I even wrote back and declined but the Don would not let go. He said he wanted me to captain the side so that he could have a look at Dennis Lillee and a few others before they went to England. He felt that the Sheffield Shield at that time was not a good enough way to find out their qualities and he wanted some strong opposition to test them to the full.

He knew that I had no malice as far as colour and creed were concerned and it was important, with West Indians, South Africans and Asians in the team, to have someone in charge whom they could all trust and respect. The Don asked me to give up my season with South Australia to take on another five-Test series, and as it was him, I agreed.

We didn't have a particularly strong team this time around although it included Tony Greig, Peter Pollock, Sunil Gavaskar, Rohan Kanhai, Clive Lloyd, Bishen Bedi, Faroukh Engineer, Zaheer Abass, Bob Tunis from New Zealand and Richard Hutton. Hylton Ackerman from Northants and a fellow named Massoo from India who had never played Test cricket. We tried for Barry Richards, Graeme Pollock and Mike Procter so that we would have a similar team to the one we had in England, but with no luck. This one was not quite at the same level.

The first game was in Brisbane and I was talking to Ray Lindwall whom I hadn't seen for some time. We were standing outside a little coffee shop watching Dennis Lillee go back 20 yards or so and I said to Ray, 'Why is he running from so far?' Lindwall gave me a look that said, 'You'll see.' I did. That first ball was so quick I scarcely saw it. I had heard all about him but he was even quicker than I expected.

The Queensland wicket was a lot slower than the others and we made a good total through Ackerman and Gavaskar. I went in quite late and made 30 or 40.

The next game was in Perth. Now that was a quick wicket where bowlers such as Michael Bevan and Sam Gannon, ordinary little medium pacers, seemed like Wes Hall and Charlie Griffith. It didn't take much working out that Dennis was going to be real quick on his own track. The point was proved when I walked out to the middle of the WACA with Hutton before the game began and watched Richard bounce the ball higher than his head. 'If I do that at Headingley,' he remarked ruefully, 'I have to send for a shovel to dig it out!' He couldn't believe that a ball could bounce that high, it was more like a tennis ball.

Australia won the toss, batted for a couple of days and made around 400. We began our innings that night and went to the ground early the next morning, well before play resumed. They had covered the wicket with tarpaulins followed by heavy plastic and then canvas. I know from my own experience that where you have temperatures of 100 during the day dipping to 60 in the evening, there are going to be changes.

Add to that the wind they call the Freemantle Doctor that blows in and the inevitable result is that the wicket was going to sweat.

When I looked at it after the covers had been lifted, I saw that, sure enough, it had sweated really badly, and I knew what we were in for. It was going to be a very rough ride indeed. Gavaskar and Faroukh Engineer went out to resume their innings and I called the rest of the team to the window and told them to watch the first over from Lillee.

They all wanted to know why but I wanted them to see for themselves. The first ball Lillee bowled, Gavaskar went forward, the ball took off and went past his head at an incredible rate of knots. All the fellows in the dressing room immediately started to volunteer for the 9, 10 and 11 positions in the batting order.

Dennis had 0–11 overnight and finished up with 8 for 29. I had never seen anything like it. The laws of gravity tell you that if a moving object hits anything it must slow down. You often hear a commentator saying the ball quickened off the wicket but that is only a figure of speech. But this wicket was quick and bouncy and it really looked as though the ball was taking off after it had pitched.

Gavaskar played one from Dennis down to deep third man. He called Faroukh for an easy single but Faroukh quickly held up an arresting hand and shouted, 'No, no, no.' A few minutes later, the boot was on the other foot as Faroukh played one into the deep and called for three. This time it was Gavaskar who ran two and shouted, 'No, no, no.' Neither of these two fine batsmen wanted to face Lillee on this track.

I was getting on a bit but I still possessed that competitive edge. Facing pace wasn't going to be my problem even at 36 years of age. I walked in to bat when we were just over the 100 for five wickets down. About 20 yards from the wicket, I passed a ring of fielders and as I walked past I jokingly asked, 'What are you all doing back here?' Wicket-keeper Marsh replied, 'You'll find out.'

The first ball Dennis bowled to me had gone before I got my bat up. The second reared and hit me on the glove and Ian Chappell took the catch. As I walked past him, still 20 yards from the wicket, I said, 'I always thought you were a good friend and now I know that you are a very good friend.'

In the second innings, I made a better contribution with 30 or 40 while Rohan Kanhai scored 100. But on the way he took a ball in the chest from Dennis and did not play again until the last of the five Tests. Dennis was so quick he made Graham McKenzie look like a spin bowler. He was probably the quickest that I have ever seen. Frank Tyson was consistently the fastest, but on that Perth wicket, Dennis was faster than anyone else I played against in my life.

When I played against Frank Tyson in the West Indies and he played for the Jim Swanton team, the wicket in Trinidad was a lot slower but Frank was still hustling through. I would have liked to see how quick he was on that WACA wicket.

The Rest of the World side took some media punishment for our performances, me in particular as captain. I was determined that we were going to do better when the tour moved on to Melbourne, never one of my luckier grounds. It was, in fact, the only major ground in Australia where I had not made a century. Dennis had me for that duck in Perth and obviously fancied me again. When I went in he was brought on and I played too early from memory of the Perth wicket and was out for a duck once more.

That evening I went into the Aussies' dressing room and I was sitting next to Ian Chappell with Dennis Lillee standing close by. I said to Ian, 'I hear you have a fellow by the name of Lillee and every time I come in he bowls me bouncers. I want you to tell him that I can bowl quick, too. Tell him as well that I can also bat a bit better than he can and to look out for me when he comes in to bat.'

I knew that he could hear everything I said and I had deliberately used just his surname, the way they used to do in England with the professionals, to rile him.

Australia went in to bat the next day and they had a few runs on the board when Dennis came in. I was bowling at the time and when I ran up I was trying to get him out to finish the innings, not knock him out, although I hadn't forgotten what I said. Dennis was extremely careful in the way he got behind the ball.

Tony Greig, who never forgets anything and doesn't give an inch, came up to me and said, 'Why don't you let him have it?'

'Have what?' I asked innocently.

'The bouncer,' answered Tony.

I bowled a couple more on a length and Dennis was nicely behind them. Then was the time to bowl the bouncer. I told Tony that I was going to bowl it outside the off stump and not in line. I just wanted to let Dennis know I could do it as well, not hurt him. The ball flew past his nose and he turned pink, changing colour completely. I knew that I had him and the next ball I took the weight off, he slogged and skied a simple catch to Tony at mid-off.

At the end of play I went back to the Australian dressing room, smiling as I sat next to Ian again.

'What are you grinning about?' he asked.

'You're my friend. I can't come in here and smile with you?'

He knew what I was smiling about and he laughed. 'Even before Dennis got to the dressing room he hit the bloody wall and said that he was going to show that bastard Sobers what fast bowling was all about next time,' he said.

'Ian, you know me. I have never been afraid of anything. He has the ball and I have the bat. Let him do what he has to do.'

When I came in to bat for the second time we stood at 146 for 3 with a lead of 45. The first couple of balls hit the middle of the bat and before many minutes had passed Dennis came on snorting like an enraged bull, looking for my blood. I hit him all round the field. That was the innings when I scored 254 and Sir Donald Bradman said it was the best innings he had ever seen on Australian soil, even better than the 132 I scored at the Gabba in the famous tied Test. When I walked back to the pavilion after my innings, the Aussies, as always, were the first to lead the applause and right out there in front was Lillee who said to me, 'I have had my arse cut properly today. I had heard about you and read about you and now I have seen you. I really appreciate it.'

That was the way it was in those days, and Dennis and I became firm friends from then on.

The innings was reported in Wisden:

The most distinguished innings of the season came from the captain, G.S. Sobers, 35, when in Melbourne at the New Year he scored 254 runs against Australia. It was an unforgettable display, combining such elegance of stroke play, power and aggression that the crowds responded ecstatically. It was a throw back to the dominance of Sobers in other years. On the Monday, January 3, 1972, Sobers scored 139 not out in three hours, 36 minutes and he hit 21 fours. It was majestic batting. After a rest day, Sobers resumed his great innings on Wednesday, sedately, but recovered his aggression until, obviously tired, he was dismissed for 254. He had batted in all for six hours and 16 minutes and he had hit two sixes off successive balls from O'Keefe, and 35 fours.

Sir Donald added:

The innings was probably the best seen in Australia. The people who saw Sobers have enjoyed one of the historic events of cricket. They were privileged to have such an experience.

The Don spoke the commentary on a film of my innings, going through my technique as shots were frozen into frames. For one shot in particular, when Lillee bowled me a half-volley which I hit back past him like a bullet, he said, 'The ball has come back to Lillee off the fence before he can even pick himself up off the ground. That was the best shot of the whole match.'

He used it as a coaching film because the technique was so good, and because it was an actual game and not put on in the nets so it was showing how to play in a match of that quality. To my amazement, although the Don said it was not for sale, I was able to buy one along with MCC coaching and other tapes. I was disappointed that it was made into a commercial property without telling me or offering a penny in royalties. But the innings was satisfaction enough. That was probably as close to perfection I ever came with the bat.

We went on to win that match and the series 2–1; the other two were drawn. With the unbalanced side we had for that series, we did remarkably well.

There was, however, one anxious moment during the Adelaide Test on 17 December 1971 when Clive Lloyd severely damaged his back in trying to catch Ashley Mallett in the covers. His life was in danger for a while and it was assumed that his career was over, but he battled back and was playing again by 1973 and captain of the West Indies two years later.

I averaged 48.71 with the bat in that series – and 48.38 with the ball! It would have been even more satisfying if those statistics could have been added to my Test career record.

CHAPTER THIRTEEN

365 not out

P laying cricket on and against teams from the subcontinent has provided a rich and rewarding thread throughout my career, not least of all my world record 365 not out against Pakistan in Jamaica in 1958. But there was so much more – frightening riots in Calcutta, umpires giving bad decisions against me in Pakistan, my much publicised engagement to an Indian film star, not to mention coaching the talented Sri Lankans when they were on their way to join the big boys of cricket.

But, I suppose, if anything changed my life it was that world record. The irony of it was that before and afterwards the critics kept going on about me not scoring a Test hundred and how long it took me to score my first century. The Third Test against Pakistan in 1958 was my 17th Test match and I scored my first Test century on the way to the record.

In this 'great' debate, history was completely ignored. It seems to be forgotten that I started as a bowler, not a batsman, not even an all-rounder. I began my Test career batting at number nine for the West Indies and yet the critics made comparisons between me and leading batsmen. Amazing! How can you compare someone who played his first Test as a bowler and batted at number nine with someone who was selected as a batsman and went in at number three or four?

I am constantly compared with specialist batsmen, not having scored my first ton until something like my 25th innings. I batted number nine, then seven, and although I did open an innings in the early days, it was not because I was an opening bat but because I was substituting for Jeff Stollmeyer and I was offered as a sacrifice to the new ball.

A lot of people saw my potential as a batsman; I was a recognised batsman at my club, Barbados Police, but not at Test level. In fact, I batted in front of genuine tailenders Sonny Ramadhin and Frank King.

I opened against Australia in 1955, then went back down to number seven and moved up the order in New Zealand solely because there were youngsters involved. It wasn't until 1957 when I went to England that I really established myself as a higher order batsman. Again, I opened on a couple of occasions because they couldn't find a compatible opening pair and they thought I had a bit of ability and a little skill. I didn't do too badly but it wasn't until 1958 that I blossomed when I was given the opportunity to capitalise on my increasing improvement to bat higher up the order.

Some thought I was a little impetuous because I kept playing my shots and taking chances, and didn't go on to make more runs when I had made a start. But as a youngster this happens. As you gain experience, you start to realise the value of your innings for the team and you start to improve your concentration; your batting starts to develop.

During those years when I started to come on as a batsman, I didn't have the luck that is needed. It seemed that every time I hit the ball in the air or it went near a fielder, I would be out. Others did the same thing and were dropped or the ball fell into space. At least, that's how it seemed to me. There is no doubt that you need that luck early on – when you have a let off, you are able to realise your mistake and capitalise on it. I never seemed to have chances like that in those days.

I always used to tell my critics that I needed that one stroke of luck and as soon as I had it I would go on and make big scores.

It began to happen against Pakistan in 1957–58. Berkeley Gaskin, who was one of our managers, and Roy Lawrence, a commentator from Jamaica, both said in public that when I scored my first hundred I would go on to make a double or even a treble century, and once I did no one knew when it would end.

In the series against Pakistan, I scored 52, 52 and 80 before my 365 not out in the Third Test. That was my first century but I can honestly say that it didn't bother me that much because even then I was a team player. Runs were not important unless the team benefited.

I came in at the fall of the first wicket with the score at 87 for 1 and I don't remember giving a chance for the next 10 hours. I could almost feel the relief from the crowd when I passed the first hundred, and at close of play on the third day I was 228 not out. Conrad Hunte was on 242 and all the talk was of records. I had a restless night with very little sleep.

It was only when I reached 300 that Clyde Walcott came up to me and remarked that I had 64 more runs to go for the world record and why not try for it. There was plenty of time available because this was a six-day game. He said that I was likely to score 300 once in my career so it would be foolish not to have a go.

The remarkable thing was that Conrad Hunte was run out for 260; he might have been the player to break the record and I would not have had the opportunity. We had a record-breaking partnership of 446 but we needed to be told as we came out after lunch that we needed just a run or two to break the record set by Sir Don Bradman and Bill Ponsford 24 years earlier.

Conrad's dismissal was unfortunate. He played the ball to mid-off and called me for a single that we thought would break the record. It was his call; he was running to the danger end so I took off. Aijaz Butt at mid-off scooped up the ball and hit the stumps directly. Had the ball missed, Conrad would have been home. Worse, later we were to discover that the run would not have taken us to the record – we were still five short.

Right Being
introduced to the
Queen during
the Second Test
on the second
day in June 1966

EMPICS

Below On my way to 100 as I hit David Brown through the covers in the First Test of the same tour at Old Trafford

HULTON

Left Arriving at Heathrow Airport, London, in April 1968 ready for my season with Nottinghamshire

Below The shot that brought me another world record. This time the sixth six in an over for Nottinghamshire against Glamorgan in 1968 and *(inset)* with the fortunate bowler Malcolm Nash afterwards. He has been in demand to speak at dinners ever since

Right My wedding to
Pru in England on 11
September 1969

Below left I spent
many happy years in
Australia and here
I am coaching
youngsters during
my stint with South
Australia

Below right New
Zealand was never
a happy hunting
ground for me but
I hit this one well
enough when they
visited us at Sabina
Park in 1972

DAVID FRITH

DAVID FRITH

WILLIE ALLEYNE

Out for nought in first innings — with a smile!

Swoosh — and away goes this sweep for three.

No doubt about this drive — it's six runs.

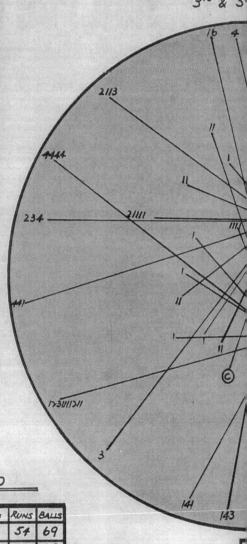

1st INNINGS

c STACKPOLE b LILLEE 0

BOWLER		1's	2's	3's	4's	6's	RUNS	BALLS
LILLEE	D.K.	13	3	1	8	–	54	69
MASSIE	R.A.L.	14	2	1	7	–	49	68
WATSON	G.D.	7	1	1	–	–	12	21
JENNER	T.J.	9	1	3	6	–	44	49
O'KEEFFE	K.J.	17	4	2	10	2	83	103
STACKPOLE	K.R.	1	1	–	1	–	7	5
CHAPPELL	G.S.	1	–	–	1	–	5	8
TOTALS		62	12	8	33	2	254	323

ERS

NE CRICKET GROUND

AUSTRALIA

RY, 1972.

213244

6

4

41414
244124

41

III

34

2

12

444

I

VIIII

4414

4411

III

Off the toes, oh so gently, and it's four more.

Rest day — and time for golf with Ian Chappell.

The wrists are working and more runs . . .

2nd INNINGS

c WALTERS b CHAPPELL G   254

PARTNERSHIPS						
WKT	PARTNERS			SNDY	SOBERS	TOTAL
4TH	POLLOCK	R.G.	8	–	23	31
5TH	GREIG	A.W.	3	2	32	37
6TH	ENGINEER	F.M.	14	–	20	34
7TH	ALAM	I	15	6	50	71
8TH	POLLOCK	P.M.	54	3	129	186

COMPILED BY M.P. RINGHAM
V.C.A. VISITING TEAMS' SCORER

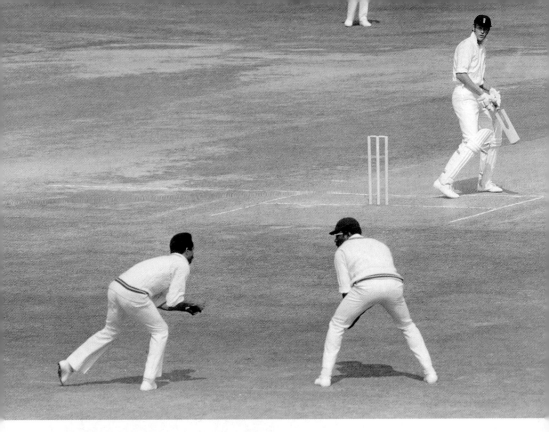

Above A quick eye and quick hands at first slip to dismiss the dangerous Tony Greig off Keith Boyce at Lord's in 1973

Left My final moment in Test cricket – bowled by deadly Derek Underwood in my last Test, against England in Trinidad in 1974

DAVID FRITH

PATRICK EAGAR

DAVID FRITH

Above My great love – golf!

Right I'm no Michael Jordan but I enjoyed playing basketball

Below Serious stuff – listening to the horseracing with fellow gambling enthusiasts Denis Compton and Ted Dexter

Overleaf How to pass the time on a rainy day. A game of cards and an, in those days, acceptable cigarette

HULTON

When Clyde told me how many I needed, I decided to get my head down. I thought to myself that the only way I was going to do it was to forget about the 300 and pretend that I had just come in and the West Indies needed me to score 64 for victory.

My only real moment of anxiety came when I played Khan Mohammad to midwicket and called for a run, only to see Everton Weekes staying firmly where he was. Fortunately, substitute fielder Waqar Hussain threw the ball to the wrong end.

The bowling was reasonably good but they had lost one or two of their players to injury. Opening bowler Mahmood Hussain bowled five balls in the innings, but there was Fazal, Khan, Nasim and Kardar. If you play on bad wickets, the bowlers take full advantage; so when the roles are reversed, my attitude is that a batsman should not spare the bowlers.

The main bowling burden fell on Fazal, who was quite a useful quick bowler, and Khan who, between them, bowled almost 140 overs.

When I reached 363, one short of the record, captain Abdul Kardar brought on opening bat Hanif Mohammad. I scored a single off the first ball and Clyde took a single off the second to leave me on strike. Hanif, not a bowler of note, asked the umpire if he could bowl left-handed, as I just needed that one run for the record. The umpire, in turn, asked me and I said that it was all right and he could bowl with both hands if he wished. I pushed the first ball out into the covers and before I could think Clyde had called, was down on me and I had to go. So I broke Sir Len Hutton's record.

I don't think that our captain Gerry Alexander was ready to declare as we still had an hour or so to go but he was left with little option as the crowd erupted. More than 13,000 spectators, well over the ground's true capacity, went crazy. They invaded the pitch and were all over the wicket. It was some 15 or 20 minutes before the ground was cleared.

This presented a great opportunity for Kardar. He pointed out to the umpires that little pieces had been taken out of the wicket by the galloping fans and the Pakistanis said that they would not bat on the wicket until it had been repaired.

That bothered me at the time because I feared that in going for the record, I might have cost my country the opportunity of building on our one-Test lead. It was important for me that we went on to win the match by bowling Pakistan out for 288 the next day to win by an innings and 174 runs. The record would not have meant the same in a drawn game.

I have to say that I enjoyed every minute of it. To score 365 in 10 hours compared very favourably with Len Hutton who took three and a half hours longer. Brian Lara, who went on to take the record with his 375, took 12 hours – and he is no slouch with the bat. In all I batted for 10 hours and 14 minutes and that was six hours quicker than Hanif's 337 in the First Test of the series at Bridgetown. But then his concentration was legend, having scored 499 in a domestic match in Karachi.

Most players who score a triple hundred take well over that 10-hour milestone, but I never poked around to try to reach 300. I was able to play my shots because once I had scored that first ton, I had no thoughts of double hundreds or records on my mind. It was only when Clyde mentioned it that I even thought about it while I was batting. Had the captain declared it would not have bothered me at all. It was only when I spoke to Clyde that I realised that the captain was going to let me try to score the runs. He knew that I wasn't going to plug around for the rest of the afternoon and into the next morning.

The joy of passing 300 and then the record took away all of the tiredness. The adrenalin was pumping and I felt that I could have gone back out and opened the bowling if we had been able to carry on.

In fact, I did bowl next day albeit only 15 overs. The wickets were shared by Roy Gilchrist, Tom Dewdney, Dennis Atkinson and Lance Gibbs. Neither Nasim-ul-Ghani nor Mahmood Hussain batted in that second innings and the Pakistanis folded with their nine men.

If we had drawn that game I would have felt guilty that the captain had let me bat on at the expense of my country. That is one of the reasons why I have always scored my runs quickly. That has always been my approach. I can never remember making runs just for the sake of making runs; the energy you use scoring those runs could be better used further down the road when it becomes important. It was just a typical Garry Sobers innings – although I had not had that many innings for it to be typical of!

That innings brought me worldwide recognition, but it also meant that every time anyone went past 250 anywhere in the world, I would take telephone calls asking me how I felt about my record being under threat. Records are made to be broken; that's what they are for. I remember when Graham Gooch scored 333. It was lucky that I was on the golf course as the English press tried to telephone me every few runs to ask me what I thought. I tried to tell them it didn't mean that much but I don't think they believed me. They kept calling back until Graham lost his wicket 32 runs short.

Whenever I broke or set records, we went on to win. It was never a selfish thing but when I came off after breaking Sir Len Hutton's record, I admit it was a wonderful feeling and we celebrated with a fabulous evening. I had messages of goodwill from all over the world, including a telephone call from Sir Len Hutton himself congratulating me. A few years later, I was at Leeds watching Australia play England when Sir Leonard walked by. 'Do you remember Sabina Park?' he said. I even received the key to the city of Kingston. It's still on display at home – I'm proud of it.

When I returned home to Barbados, the Cricket Association and the government had a motorcade waiting for me at the airport and we drove through the crowded streets. It was as joyous an occasion for them as it was for me, to think that their own 21-year-old should have broken this record.

The innings undoubtedly changed my life but not my bank balance. Suddenly I was a celebrity, not just in Barbados and the Caribbean, but around the cricket-playing world. Even *Wisden* went overboard by describing my innings as 'monumental'.

We won the Fourth Test in Georgetown, British Guiana, and far from finding a reaction setting in, I opened the batting and scored 125 in the first innings and an unbeaten 109 in the second. Oddly, for the second successive Test, I failed to take a wicket, just as I did in the Fifth and final Test in Trinidad when we lost by an innings.

Before the end of that year we were off on a tour of the subcontinent, my first, taking in five Tests in India and a further three in Pakistan starting in November and finishing in March.

I had heard a great deal about the trials and tribulations of the previous trips to the area, mostly from Everton Weekes, and all about the conditions and how they were not always satisfactory for visiting teams. But things were getting better and there was no denying the enthusiasm for the game. The atmosphere everywhere was uplifting.

We still had to have any number of inoculations. Injections were not so sophisticated then, either, and there was always a slight concern about any after effects. When I went with Ron Roberts' Commonwealth team in 1963–64 under Richie Benaud, I had the usual cholera injection and promptly forgot all about it, drank a few beers, had a few Scotches and went happily off to my bed. When I woke up the next morning, I couldn't move my arm. At first I thought that I had been sleeping awkwardly but then I remembered I had been drinking on top of the injections, something we had all been warned not to do.

The best ground was undoubtedly the CCI in Bombay because everything there was on the spot, including the accommodation. You could lie in your bed and watch the cricket; you could even put on your pads and go straight from your room to bat on that lovely wicket if you wished. The club was used by the very rich who used to take their vacations and play bridge there, so you can imagine how well we were looked after and the quality of the service.

When we played the First Test there, it was not long after I had undergone an operation for appendicitis – I was awake during the operation and watched the entire proceedings – and I needed a spinal-cord injection to enable me to play. I remember halfway through the innings my back went into spasm and I was in tremendous pain. To make matters worse, it was 110 degrees but I batted right through for 142 not out. When I came off, I was in so much agony they sent me straight to the Breach Candy hospital to have another pain-killing injection. I wouldn't want to go through that again. The needle looked like something they jabbed horses with; it was huge. There was no anaesthetic so they gave me a pillow to bite on but when that needle went into me it must have caught a bone, a nerve or something, and I almost blew the roof off the hospital with my scream.

It did some good. I was back in the field the next day, although I was limited to bowling three overs. In total, I bowled six overs in the entire match as the First Test petered out to a draw.

India were not hugely rated in international terms in those days but there were distinct signs of things to come. They have always been blessed with very good spinners but they also had an opening bowler, Surendranath, who played some of his cricket in England, and he could move the ball around. Another opening bowler, a little man named R.B. Desai, took four wickets in the Fifth Test in Delhi when we scored a massive 644 for 8 with all of us scoring runs. But it was the spinners who really caught the eye led by Subhas Gupte, a truly outstanding bowler. Then there was Chandra Borde, another who had played league cricket in England, with his nice loopy leg spin. He was a useful bat as well. With Polly Umrigar, V.J. Manjrekar, their captain Ghulam Ahmed, Pankaj Roy and Nari Contractor, it was quite a useful team but we won the series 3–0 with two drawn.

Eden Gardens in Calcutta was the wicket I really enjoyed. That was where I scored 106 in a team total of 614 for 5 with Rohan Kanhai scoring a double century and Basil Butcher a hundred. We bowled them out for 124 and 154. They failed to master the pace of Roy Gilchrist and Wes Hall who took 15 wickets between them as the ball moved about on the green wicket.

The living conditions were good for that Test because we stayed at the Great Eastern Hotel. Some of the places where we stayed were little more than guesthouses and some of the rooms were not pleasant to live in at all, but we had been warned and were prepared for it. The food wasn't too bad except for the meatless days and the lack of drinks – the sort of drinks that I enjoyed when I relaxed. We were issued with coupons every month that permitted us to buy alcohol. We could have a drink when we were invited to one of the Maharajah's palaces, but the prohibition that had been imposed after their split from Pakistan curtailed most everything. Going out with the local girls was out of the question. The Indians loved entertaining and there were many social gatherings, but even there mixing with girls was difficult because of their religion and the fear that their reputations might be damaged by rumour and innuendo if they were seen with fit, healthy young cricketers.

But on that first tour, the social side was secondary. I was happy to concentrate on the cricket. It was in India that I learned how to play spin. I enjoyed a successful tour and it was pointed out to me that in my first 16 Tests I had scored 856 runs for an average of 32.9 while in my next eight I scored 1,192 with an average of 137.1. A lot of those runs were scored against India.

We saw a great deal of the country, and were aware of the poverty, because we had to travel everywhere by train, and that was some experience. There were people all over you and hanging from the outside of the carriages. Mainly we mixed with the upper classes of society but when we drove through the streets, we could see the people sleeping rough, the deformed beggars and the young children asking for help. It was hard to take, considering the comparative luxury we were enjoying. We just had to grin and bear it because there was little we could do.

The food was no problem – I have now been to India on about seven occasions, and I can honestly say that I have never been ill through the food – but one of the things you had to be careful about was the water. I was a Scotch and soda man at the time and I was as happy and healthy as you could get. The alcohol would kill most of the germs but I kept off the water and didn't have ice in my whisky. I stayed with bottled soda. I also cleaned my teeth with the soda.

Nowadays the food and the service are fantastic. You can order a full meal at four o'clock in the morning and sit back and watch sport on television in your hotel room with cricket from all over the world. That and English football seem to be the most popular events.

I found Pakistan fascinating but frustrating. I was looking forward to going there straight from our successes in India. I had averaged 114 and scored over 700 runs; I was playing really well and was on top of my form. But instead of building on that excellent platform, it turned out to be the trip from hell. I was so disappointed and didn't know what in the world was going on.

We won the toss in the First Test at the National Stadium in Karachi and Gerry Alexander decided to bat. When I went in at number four I was in confident mood, even though we were 62 for 2 and Fazal Mahmood was bowling big leg-cutters. I played down the line; the ball missed the bat, hit the pad and Fazal appealed. I knew where my leg was in relationship to the stumps, outside the leg stump, so imagine my surprise when I was given out lbw. I was puzzled but said nothing. But then came the second innings and the same sort of rank bad decision. This time there was a distinct inside edge on to the pad. Leg slip Ijaz Butt dived only for the ball to fall well short of him, but Fazal appealed anyway and once again up went the umpire's finger. I looked at Ijaz in surprise and he looked at me and said, 'What's happening?' We both knew I had not been caught, and the only decision it could have been was lbw again.

I shrugged my shoulders and answered, 'It looks as though I'm out.' As I walked back to the pavilion, Collie Smith, who had watched in amazement at the non-strike end, made some angry comments to Fazal.

When I reached the dressing room I started packing my bags. I had decided that there was no point in hanging around and that I was going home. Berkeley Gaskin, the tour manager, came up and asked me what I was doing. I told him I was leaving, going home, back to the Caribbean. When he asked me why I replied that there was no chance of me getting any runs in Pakistan, therefore there was no point in me hanging around. I couldn't play cricket this way.

Gaskin sat me down and told me that they knew in advance what was going to happen. A Pakistani player had boasted to him and some of our senior players when they arrived that I wouldn't score a run on the tour and that wherever I was hit, they would appeal and I would be given out. I demanded to know why he hadn't told me this before I went out to bat. I'm not sure how true all this was, but there was a second strange decision in Dacca.

I eventually cooled down and was persuaded to play on. We lost that First Test by 10 wickets and then went on to Dacca. This time I came in at number three and was feeling quite good as I moved on to 29 on a really bad wicket. But then on came Fazal again. He bowled an off-cutter and I went to play him through midwicket, missed and the ball hit me well outside leg stump – that was my opinion and that of most of those in a position to judge. There was an immediate appeal and up went the finger again. It struck me as an appalling decision. I was philosophical about it by now and when I went back to the pavilion I said to the rest of the team that if that was what it was going to be like, I would accept it, and if they still wanted me to stay, I would.

We lost by 41 runs, even though we bowled them out for 145 and 144 with just one lbw decision going our way. In turn, we were bowled out for 76 and 172 and I top scored in both innings, keeping my pads out of the way in the second innings until I was caught, ironically, by Fazal off Mahmood for 45 – the second highest score in the entire match!

But it was still hard to take. I was seething inside at the injustice. It helped relax me when I met a huge Texan in a big hat who introduced himself to me at the ground by telling me that he had heard that I thought I could drink. He told me that since he had been in Dacca he had found no one to have a session with. He invited me to bring some of the guys along for fun but that he and I would have our own party. I asked Collie Smith, Tom Dewdney, who was a bit of a nut, and Jackie Hendriks to accompany me and no sooner had we arrived at the American's apartment than he sat me down and poured me a large Scotch and then another and another.

The man was a good drinker and later on I felt the need to go and have a lie down. About two o'clock in the morning he came and woke me up with a bottle of beer in his hand and invited me to start again. So I had a few more drinks with him. Next day, the others went off on a riverboat trip and when they came back we were still drinking and we carried on until the Texan's wife dropped Collie, Jackie, Tom and me back at our hotel later that evening. What else was there to do? They certainly wouldn't let me play cricket.

I suppose these days there would be a strong suspicion of there being some sort of gambling coup being worked but I honestly do not believe that was the case. I had scored 365 against them in the West Indies and I had scored a lot of runs in India just before we arrived. Clearly they had decided that I was the man they wanted out.

We moved on to Lahore with the series already lost and won by an innings. That was played fairly and Rohan Kanhai scored a double century. I added 72 before being bowled by Nasim.

I discovered that some of the Pakistan players knew that I wasn't going to make runs in this series. One or two have subsequently told me that they knew what was going to happen. That is why I can talk openly about it now. That was against everything cricket stood for and everything I believed in. In three innings, I was never near out but they have gone down in history as three failures against me. I don't worry about the scores but I do worry about the morals and the fact that some Pakistani players knew what was happening and did nothing about it.

It was the worst umpiring I ever came across in my career. I can understand and forgive umpires for making honest mistakes but I feel sure that hadn't happened here. I never felt the same way again, thank God.

It was such a pity because I was on top of my game. West Indian cricket was resurgent and we were looking forward to winning another series.

We had somewhat weakened our attack when Roy Gilchrist was sent home from India at the end of that leg of the tour because he had behaved badly, defying the captain Gerry Alexander who had continually warned him about his behaviour. He had bowled beamers and told the captain that he chucked them with intent to hurt. Alexander told him never to bowl them in any match he was in charge of again. His warning fell on deaf ears.

We went to play at Amritsar in a three-day match for the final game of the tour. They had a player named Saranjit Singh who had been at Cambridge University with Gerry Alexander. Singh reckoned he was a good cricketer but was being overlooked by the Indians for their Test side and he saw this as his chance to impress the selectors. Before the game, he went round criticising Gilchrist, asking who he thought he was, that he was nothing to be scared of and that he would see him off and show him who was the master when they came face to face. It was pretty inflammatory stuff. Had I been Gerry, I would not have played Gilchrist and avoided the inevitable trouble. We lost the toss and Saranjit Singh opened the batting, putting him in immediate conflict with Gilchrist. Before a ball was bowled, Gillie was warned by the skipper to be careful and not to let what had been said affect him.

But Gillie wasn't the sort of fellow to listen to advice like that and when he ran in to bowl to Singh, he just turned his arm over at half pace, the batsman came down the wicket and drove him through the covers to the boundary. As he walked back, the batsman turned to our bowler and said, 'Gillie, that was a lovely shot, wasn't it?'

Two balls later, Singh did it again, saying to Gilchrist at the end of his follow-through, 'Gillie, that was an even better shot than the first one.'

Gillie said nothing but made his way back to the sightscreen, put his foot on it, turned, ran in and fired in a vicious bouncer that literally took the turban off the surprised Singh. His hair fell down and he raced off the field to tuck it back.

When he returned to the crease, the very next ball the umpire no balled Gillie – he went through the crease and delivered a beamer straight at Singh's face. Only God saved the Indian that day, it could have been no one else. He couldn't have moved his head that rapidly on his own; reactions just aren't that quick.

Having already warned him, Gerry called Gillie over and sent him from the field. He had tried to have him sent home earlier for his bad behaviour but the committee knew that the Indian batsmen were afraid of him and Wes Hall, and he stayed on to take 26 wickets in four Tests at an average of 16. But this was the final straw and Gerry told the committee that it was no longer a matter for discussion and that if Gilchrist was not sent home then he, the captain, would go. So Gillie was sent home and missed the Pakistan tour that followed, and he did not play Test cricket again. He had made just 13 appearances and carried on getting into trouble wherever he played.

When Gerry saw what the Pakistani umpires were doing to me he said that he wished he had kept Gilchrist to even the balance. If we had had Gilchrist in the side, we would have won the series. If the umpires hadn't given their batsmen out, he would have knocked them out. He wouldn't have had to bowl beamers or any other unfair balls; he would have been too quick for them, and the bouncers would have frightened them.

I went back to Pakistan to play in a relief fund match and was made very welcome but there was no other tour of Pakistan during my playing days. The West Indies did not go back there until 1975. But despite all that happened to me, had I still been playing then I would have gone back.

CHAPTER FOURTEEN

Reluctant tourist

I returned to India in 1966–67 for a three-Test series and, quite frankly, I did not want to go. At that time, the Indians were still not considered a really top cricket-playing nation despite having a lot of good players, and I felt it should be treated as an opportunity to groom some of the younger ones rather than sending all the top players. I had been playing a lot of cricket and I recommended that they send a couple of youngsters and give me a rest. The Board were having none of it and told me that, as captain of the West Indies, I was public property. India wanted me over there, they had requested me and I had to go.

As much as I was charmed by the country and its people, I had already been there with the Ron Roberts Commonwealth team as well as with the West Indies and I would have loved a break. But, in the end, I was glad that I went.

Living conditions were not very good but the wickets were excellent and so was the cricket, except for the occasional dodgy umpiring decision. These were not as bad as some players tried to make out.

There was nothing sinister about them. I put it down to the Indian umpires' lack of exposure to international cricket compared with other nationalities' umpires. English, Australian and West Indian umpires had far more chance to improve their skills with five Tests at a time whereas most teams on the subcontinent played only three.

All Indians seem to be cricket mad. It was brought home to us how seriously they take it when we were involved in a riot at Calcutta on New Year's Day 1967. It was the Second Test. We had won the first in Bombay by six wickets and the Indian supporters were expecting the likes of Bedi and Venkat to spin us to defeat to level the series and restore pride.

There are so many people who want to watch cricket in India that the ground was full long before stumps were pitched. It was said that an extra 10,000 tickets over and above the capacity of the ground had been given out by political parties trying to gain votes before a big election that was imminent. This was in the days before the Eden Park ground was expanded to the splendid arena that it is today.

The trouble began to brew when the crowd started to spill over the boundary. We were batting and, gradually, the playing area was becoming smaller and smaller with the police trying in vain to force people back. There was nowhere for them to go. There were just too many people inside and outside the ground and all of them seemed to have tickets and the right of entry. Maybe the ground could have taken an extra 1,000 people but not 10,000. We could all see something was going to blow.

The spark came when one of the exasperated policemen took out his baton and lashed out at one of the spectators. When the fans around the injured man saw what had happened and the blood that flowed from the head wound, they just went crazy.

The players ran off the field as the enraged spectators started to set fire to the stands, paper, furniture and anything else flammable that they could lay their hands on. I remember being grateful that we weren't in one of the stands with a canvas roof; at least, I was until they started to attack the dressing-room area. In the midst of all this trouble, Conrad Hunte went to the top of the pavilion to take our flag down to save it from being damaged. He asked me to help but I told him he must be mad and so he did it on his own.

The police used tear gas on the fans and it started seeping into our dressing room. It was horrible and we were choking and gasping. The tear gas was supposed to protect us from the fans. We had to wrap wet towels around our heads and those who leant out of the windows at the back for some fresh air were abused and threatened. The fans didn't pick on us particularly but just anyone who was in their way. Eventually, they brought cars round to the back entrance. Charlie Griffith broke down the galvanised sheet of metal that protected the back door from the street behind the pavilion and we spilled out into the fresh air.

It was very frightening. When we made our escape on to the road, five of us plus the driver were levered into a little Ford Prefect, a car that normally held three passengers at a squeeze. While we were piling into the car, Charlie Griffith raced past shouting that he didn't want a lift and he ran all the way back to the hotel, a good two miles.

It was a desperate scene as the rioting fans carried on outside the ground, burning buses and police motorcycles. Our team bus was stoned and we decided we would get the hell out of it the very next morning and take the team back home to the West Indies. But the Indians told us that was the worst thing we could do. It was explained to us that if we went back the next day and continued the match, nothing would happen, but if we were to leave, we could be seriously hurt; the bus would never reach the airport. They advised us to go back and play.

It was eventually decided that we should not play the next day while they cleared up the ground, but we eventually resumed amidst the charred remnants of the stand and continued to play the Test match. I scored a quick 70 and then we bowled them out twice to win by an innings. I picked up seven wickets.

The advice to stay was good. These are not usually violent people but they say they have the worst tempers in the world and once started, they cannot be stopped. It takes a lot to get them going but once the trigger is pulled, watch out. I have seen Indians cursed and abused and all they do is laugh. Push and they won't retaliate, but hope and pray to God that you don't push once too often because you would not like what you see. They can be the most violent people in the world and that is what Mahatma Ghandi fought for, to teach them to turn the other cheek. He took all that punishment because he wanted them to understand that to rebel wasn't the way and that they must not fight back. There was no more trouble on the tour. It was as though nothing had happened.

We drew the Third and final Test in Madras to clinch the series. Charlie Griffith and I saved the match with an unbroken stand of 77. Charlie was undefeated on 40 at stumps while I added to my 95 in the first innings with 74 not out in the second.

I remember Chandrasekhar taking the second new ball and bowling Charlie one of the fastest bouncers I have ever seen. It was quite deliberate, as Charlie had bounced him a time or two. Charlie was such a clever cricketer. He was trying to kill time and play as few balls as possible. He played forward on one occasion to Prasanna, a very slow bowler, and the ball gently looped up over his arms and hit him on the chest. Looking up at the clock and knowing there was only Wes Hall and Lance Gibbs to come in, he lay on the pitch for around five minutes before he 'recovered' and was able to carry on.

Charlie knew how to play the game. Every minute of that charade was for the benefit of the team. He sat up and immediately fell down again. It was hard for me to suppress a grin although it was not something I would have done.

It was a profitable series for me. Even though I did not score a hundred this time, I averaged 114 and I was second in the bowling with 14 wickets to Lance Gibbs's 18.

The entire tour, however, was overshadowed when Frank Worrell, in India on university business, was suddenly taken ill and flown home. He was diagnosed as having developed leukaemia and he died shortly afterwards in the University Hospital of the West Indies, aged just 42, a loss not only to the West Indies but to the entire world of cricket. We learned of his death when we arrived back in Jamaica.

It was during this tour that I became engaged to a beautiful young actress, the 17-year-old Anju Mahindu. It was one of those things that happen when you travel on tour. I was never a person who even thought about marriage and settling down in those days. I met lots of nice girls and their families. I would be a liar if didn't admit that meeting females on these tours was a pleasant part of life – of course it was. I liked being with them, going out for dinners, dancing and that kind of thing. But marriage was a different matter altogether and would have been difficult to say the least with my constant travelling around the world.

But I just took to this girl and she to me. Becoming engaged seemed to be the right thing to do at the time. She was so beautiful and such a nice person, I fell head over heels in love. When the engagement idea came up, I thought, 'Why not?'

The engagement party was one of the best social gatherings I have ever attended. There must have been 500 or 600 guests, most of them actors and actresses. It was big news, flashed around the world on the newsreels. She was a celebrity and I was treated in the same fashion in India. Obviously, to the media it was a great story and a perfect union. Fortunately, I got on well with her mother and her sisters and everything looked very good indeed. The people in the West Indies must have wondered what was going on.

I even made a 40-minute film with Anju. Every morning in our Breach Candy Hotel, where all the stars stayed, I used to pass Djulip Singh, one of the top Bollywood actors, and he would shout out for me to join him for breakfast. Everyone was incredibly friendly to me and couldn't do enough. I never saw the film and don't know whether it was released or what happened to it.

I was at the top of my career at the time and no doubt the publicity was good for Anju as her first film was coming out at the time, especially since the Indian captain, the Nawab of Pataudi, had also married an Indian actress a year or so before our engagement. I never looked at it that way.

There may have been some question marks over my intentions but I was deadly serious about it all. I fully intended to marry her. I was keen for her to travel to England for our marriage ceremony. I now know that behind the scenes there were all sorts of problems. For one thing, if I had taken her to England, I would have had to deposit a certain amount of money in the Reserve Bank as a sort of dowry, something I did not understand at all at the time. I was due to return to England and she was keen to come with me, but in the end she stayed behind.

The distance between us proved to be the real barrier and it eventually became obvious to me that the marriage was not going to happen. When I became engaged to Australian Pru Kirby a couple of years later, I had to telephone my Indian fiancée for her consent. She had to write to me and say in the letter that she released me from my proposal to her so that I could marry someone else. It was all done very properly. Anju had a sister Annu and a lot of people told me later that she thought a great deal of me. She was probably the most upset of all that I wasn't to become part of the family.

Cricketers hold a very high status in India and to this day I regularly receive letters asking for autographs. I love the country and still go there quite often, commentating when the West Indies play there and also when Sri Lanka play a series. Today it is a fantastic place. The hotels are incredible and the food is great and, thankfully, there is no longer the need for all those injections before you go.

The Indians did not like coming to the West Indies as much as I liked going there. For a start they didn't like the pace of our attacks. They were unused to that sort of speed. They did not have the experience of it on their own wickets and it was difficult for them to handle genuine pace at home or away.

Freddie Trueman would have had a lot more wickets if he had toured India. If he had gone on the two tours to India he missed, and the other one he was banned for in South Africa, he could have easily reached 380 wickets instead of his then record of 307. Most of the really quick bowlers who went to India took a lot of wickets.

Things haven't changed. I remember Bishen Bedi calling his team off in Jamaica, saying that he did not want them seriously hurt. I don't blame him. In those days, West Indies didn't have fast bowlers . . . they had express bowlers! A lot of teams tolerated it but few of them could handle the pace and power of Michael Holding, Colin Croft, Andy Roberts and Joel Garner. There was never any relief and even today they look back on batting against them as a form of suicide. It was consistent pace, over after over. I can imagine what it was like when Test batsmen were used to two fast bowlers a medium pacer and then maybe a couple of spinners. Here were four bowlers in one team who bowled at over 90 miles an hour. It was relentless and must have been unbearable with no limits against bouncers.

India did, however, overcome the odds in their 1971 tour of the West Indies. This was largely due to the emergence of Sunil Gavaskar who scored a total of 774 runs with a top score of 220 and 124 in the Fifth Test. With Hall and Griffith retired, we boasted no true pace and India's win in the Second Test in Trinidad was enough, as the other four Tests were drawn. I made three centuries in that series including 178 not out in the Fourth Test at Bridgetown, and scored 597 at an average of 74.62. With our attack blunted, I also bowled 219 overs in that series and took a dozen wickets, this despite the fact that I damaged a muscle and played virtually on one leg.

I had the great fortune to be in Sri Lanka, coaching their national cricket team for a two-year period, when they attained Test status, and I took them to England in 1984 for the World Cup.

It all happened through the president of the Sri Lankan Cricket Board, Gamani De Senaka. He went to England in 1981 to clinch their promotion to full Test status, which became operative two years later, and returned home via Australia. He came to see me where I was living in Sydney and invited me back to Sri Lanka to have a look at their cricket. I was pleased to accept his invitation and a couple of months later, I went to Colombo where I was immediately entranced by the young batsman Arjuna Ranatunga. What a beautiful little player he was – still a teenager but so accomplished. When you see a youngster of that age playing with correctness of technique, not afraid of anybody and not afraid to hit the ball, it is a great thrill whatever nationality he may be. His mannerisms and characteristics immediately attracted me.

The following year, I was invited to coach them before they played Australia in a one-day game, followed by a Test match. The first thing I asked when I arrived was what had happened to the young Ranatunga and I was told he wasn't in the team because the chairman of selectors, a former off-spinner, didn't rate him.

I had been asked to attend the team selection as an observer. When Ranatunga's name came up, it was immediately dismissed, but before they could move on to the next player, I interrupted and said that this particular player must play in the next game. They were amazed at my intervention and the chairman told me that I had no say in the selection. I responded to the effect that whether I had any say or not, if this cricketer wasn't in the side, I would be speaking to the president about it. I pulled rank and it worked, not just for the young batsman, but for the future of the game in the country. He was picked and responded by scoring a century against the Australians in the one-day game. He then played in the Test match, scored 90 and never looked back.

It not only helped him, it also helped me because it was realised that I wasn't going to stand any nonsense or get involved in their internal political squabbles. I was out there to do a job for the president and I was going to do it to the best of my ability. Ranatunga never forgot my intervention as he went on to lead Sri Lanka to great things, particularly in one-day cricket.

What a pleasure it was to coach them! They had lost a lot of their best players to a ban following a rebel tour to South Africa and this was a fresh, largely untried bunch of young players. But when I saw the quality of the players in the nets for the first time, I couldn't understand what I was doing there. Their technique was so good it looked as though they had already enjoyed the best of coaching. Van Silvas, their coach, had done a great job with the youngsters, including Aravinda Da Silva, who was also a teenager. I immediately thought that I would have to forget about the basic techniques, in which they were so well versed, and look at something different, advanced techniques and ways to help them into this high class of cricket. I decided that the way to tackle it was to brainwash them. I knew that there were plenty of good cricketers from the days when I had played against Ceylon. They were an unsophisticated team and I always used to do well there, scoring 100 every time I played against them. That gave the youngsters respect for me; they looked up to me and listened to what I had to tell them.

Their biggest problem was that they were not so good against quick bowlers and every country was looking for really fast men at the time. I had to ask myself how I could get it into their heads and minds that if they wanted to play cricket at this level they had to learn to play the quickies whether they liked it or not.

I searched out their fastest bowlers, including Asantha de Mel and big V.B. John, to see how they faced up to them. At the same time, I had to explain that their fast bowlers were not even quick by international standards, and if they were going to back away from them, they had no chance against the really fast men and they might as well forget all about playing Test cricket.

I asked them how would they play against Joel Garner, Michael Holding and Colin Croft of the West Indies, or New Zealand's Sir Richard Hadlee, or Australia's Jeff Thomson and Dennis Lillee, or England's Graham Dilley and all those fellows. I told them if they didn't get behind the ball to forget all about winning Test matches.

I tackled the project from the aspect of coping with fast bowling using advanced techniques and started to get results, really good results. They always remembered that, and I told everyone that within 10 or 12 years this would be a world-beating team.

We should have done far better than we did in England when we went there for the 1983 World Cup. Sri Lanka played Pakistan, one of the top teams in the competition, at Leeds and had them gasping at 34 for 6 and looking as though they would bowl them out for under 70. Imran Khan steadied Pakistan and they eventually finished with over 200 runs and knocked it clean out of our hands. Although we had good players, we were not going to score that many runs in English conditions. Had we needed 80 or 90, we would have walked that and gone into the semi-finals. Who knows what would have happened after that.

Shortly afterwards, New Zealand came to Sri Lanka and although we gave them a good fight, Richard Hadlee made the difference and they were just too good for us. Sitting in the pavilion, I could see how he was going to work out certain of our batsmen. I would sit down with the players and tell them to watch how he was going to get Dulip out. He would set him up with a bouncer, which Dulip would hook, then he would bowl him another to keep him on the back foot. Then it was two coming into him followed by the one that went away and he would be caught in the slips. He did it all the time, so consistently.

Hadlee was one of the bowlers who could judge a batsman almost as soon as he came in. He watched how he shaped up against him and if he wasn't good enough, he would be out in the next three or four balls. Richard would carefully adjust his field, bowl the right ball and sure enough, he would take the wicket. I saw him work out so many batsmen.

I never played against Hadlee but I was very appreciative of his qualities and would have enjoyed batting against him. He was a great bowler and I rated him right up there among the very best. He bowled very quickly when he started but slowed down and concentrated on movement. You could tell the batsman what to expect but as soon as they shaped up, you knew that all your advice would be of no use.

I could see the potential in these young Sri Lankan players and it didn't surprise me at all how well they did in the years that followed. They are exciting players and play the game the way I like to see it played. They asked me to go back but with all the political problems and the violence, I felt that little bit apprehensive. I am an easygoing person and like to live my life without restrictions and without being told that I cannot go here or go there because something might happen to me. With my lifestyle, I never know where I may stray one night.

The day I was leaving there was an explosion of trouble and they had to drive me through the back streets to get me safely to the airport. The driver had to tell people it was me in the car to get through the roadblocks. I have never been afraid but I stay away from trouble. Cammie Smith goes regularly to Sri Lanka as a referee and says he has seen no trouble and I am, of course, delighted that no cricketer has ever been caught up in the violence.

I hope I have the chance of going back before I die. There was a benefit for Ranatunga recently and I would have gone then but the invitation came too late and I was away at just the wrong time.

It would have been nice to do the same thing for the West Indies that I did for Sri Lanka – but I don't have a coaching certificate. Only people with coaching certificates qualify for the position where I come from, no matter what you might have achieved in your career.

CHAPTER FIFTEEN

On batting

My philosophy with batting is fairly simple. I liked to attack and, to be honest, I can never remember being bogged down at any level. I was always a free scorer in even the tightest situations because I looked at the game knowing that you have to play shots. Once you have your eye in and you are set, no matter how good the bowling is, you should score your runs quickly, especially on the types of wicket that are prevalent these days.

It was different when I first moved to play in England. I had to be careful on a green top, batting somewhere such as The Oval on a turning wicket when I didn't have the necessary experience. It took a little time to develop the skill of playing a variety of shots, to learn how to explode. But even on the worst wickets and in the most difficult situations, I was always able to play shots once I was in and seeing the ball.

The wicket at Sabina Park was not everyone's favourite but it was good to me. It was fast and bouncy and I liked the ball coming on to me so that I could play shots. On slower wickets, I wasn't so good; I could stay there but shots were difficult until I learned to cope. This was one of the problems I had in New Zealand when the ball just wasn't coming through and I never scored runs. Jamaican wickets were like those in Perth where, if you could play back, you would usually make runs. I can't ever remember really failing in Jamaica. After the world record 365 against Pakistan, which included my first 100 in Test cricket, I made regular centuries in Kingston. In 11 Tests and 18 innings there, I scored a total of 1,354 runs at an average of 104.15 with five 100s and four 50s. I also took 27 wickets and held eight catches. It is easy to see why I liked it so much!

Another good ground for me was Bourda in Guyana. It wasn't as quick as Sabina Park; it was a placid, beautiful wicket and the outfield was like lightning. Once you beat the in-field, you knew that it would be a boundary. I scored five centuries there, including two in the same game, and averaged 94.7 in seven Tests.

My home track at Kensington Oval in Barbados was also an excellent wicket where the ball used to come on and I averaged 76.16 there. The Queen's Park Oval was more often than not a slow wicket and consequently I made just one century in Trinidad in 17 Tests and averaged 35.33. The ball never really came on there as it did on other Caribbean wickets or in Australia.

Of the English grounds, I always enjoyed myself at Trent Bridge but I did like the way the ball used to come on at Lord's where I more often than not batted well and averaged almost 100 in my five Tests.

But there was nothing quite like Jamaica where I first played for the West Indies, at an age when all the people love you. Their hearts went out to the skinny lad just out of short pants. Whenever I went back I was welcomed and the expectancy was always high. The Jamaicans really took me to their hearts.

Fear is the worst enemy of every cricketer. I decided from an early age that I could not afford to be scared of a bowler or a batsman or fielding in any position, no matter how close to the wicket. So I built my cricket around myself, and I went out there fearless, whatever I had to do, but especially when I was batting. They had the ball and

I had the bat, and I was always determined that they were not going to dictate to me. Of course, there were bowlers whom I would watch more closely than others, those against whom I wouldn't take as many chances. England's Fred Trueman was one, especially when he was holding a new ball. That was the time when I would look and think that much more. The same applied to Dennis Lillee, especially on his home wicket at the W.A.C.A in Perth.

When I faced world-class spinners such as Subhas Gupte, Richie Benaud, Bishen Bedi, Prasana, Jim Laker, Tony Lock and Lance Gibbs, I watched them closely, too, because they were clever, expert bowlers and you knew what they could do, especially on a wicket that suited their special skills. I studied them carefully when I first arrived at the crease but, when I was at my peak, once settled, I would treat those same bowlers as you would any other.

No matter how great a batsman you think you may be, there is always an initial period, usually in the first 20 minutes, when you are very vulnerable and that is the time the bowlers have to claim your wicket. There are many things you have to weigh up when you go in to bat – the position of the game, what needs to be done for your team, what risks you should or shouldn't take, how you are going to plan your innings. It is not just natural ability that makes a batsman great; the planning in those early minutes is crucial.

There were days when I would come out of the nets feeling good. I would look at the wicket and from the first ball hitting the middle of the bat, I would know that the only way I was going to be out was if I gave my wicket away.

I guess I was unlike most batsmen in that situation. I would weigh everything up, decide the most likely way I was going to get out – and eliminate it. I may have thought that the only way I could give up my wicket on that particular day was by being caught in the slips, so everything outside the off stump I would leave well alone. I admit that it was a strange way of going about things, which is why I have not talked about it before, but it was my way of focusing and keeping my concentration.

Concentration is vital. A player with an injury can surprise even himself by performing above his expectations because the injury focuses his mind. Gordon Greenidge in particular was like that. When he was hurt, he would become like a wounded lion, really dangerous.

I found that I could judge a quality batsman by the balls he left alone. I often hear a commentator saying a batsman knows where his off stump is. I have spoken to a lot of players about that and have never been given the right answer. I knew the answer. The only way is if your back foot is level with the off stump. If the ball pitches outside that, you know it cannot hit the stumps unless it comes back, and then you know you have to play it. If you are standing on the leg stump, you have to play the ball even though it is wide; you are not covering the stumps.

Cricket is a simple game. Once you cover the stumps and the ball is outside your body, there is no way it can hit the woodwork. The only way you can be out is by making a mistake. That is how you know where your stumps are; that is how you know what shots to play to which ball. If it is on your stumps, you know you have to play it because if you don't you will be bowled or lbw. If it is out there, you decide whether to hook it up, hook it down or leave it alone. That is why you should always move and cover your wicket; that is how you know where your ball is. It doesn't necessarily mean that you know where your stumps are unless you cover them.

I learned a lot playing in England in the changing conditions, and from the quality of the players I played with and against. The variety was immense. Some of the bowlers I played against were very good and some were hopeless, but if they were bowling now under those same conditions, they would give a lot of players who call themselves batsmen all sorts of trouble because few of them can handle the ball that moves about. We see that so often at Headingley where small totals are the order of the day. The ball moves around and does too much for batsmen unused to those conditions.

I didn't need convincing to go. I wanted to play wherever I could, but England more than anywhere else in the world because we had always been told that this was the home of cricket with different conditions from anywhere else. In those days, it presented the biggest test for any cricketer. I'm glad that I played in England when I did. It taught me how to play the ball on its merit. It taught me to watch the seam bowler off the wicket, not just from the hand but right up until the last split second.

When I arrived, I still played off the back foot and a lot of the English players used to tell me that I had to get on the front foot to narrow the angle of the seam and ball. My attitude was that if you played off the back foot, by the time the ball reached you it had gone so far you could leave it as you watched it move. If you were on the front foot, there was no time to adjust and it could hit the edge. If you were back and it cut away, you could leave it alone and if it came back in there was time to play it.

Tom Graveney never committed himself on the front foot. I once asked him why most Englishmen did and he couldn't tell me. That, to me, was just about survival whereas most great batsmen don't push out the front foot; they are back-foot players.

I once batted with Colin Cowdrey on a wicket that had a bit of green in it and looked somewhat dangerous. It was on the Ron Roberts' tour of India in Calcutta. We both scored tons and when he reached his 100 I wandered down the wicket to tell him how magnificently he had batted and asked him why he did not bat this way all the time.

'Why don't you put the bat to the ball as you have done here,' I wondered, 'instead of the pad to the ball?' He answered that he wasn't as good a batsman as I was.

'Don't give me that,' I said. 'That's just a diplomatic answer, that's sarcasm, man. It is nothing to do with how good I can play or how good you can play.'

He was so much a team player for England, with so much resting on his shoulders, that he had to find the safest way to stay at the crease, and in those days the umpires weren't giving you out on the front foot. His attitude was that as long as you stayed at the crease the runs would come. In today's cricket he would be a magnificent player because he wouldn't be able to push the pad at the ball. If he did, he would be given out. He could play with the bat magnificently when he put his mind to it. It was because of his dedication to the England team that he batted the way he did.

England was home from home for me. Most of my adult cricket was played in England. I went there in 1957 and played every year until 1975, either on tour, or league or county cricket. I played much more cricket in England than in the Caribbean where I played inter-colonial cricket and in the Shell Shield.

In England the game was more psychological than in the Caribbean, much of it played in the mind because every day brought different conditions and different wickets. There were too many batsmen who were, and still are, worried about the previous ball that had just beaten the edge of their bat, anxious about what the next ball might be going to do. You could almost hear them thinking is it going to be an inswinger, a bouncer or an outswinger? That's a waste of time and energy. Once the ball has gone it's gone, it's history.

I never used to worry about the last ball or what the one after next might do. The only ball that matters is the one to come. I relaxed until the bowler started his run-up, waiting until he was ready to bowl, and then I started to concentrate. With some bowlers you can anticipate what they are going to do, others are more unpredictable. Your experience will tell you that certain fast bowlers, after you have hit them to the boundary, will bowl a bouncer next ball up. It was so obvious, yet some of those bowlers did not realise that the batsman knew exactly what was coming. With others, you can spot in their run-up that they are about to bowl something different. They increase their pace, run wider or cut their stride. If you can spot those idiosyncrasies, it gives that little bit of edge, a head start to be in the right position against bowling that's truly fast. When that bowler runs up, you have no friends, no one you want to talk to. If he still wants to be your friend after you have hit him for another boundary, that's fine, too.

Wes Hall was a classic example – when he reached the last three or four strides he used to break into shorter steps which meant he was trying to leap higher. With his huge strides he had difficulty gaining the elevation he needed and by the time you saw those shorter strides it was obvious he was preparing to bowl a bouncer and you were looking for it, getting into position that much earlier to play the shot. That extra fraction of a second was crucial at Wes's pace.

I don't think he realised that I had found him out until after we played against each other in Australia. It was South Australia against Queensland. To his surprise, I told him that he was one of the easiest fast bowlers to play against because I always knew when a bouncer was coming well in advance of the delivery stride. I explained to him how he telegraphed the message to the batsman when he cut his strides. When I played against great bowlers like him with lightning pace, I always looked for an advantage, anything to gain that little edge. That, I told Wes, was my edge on him. By then it was too late in our careers for him to change to any great effect against me.

If you go in to bat without any kind of planning, you have little chance of building an innings of any significance. If you look at a wicket and say to yourself that you can't bat on that, you cannot succeed. I know because it happened to me in New Zealand. I looked at the wicket and couldn't see how I could score runs. With that negative thinking, it became a self-fulfilling prophecy. On wickets like that you have to chance your arm, and if you see the ball in a certain area, you have to attack it. If something bad or unexpected happens, tough luck, but if it doesn't, you have your four.

A number of critics in England said of me, 'He's a back-foot player with a lot of skill and a good eye.' But there was a lot more to my cricket than good eyesight and skill. There was thought behind everything I did, no matter how trivial or insignificant it may have seemed. It saddens me that some people aren't prepared to give me that credit. If they believed that no thought went into it because it was made to look so easy, nothing could be further from the truth.

Sometimes, as happened to me when I was a youngster and batting down the order, you have to go out there and do the best for the team and forget about the rest. You may not think you have the talent of those who have batted previously but you have to have something to be there in the first place, and if you use that knowledge and think the right way, it will pay off in the long run. This is how I have always approached my cricket, whether I was bowling, batting or fielding.

Cricket at the top level is very much like golf with 99 per cent of it above the shoulders. It doesn't matter how much ability you have; if you don't channel it in the right direction, you will never be successful – reasonably good, maybe, but never able to reach the heights. To do that you have to have the mental capacity to match the skill and ability. If a player can work the two together, there is a chance of being a world-beater.

I was never a superstitious cricketer because I was a thinking cricketer. I never minded whether I was first out of the dressing room or the last, whether I put my right pad on first or my left, whether I batted at number one or number nine. In 1957 I opened the batting and when I made my 365 I batted at number four.

I never believed that I was any more gifted than anyone else. I just loved the game and was prepared to give some thought to it. Others said it was a gift but I realised soon enough that my ability was not going to be enough on its own. I had to work with it and I had to do something to bring it out. I knew that I couldn't just go out there, throw the bat at every ball and expect it to happen. If it were that easy, everyone would make it to the top.

Out in the middle, I would look at certain things when the bowler ran up. There is a lot going on before the bowler lets go of the ball and before it reaches the batsman. All these things need noting and assessing, enabling you to pick up the ball early and to be in position to make a shot. When someone is bowling at more than 90 miles an hour, you have a split second to pick up the ball and get into position to play a shot. You need every possible advantage. How can you cope if you are not prepared?

I played against Frank Tyson, Fred Trueman, John Snow, Brian

Statham, and Dennis Lillee when I was getting on in years. Even when the reflexes begin to slow down, you retain that built-in reaction that makes you move when you see the ball. I never moved until the ball was in the air, no matter how fast they bowled. I stayed still and when it was out of the hand and in the air, that was when I made my decisions.

I used to read a lot from the hands. Some said that I didn't read the googly but my answer to that was if I could score runs off it, did it matter whether I was reading it or not? I made more runs against good spin bowlers than any other bowlers. I always wanted to measure myself against the best there was, whether it was bowling or batting.

I never suffered from nerves but there was always that little bit of tension because you want to do well for yourself and your team. It is that tension that keeps you safe from doing something stupid. But if you go out with too much confidence, you will make a mistake, especially if you are playing at the very highest level.

No one told me or showed me what to do; I was completely self-taught. I watched and listened, took in what I thought would benefit me and rejected the rest.

Nets were very important to me when I was a youngster and I took one whenever and wherever I could. That was the place to sort things out, to develop, to improve all aspects of your game, not just batting but bowling and fielding as well. When I batted in the nets, I approached it as if I was actually playing in a match out in the middle. Every evening as a youngster I would go into the park and bat and bat, never giving up my wicket and never retiring. I worked very hard on my game then, but once I reached the top, I used to top it up and never used the nets a lot. All the practice and hard work came when I was young and developing.

I batted in the middle order for most of my senior career, and my innings was often important to the team. We would be chasing quick runs or trying to recover after a bad start. That was the situation I relished most and many of my best innings came with adversity staring me in the face. One such was in the Third Test against New Zealand in

Barbados in 1972 when Charlie Davis and I came together with the score at 105 for 3, leaving us almost 200 runs behind in our second innings. If we didn't stand up and bat, we would lose the match and the series. I had a bit of luck when I was dropped in the slips early, and I made use of it. We both went on to make hundreds, Charlie with 183 and me with 142, one of my rare high scores against the Kiwis.

Then there was the innings in Australia on the 1960–61 tour when I scored 132 in a very difficult situation in Brisbane when Frank Worrell and I put on 174 runs. There was the similar recovery when Frank and I batted right through until the evening against England in the First Test in Bridgetown in January 1960, putting on 399 for the fourth wicket. On the tour of India in 1968, I had to bat to save the day in almost every innings in all three Tests.

Batting is psychological at that level. The mind games are important and you have to be prepared to appreciate what the opposition captain and bowlers are thinking as well as having your own plan of campaign. It isn't always necessary to thrash the ball round the field in a frenzy; sometimes batsmen need to occupy the crease as well as score runs to make the equations work.

I was lucky because I rarely ran out of partners even though I was usually batting at five or six. To score 8,000 runs batting largely in the middle order, you cannot do it all by yourself. How many players batting in that position make that many runs? Not many, as history and *Wisden* show. A big score lower down the order usually means that the team is in difficulties. If you go in at five or six with the score topping 300, you are not going to score many centuries, but if you are 100 for 4, you are going to have to bat.

The average is not that important because of the number of not outs, but the number of runs is significant when you consider that the top order included batsmen such as Conrad Hunte, Frank Worrell, Everton Weekes, Clyde Walcott, Rohan Kanhai, Joe Solomon, Seymour Nurse, Basil Butcher and all those other good players. The fact that I made 8,000 runs shows that there were some problems along the way.

When you look through cricket history, all the record-holders are those who batted at the top of the order for a long time – Sunil Gavaskar, Allan Border, Len Hutton, Graham Gooch, Colin Cowdrey, Viv Richards, Gordon Greenidge. It is impossible to call two players who batted as low down as I did who scored a similar number of runs.

Certainly all of the batsmen I admired tended to be high-order batsmen. England's Colin Cowdrey was a regular adversary, a tremendous player. I enjoyed watching him enormously when I played with him in India, and also the way he handled the English wickets, except when he preferred his pad to his bat. He was a team man, like me, who wanted to do well for his county or his country rather than just for himself. I knew him as someone you could talk to, a marvellous, genuine, sincere person. I knew him as a cricketer, but later on in his life I saw a lot more of him off the pitch. He came with Ted Dexter to speak at a benefit dinner for me. I found him a wonderful person to talk to after we had both retired.

Peter May was an elegant, beautiful bat but he had the same chink in his armour as Sir Frank Worrell – anything too fast and too short and Peter wasn't totally happy with it. But in playing in the V, in terms of correctness and getting behind the ball, he was supreme. I didn't see him hooking that much and I have always believed that great players should have all the shots and not be limited in their play. Colin could hook when he wanted to, but I rarely saw Peter May hook in Test cricket. Maybe he was more adventurous in county cricket. However, he was a lovely driver through the covers, mid-on and mid-off, beautiful to watch.

Ted Dexter and Tom Graveney were two of my favourite English batsmen. Tom was glorious off the front foot. It was amazing to me that a player of such talent missed so much Test cricket. After being in the wilderness for five years, they brought him back against us in 1966 and he did very well, scoring 96 and 30 not out at Lord's; 109 and 32 at Nottingham; 8 and 19 at Leeds and finally 165 at The Oval.

Tom had suffered through his brushes with the authorities, including a ball-throwing incident in Barbados after taking a slip catch that was not given out. During the First Test of the 1969 tour, at Old

Trafford, there was another 'serious breach of discipline', this time for keeping a promise. He had pledged to appear in a sold-out benefit match at Luton Cricket Club and he felt that he could not let them down, even though the game fell on the rest day in the middle of the Test match. He had been promised a minimum of £1,000 and at the time his entire fee for the five-day Test match was £120! Money was poor in cricket in those days all over the world, and it was criminal that Graveney was punished for helping to secure his future after he finished playing. After being ignored for five years, who could blame him for fulfilling obligations made long before his selection.

He had checked the date with Alec Bedser, the England chairman of selectors, and been told that he could not play in the two matches. Tom said he would reluctantly miss the Test unless an arrangement could be made. When he was selected, he assumed that it had, but he was promptly banned for three Test matches and never played for his country again. His last innings was 75 in a big England total that led to a 10-wicket win.

I would have done exactly the same thing as Tom. He was right and I admire a person like that for sticking to his guns. There cannot be a cricketing reason for the way Tom was treated throughout his entire career with England. He was definitely among the top players with Peter May, Colin Cowdrey, Ken Barrington and Ted Dexter. That was a fantastic batting line-up. It puzzled not only the people in England but cricket fans all over the world. His ability was admired and respected. He had true class, and a good pair of hands in the slips. What made it even more mysterious was that Tom was such a nice man, always smiling and invariably with something witty to say. I often played golf with him.

Ted Dexter was another great character. No matter how well he performed, there was always something missing for him; it was never quite 100 per cent. I played golf with him one Saturday at Wentworth, right off the back of the tee. He shot a 68, a round of which any professional tour player would have been proud. The following day we were playing again, this time at Sunningdale, and he went straight to the professional Clive Clarke for a lesson because he had missed a shot. Can you imagine shooting a 68 off the back tee at Wentworth and then less than 24 hours later asking for a lesson before playing again – and this was an amateur! He was so meticulous. One bad shot and it spoiled his entire round. On the course you could hear him muttering, 'Keep your head down . . . concentrate . . . come on . . . come on . . . take the club back slowly.'

He was the same when playing cricket. He talked to himself all the time at the crease. He was beyond a perfectionist – and he was very methodical, quite different from me, but we got on well.

Some people had the wrong impression of him because of his 'Lord Ted' nickname, thinking that he was a snob who would pick and choose to whom he would speak. One day I sat talking with him in the dressing room when someone shouted some comment to him as he walked past. Ted just ignored him. I mentioned it and Ted explained, 'It's like this. Some people think I'm snobbish and if I stop and talk they will think I'm putting it on, trying to prove I'm not that way. If people really want to talk to me they can and they will find out exactly who I am. I would never stoop to stopping and talking just to prove I'm not that way. I would rather they thought I was snobbish than do that because if they want to think that way they will.'

He is one of the nicest gentlemen you could ever meet and he and his wife Sue are great company. Whenever I came to England he would arrange to meet me and take me to play golf or to his home for a meal. When I married Pru, we were travelling through England on our honeymoon and he and Sue invited us to spend a few days with them. They were happy days. He has a good sense of humour. I agree with him about people. If they feel a certain way, it is no use bending backwards to try to make them change their minds. Let them find out for themselves.

The ability to improvise is a talent that can lift a batsman out of the ordinary and make him something special. This was certainly the case with my compatriot Sir Vivian Richards, who was blessed with such a quick eye that he could pick up the ball extremely early. This allowed him to hit across the line. He was able to pick up a ball outside his off stump and hit it anywhere between mid-on and backward square leg.

He was such an exciting batsman to watch when he launched into his attack although I felt that in his earlier years his defensive technique was a little lacking and offered bowlers opportunities, especially early in his innings. The problem of not playing his defensive shots with a straight bat was righted later on and he offered the game so much.

Apart from the three Ws, the West Indies has always been blessed with world-class batsmen right up to the modern day with Brian Lara. Of those I played with, Conrad Hunte was beautifully correct; Rohan Kanhai had a sound defence and brought his trademark falling sweep shot to the party; and Lawrence Rowe was a superb talent. This was amply displayed when he scored a debut Test century and, as if to show it was no fluke, scored a double century in his next innings. Then, of course, there was my friend Collie Smith whose tragic death prevented him from fulfilling that phenomenal promise.

Among the Australians, the Chappell brothers were different. Greg was not such a good hooker as Ian. Greg would force it down or just drop it in front of him very much like Bobby Simpson who was another not so hot at coping with the bouncer. The same could be said of the South African Graeme Pollock, although Gregory Armstrong told me that on the rebel tour of South Africa, he hooked Sylvester Clarke and Franklyn Stephenson all round the park. Maybe he learned from fellow South African Barry Richards who not only hooked but displayed fine technique in all areas of the art of batting.

One of the very best batsmen I ever saw was India's prolific Sunil Gavaskar who piled up his runs against some of the best bowling of all time, scoring over 10,000 runs and compiling 34 Test centuries. He scored his runs regularly wherever he played, on any wickets, and boasted the full range of shots, dictating to the bowler what he should bowl rather than the other way around. He was still making centuries when he retired at 38 years of age. He was only tiny but that is no deterrent to being a good batsman and he was in outstanding company

– Don Bradman, the best of all, Hanif Mohammad, Rohan Kanhai, Neil Harvey and Everton Weekes.

Hanif Mohammad was one of the greatest run-gathering machines of all time with almost perfect technique and immense concentration. He treated every good ball with respect while despatching every bad ball. He rarely gave a chance and God help you if you missed an opportunity because he would punish you for it over and over again.

CHAPTER SIXTEEN

On bowling

It all began for me as a bowler. It was as an orthodox left-arm spinner that I forced my way into the Barbados side and then into the West Indies team as a teenager, both times against India. Wickets in both, particularly four wickets for 72 in my Test debut, boosted my early hopes, but it was difficult to break through with that orthodox style because world-class spinners such as Sonny Ramadhin, Alf Valentine and Lance Gibbs were around in the West Indies at the time.

I was still bowling in the same fashion when I went to England with the West Indies in 1957, and had a reasonably good tour with the ball throughout the county games and one or two of the Tests. However, it wasn't until the next season, when I started playing league cricket with Radcliffe, that my bowling began to develop. I was able to experiment because I wasn't bowling to too many top-class players, and even if I pitched a bad ball I was likely to get away with it. On the other hand, I have seen quality leg-spinners hit all over the place in league cricket because many of the players have no respect for who you are. They weren't bothered about which way you were going to turn the ball because they would be hitting cross bat anyway, and if they got hold of you they would smash you all over the place.

Playing at that level taught me how to bowl and helped me gain confidence. That was when I started experimenting with chinamen and googlies, and my fast bowling. To achieve versatility with the ball meant a tremendous amount of work but I relished every moment. I was never happier than when I was involved. In the League, if the professional could bowl at any pace at all, he would open the bowling. Often I would bowl all through an innings with fast, orthodox left arm and unorthodox. The more ways I bowled, the more chance I had of taking those magic five wickets and receiving a much-needed collection from the crowd. It was an education and stood me in good stead for the rest of my career.

In Test matches, too, I would bowl all three styles, occasionally even opening the bowling. The first time I bowled with the new ball was on the 1960–61 tour to Australia. Frank Worrell was skipper and he knew I could bowl quickly and could swing the ball in the right conditions. In fact, fast bowling had always been in my blood, from the days when, as a boy, we played 'firms' and the only way to earn the right to bat was to knock the stumps over or take a catch. It was no use bowling spin because all that did was to give other people catches, so I learned to bowl fast to ensure I had a knock. That was where it started but I learned to bowl fast, slow, medium and everything else when I played in the English Leagues to fit the circumstances of the day.

I must have made an impression as a fast bowler because that fine Australian batsman Neil Harvey said to me that at times I bowled a lot quicker than Wes Hall. He added that my bouncer was more difficult to pick up because I did not change my action or my run-up to the wicket. My bouncer was rapid and consequently not many batsmen could hook me with any certainty. It was an interesting point. With some fast bowlers, you could tell when there was a bouncer coming your way. Being an all-rounder, I had the double advantage of understanding what a batsman was looking for and of knowing what a bowler should do. I was certainly in a better position than most fast bowlers.

In that 1960–61 series against Australia, as an opening bowler, I bowled something like 41 eight-ball overs in succession in the Fifth Test in Melbourne. It was very satisfying but, naturally, I was extremely tired after the game and I went back to the hotel for a lie down. A couple of newspaper reporters and photographers came to see me, wanting to know if I had some magic potion or if I was a strong man lifting weights every day in order to bowl so many overs non-stop except for lunch and tea breaks. There was no secret other than my love for the game and wanting to keep involved as much as I could. Frank had wanted me to stay on to keep the Australians quiet and stop them running away with a big first-innings total. It was a ploy that worked.

I enjoyed bowling; I always enjoyed what I had to do for West Indies cricket. If it meant bowling all day, I would do it; equally, if it meant fielding at short leg under the batsman's nose without a helmet, I would do that, too. I always wanted to be in the game. That's probably why I developed the three different styles of bowling; it meant there would always be a chance of the captain using me at some stage in the game, whatever the conditions.

When I went back to Australia in 1962–63 to play for South Australia, I was used as three different bowlers in the state matches. I would be handed the new ball to open the bowling and the captain Les Favell would say out loud, 'New bowler, Sobey from the other end, bowling orthodox spin.' A little while later he would say, 'New bowler, Sobey from the other end, bowling chinamen and googlies.' The boys used to talk about it because I was always bowling. When things got tight, it didn't matter how I had bowled my quick stuff, Les would come to me and say, 'A little bit of chinamen? Just a few overs?' I would go on and if I took a few wickets I would find that I was bowling eight or nine overs. I would have a rest and when things got tight again, up he would come and say, 'Sobey, I would like you to give me a little bit of orthodox.' And then when the new ball was due I would be back on again.

I loved it and had good seasons in Australia with both bat and ball. It was probably the best time in my career as an all-rounder. My bowling came on in Australia, particularly my quick bowling.

My original orthodox bowling had faded a bit because I was more of a controlled spinner, hardly a big turner of the ball. I would beat batsmen with flight and with the straighter one. Of course, I would get turn on the right wicket, but on a normal placid track where not many spinners turned the ball, neither did I. It required a Jim Laker, Tony Lock or Lance Gibbs to turn it more than most because that was their job. I didn't have the luxury of that sort of movement off the wicket, but I could keep batsmen quiet. My chinaman/googly, which wasn't always that accurate, was the one that took the most wickets and I enjoyed bowling it more than the orthodox.

Although it was serious cricket, I would have a lot of fun watching the batsman go in the wrong direction and I used to have a little bit of a laugh to myself when they had it all wrong. On the 1966 tour to England, I remember Seymour Nurse fielding at first slip when I bowled a couple of chinamen and then a googly that sent our wicket-keeper Deryck Murray the wrong way. Seymour watched in amazement and then went up to Deryck and said with a grin, 'You take the chinaman and I'll take the googly.'

My shoulder went through bowling the googly too often. I had terrible trouble for years and went to many specialists including Mr Goldstein from Jamaica, a top orthopaedic surgeon, who told me that he thought it was a lactative tendon. He explained that the tendons had stretched and were no longer holding the ball in the socket; it was too loose. When I reached a certain position in my bowling action the shoulder would come out and throw me to one side. It was very disconcerting, particularly when bowling a chinaman. When I bowled the other stuff it didn't matter so much because I kept the shoulder firm and followed through but it certainly stopped me bowling chinamen/googlies for a long time. I would try it now and again but always with the same alarming result.

So I persisted with my left-arm orthodox spin and my quick

bowling, and the fast bowling gradually took over because I was having more success with it than with the other.

I had plenty of opportunity to bowl at international level and at one stage I had bowled more overs than anyone else in the West Indies team. Lance Gibbs eventually overtook me. In England in 1963, Frank Worrell would often ask me if I wanted to bowl. In one Test, our innings was over with half an hour or so to go and he asked me what I would do if I had to make the decision. I told him, 'I know what I would do, Skipper. I would open the bowling with me and then Wes.'

'That's all I wanted to hear,' he said. 'You've got it.'

He wanted to bowl me but he wanted to hear what I thought. He gave me the ball and I did the job for him.

As a captain, you have to use strategy. You must apply your knowledge of the game and try to understand how the opposition thinks. In that way you can put pressure on the batsmen. You can also put yourself on to bowl whenever you think it is right! When I was captain, I was never afraid to open the bowling. I did it in 1966 at the Nottingham Test and carried away Geoff Boycott with a little inswinger, catching him plumb leg before. It worked well because with a much shorter run, I swung the ball a lot more than Wes or Charlie or anyone else in the team. Sometimes swing was more important than pace, especially in England.

Bowling off a short run also affects the number of overs bowled in a session, and that can put pressure on batsmen. Often the openers will sit in the pavilion and work out between them how many overs they will have to play. With a short session until the close of play, and with the pacemen's long run-ups, the calculations will be fairly specific. If they arrive at the wicket and discover that all of a sudden they are facing spinners, that changes the mindset. Apart from readjusting to different bowlers, they also have to face more overs than anticipated. The batsmen may think that the pressure is off them and they may decide to go for runs to get the best start before having to face the fast bowlers in the morning. In that case, they are going to take chances. The bowlers have nothing to lose and could take a wicket, as happened in the Fourth Test at Headingley in 1966 when Peter Lashley and I opened the bowling and Peter picked up Geoff Boycott late in the evening. Peter wasn't a great bowler but I knew he could hold a line, swing the ball a lot, and he wouldn't just run up and bowl to cram the overs in.

One bowling performance I remember fondly was for the Rest of the World at Lord's. The inswinger, my natural ball, went quite a way so the outswinger didn't have to do that much, just straighten up or leave the bat enough to have the batsman in two minds or playing the wrong line. I was bowling from the pavilion end down the hill and I was getting the ball to leave the bat; that was where the danger was rather than with the one coming in. I took 6 for 21 in England's first innings and many people said it was the best they had seen me bowl but, to my mind, I bowled twice as well at Leeds for no wickets. I was beating the bat four times an over and they couldn't get a touch. All the fielders kept gasping. Bowl it too well and it misses everything and you don't get a chance to hit the edge, or they say the batsmen were not good enough to get a touch.

Those were probably two of my best bowling spells. The ball was moving around and I could bowl how I wanted to, set up the batsman, see how he shaped and work on him.

As a bowler I was mean with extras. I doubt very much whether I bowled a dozen no-balls in my entire professional career – if that many. This was a great asset and it meant I was able to keep a good length, hold a good line, and bowl fairly accurately. The art of good bowling is to bowl good line and length and move the ball around.

I was 32 by the time I went to Notts in 1968. I'd played a lot of cricket by then and was getting on towards the end of my career. A hundred wickets in a season were beyond me. It was hard work playing the county game after the amount of cricket I had played. Although I carried on for another seven years and was very fit, I had put an awful lot into the game. It was good that I kept as fit as I did – the first muscle I pulled was in Australia 18 years after I started playing!

I was able to bowl so much because I rarely left the field through injury. I had niggling disabilities such as damaged fingers and the usual bumps, bruises and the odd strain, but I would rather be out there playing than fiddling about in the dressing room. I never liked watching other people play cricket because I wanted to be in the thick of the action myself. I always felt that my job was to be out there helping my team. I always thought that I could help swing a game one way or other because I could contribute in so many departments.

I would have loved to have played more Test cricket between the ages of 17 and 26 and would have relished being involved in the modern-day scenario where a top international plays 15 Test matches in a calendar year and twice as many one-day internationals. I'm not saying I wouldn't have become tired or jaded, I'm sure I would, but I was never happier than when playing. I played every sort of cricket but not at that same consistent high level. It was non-stop but the quality roller-coasted. I'm sure that I would have enjoyed mixing one-day with five-day international cricket because as a bowler I always attacked the wickets. Whether I would have been successful is another thing.

One thing I would not have done in a one-day game is bowl outside the off stump or down the leg side, being negative. I was always positive and I believe that helped me in my bowling. I took 235 Test wickets but simple statistics do not tell the whole story. They don't always show how well I bowled, and there were times when I didn't bowl as often as I should have done. The concentration involved in batting for a long while and then fielding at short leg could be both mentally and physically tiring and sometimes I would bowl just four or five overs in a spell because I was so shattered. Even so, there was rarely a day's cricket I did not relish.

I am often asked which type of bowling I enjoyed most and whether batting was more important to me than my bowling. It's impossible to say. When I batted I tried to make runs, especially when the team needed them, and I bowled to the best of my ability to take a wicket and maybe break a big partnership.

I enjoyed bowling against the better batsmen because I felt it gave me more chance. Sometimes a top bowler struggles against lower-order batsmen, hence the expression not good enough to get a touch. The Fifth Test at The Oval in 1966 is a case in point. John Murray, who was a much better player than he was given credit for, Ken Higgs and John Snow put on over 260 runs for the last couple of wickets and from a winning position we lost by an innings!

It is more enjoyable to bowl against top-class batsmen because you have to work at them, look for their weaknesses, and if you are keeping them quiet you know you are bowling well. Bowl to tailenders and just because you keep beating the bat doesn't mean you are bowling well, far from it. You should be bowling them out and hitting the stumps.

When a good batsman is in, seeing the ball well and on top of the bowlers, that is the time to try to pin him down. It does not mean being negative; in fact, it is often the time to attack, not necessarily aggressively, but to be on the offensive. They are two different things. Bowling bouncers is considered aggressive but short-pitched bowling will suit the good batsman. However, if you are attacking him, you have a chance of getting him out. Also, if you were keeping batsmen of the calibre of Len Hutton, Ted Dexter, Peter May, Rohan Kanhai, Colin Cowdrey, Everton Weekes and Clyde Walcott quiet, you were bowling well. Great players turn good bowling into bad bowling. They don't respect bowlers when they are seeing the ball. Become aggressive and they will tear holes in your bowling if it is slightly out of kilter.

I liked bowling to that kind of batsman best because when you beat the bat you know you have earned it. Kanhai and Dexter were good to bowl to because they hit the ball so well and always gave the bowler a chance, but I didn't enjoy bowling to Cowdrey so much because he played with his bat and pad.

Ian Chappell was another I enjoyed bowling against. He was completely different from Bill Lawry who was something of a plodder. Keith Stackpole, Doug Walters, Norm O'Neill and Alan Davidson would punish you if you went off line. They would not spare you if you were out of sorts and I knew it.

In Australia in the 1968–69 series, a number of us West Indian bowlers took a lot of stick because there were some heavy hitters in the

Australian side at the time. To add to the problems we did not always take our catches and that is something that doesn't show up on the records.

The current crop of Australian bowlers, Glenn McGrath, Shane Warne and Gary Gillespie, are rated the most potent in the world and as a unit they are very effective but individually I believe I played against better. Watching someone and playing against them are two different things, but to me Gupte was a better bowler than Shane Warne. One reason is that Gupte had a far wider variety, and his disguised googly was far better than Warne's. Warne is a big spinner of the ball and not many turn it that far although another Australian, Stuart McGill, seems to be able to. But turning the ball is not always the biggest criterion; length and line are just as important.

However, I do believe that Warne has improved. When he played in Australia against the West Indies after his injury break, he looked a much better bowler because he seemed to have a bigger mix. The fellows did not pick his googly as well as they used to. He doesn't spin it away from them as much as he did. I was impressed with what I saw; he certainly looked a lot better than when he was turning it too big. He took a lot of hammer from Brian Lara but he also had him in trouble.

Lara and India's Sachin Tendulkar usually seem to have the measure of him. It's the English batsmen who appear to have the most trouble with him. They are beaten before they face him because they are so concerned by his reputation. That's an ongoing problem. If the English cannot play a bowler, he instantly becomes the greatest, no matter how he does against other countries. Ever since Warne bowled Mike Gatting round his legs, the press and the players would have you believe Warne is the best. Another Aussie, David Sincock, bowled me with a chinaman like that once but people didn't go on about it forever. One ball doesn't make you the king and this dismissal was as much Gatting's fault as it was Warne's ability. If a player bowls a ball outside the leg stump on a turning wicket, you should cover your stumps – that's basic. You cannot be out leg before wicket. If Gatting had gone across instead of trying to play the shot or stand up, it would have been no problem. The same principle applied to me when I was bowled by Sincock. It was my fault. I was taken by surprise because he had never bowled like that before.

Gupte was always on the spot, bowled a good googly and a good leg break and had some of the best batsmen in the world confused. The Weekes, Worrells and Walcotts made runs against him but he also had them in trouble. Wickets in the West Indies were very good in those days, and spinners found them difficult, but Gupte came to the Caribbean and took 27 in the 1952 series. He didn't play a lot of Test cricket but he took a lot of good wickets. He was so accurate, varied the flight and pushed it through, and he could bowl two different googlies. You had to watch him carefully to play him because of his wide variety.

Warne, by contrast, is a lot flatter. He bowls the flipper well and, as I've said, his googly has improved. As far as I'm concerned great leg-break bowlers don't bowl round the wicket, which he did a lot in his early days. The great leg-spinners always bowled over because they could push the ball across the batsman and make it turn back. It's much easier to bowl the googly coming over the wicket than to bowl round because in the latter case your arm is too far out to be truly effective. Warne for many years bowled round the wicket into the rough.

I'm not saying that Warne is not the greatest bowler today although there are not a lot of good leg-spinners to choose from. He has a nice aggressive attitude and will tie up good batsmen, but I would like to see him bowl a lot more variety and improve that googly still further.

Warne arrived at the turn of another cricket cycle, at the end of an era of all-out pace, at least for the successful teams. There is no doubt that he has helped resurrect the art of spin bowling around the world.

I haven't seen a great deal of the Sri Lankan Muttiah Muralitharan, which makes it difficult to talk about a bowler of his obvious calibre. His arrival on the Test scene was greeted with great suspicion and scepticism because he bowled with an unusual action. The Australians led the way in raising the questions and complaining.

The laws of cricket say that if your elbow straightens, you have bowled a no-ball because that's throwing. If he doesn't straighten his elbow, it doesn't matter what his wrist does. You don't chuck it from the wrist, you chuck it from the elbow, and when I've watched him he's been more wrist action than straightened elbow.

Quite a few off-spinners over the years bowled with a bent elbow. The late Tony Lock, the great Surrey and England off-spinner, definitely used to ping them. He admitted that. I spoke to him about it in Australia after he had corrected his action and he said to me that if he was bowling then, he did not know what he was doing all those years before. I played against him when he played for Western Australia and he bowled quite well with his arm a lot higher and a lot straighter. Tony knew that he threw now and again and the faster ball was pinged even more. But he got away with it so what could you do?

Richie Benaud was a good leg-spinner. He didn't turn the ball that much but he was very accurate, had a nice high action and a good follow-through. He had a little googly and a top spinner, and if he had turned the ball a little more both ways, he would have been out on his own, but although he had class he wasn't quite up there with Gupte or Warne. But he was a bloody good thinking cricketer. He knew his batsmen and could work them out. He knew when to bowl the googly or top spinner and when not to. There weren't many better than him, certainly not where accuracy was concerned.

Jim Laker was undoubtedly the best off-spinner I ever saw. I played against Lance Gibbs, Eripalli Prasana and Bishen Bedi and all were high-class bowlers but Jim was certainly the best although Lance was not that far behind. Alf Valentine was one of the best left-arm spinners. He had a straight one that was really good and brought him a lot of wickets.

When you batted against Jim Laker you could hear the ball fizz as he spun it. He also had the straight one. Many spinners bowl a straight ball faster than when using spin, but not Jim. His straight one drifted and he used to snare Clyde Walcott with it all the time, more often than not caught in the slips. With Jim, the ball was always nicely flighted, well-weighted, with good line, excellent length and devastating accuracy.

Tony Lock, Jim's Surrey and England partner, was trouble on a turning wicket and I still find it phenomenal that he took just one wicket when Jim recorded 19 against the Australians at Old Trafford in 1956.

England produced quite a few good off-spin bowlers. I particularly liked Gloucestershire's John Mortimore. I thought he was better than his favoured county colleague David Allen, or Fred Titmus of Middlesex who was picked more than either of them. I assume that John was not selected because he was not such a good bat. With England at the time, there was always room for the off-spinner or the wicket-keeper who could bat rather than the genuine specialist.

The one who impresses me currently is the Pakistani spinner Saqlain Mushtaq who could turn out to be one of the best. No off-spinner has ever bowled the one that went the other way before. Valentine used to bowl left-arm spin but this boy just reverses the spin on the ball to make it go the other way, and he does it at will. It's not the straight one he's doing it to; it is one that actually turns, which is remarkable and makes him extraordinarily difficult to play. Jim Laker bowled the one that straightened or just deviated, and Lance did the same, but this boy makes it talk. It amazes me. I have seen him confuse and kerfuffle a lot of good batsmen. He must have developed and practised this on his own because I cannot recall another bowler he could have copied or learned it from. It goes to show that this great game of ours is still developing and moving forward.

Among the modern-day quick bowlers, Glenn McGrath is right there at the top. He can destroy you if you are a front-foot player but if you go back and across to him, he finds it difficult to bowl to you because his radar seems to be set on a certain length. Play a few shots to him and he can be knocked off his length, as well as making him annoyed. No bowler bowls well when he loses control of his temper because he stops thinking straight.

McGrath is not in the class of the great West Indian fast bowlers. He is accurate, has a good line and length and moves the ball nicely off the seam but he does not have the pace of Michael Holding, Andy Roberts and Wes Hall or the bounce of Joel Garner, Colin Croft, Curtly Ambrose and Courtney Walsh. But he is still in his prime and time will tell just how good he is.

However, I don't agree with talk of him as one of the greatest Australian fast bowlers of all time. I don't believe he is as good as Dennis Lillee or as rapid as another Aussie of the same era, Jeff Thomson. Thommo was outstandingly quick and we did not see enough of him internationally, which was a shame. According to Ian Chappell, in the West Indies we missed the best and quickest of him in Test cricket.

It's hard to rate the best-ever fast bowlers because there have been so many good ones. As I've said, pace is not the only criterion, as shown by Holding, Trueman, Ambrose and Lillee, all of whom did far more than just run up and bowl as fast as they could. Alan Davidson was a very good bowler, too, and another whom I would rate above McGrath. Graham McKenzie wasn't bad. In every era a new face turns up and you kind of forget those who have gone before and just how good they were. It is too easy to apply the word great to someone for taking more wickets or scoring more runs than in the past. Those are not the criteria to use because they are playing so much more Test cricket nowadays.

I did not see enough of the South African Allan Donald to judge him, but from what I did see, he was a class bowler who should be rated among the top fast bowlers of his time.

Most fast bowlers start off quick but erratic and improve as they mature. Freddie Trueman, John Snow, Jeff Thomson, Dennis Lillee, Wes Hall and even the outstanding New Zealander Sir Richard Hadlee were all over the place when they started because they were looking for raw pace. As they grow older they lose that edge and have to compensate. That's when they learn how to bowl properly and how to take wickets, how to think batsmen out instead of blasting them out.

It is a tremendous thrill for bowler and spectators alike when the quickies uproot the stumps. They are able to do it because batsmen do not always get right behind the ball; they hesitate, move too late or don't get there at all. Consequently, they are not in the right place to see any movement, that is behind the line of the ball; they push forward and edge the ball, or their stumps are flattened. Sometimes the ball will come back off the seam and that's when they are bowled between bat and pad. Bowlers are quick to realise when batsmen are not behind the ball and they will try to increase their pace, even if they are a touch wild, because they know they have the batsman in trouble.

Pakistan's Shoaib Akhtar is very, very quick. Apparently there is some doubt about his action but that always seems to be the case when someone starts to bowl really fast. People look around for a reason and come up with something or another. You have to have laws and rules but how they are enforced depends on who is interpreting and administering them.

While Trueman, Statham, Laker and Lock were among the best English bowlers I faced, I found that on a wet turner Kent's Derek Underwood was as difficult to face as anyone. I would go so far as to say that on a wet wicket there was none better. On a good firm wicket he would bowl tight but he could be worked out, and he could play a good batsman in with his accuracy so they could eventually get after him. He varied his flight on hard wickets but the ball hardly turned. I knew that when he started on the off stump he wasn't going to turn the ball much, he was going to drift it more than turn it.

One of his greatest assets was that on soft, rain-affected wickets he could still bowl a straight one, which is not nearly as easy as it sounds. There were plenty of spinners who, on a real turner, could not bowl a straight ball. At The Oval once, he bowled the Australians out after a storm, turning the ball a yard and then bowling the straight one through bat and pad. It was phenomenal to get a ball to go straight through the way he did. That's why he was so effective, that and his accuracy, and why lbw or clean bowled appeared so often with his name. It's why he was called 'Deadly'. His length and line were immaculate and he bowled at quite a sharp pace.

Johnny Wardle of Yorkshire was a great character and a fine bowler, especially in the West Indies where he bowled his chinaman/googly instead of his orthodox. I remember watching his first ball, which was a chinaman; the batsman snicked it only for the umpire to indicate not out. The next ball was a googly. The batsman played back, it hit him on the pads right in front but once again the umpire shook his head. The next ball he bowled quick and flat, knocking all three stumps over. Turning to the umpire, he remarked, 'I nearly f****** got him that time!'

His other famous remark after being turned down for a leg before appeal was, 'Missing off, missing leg – but knocking the f****** middle peg out of the ground.'

I played in a couple of benefit games in Yorkshire with Johnny, including one for Vic Wilson that I recall with great embarrassment. I was playing against Vic's side and had just started bowling my chinamen and googlies and wasn't pitching them too well. When Vic came in I bowled him what was supposed to be a full toss to get him off the mark – but it dropped on a perfect length and knocked over all three stumps. I could not believe it, bowling the man first ball in his benefit match. I could hear the crowd muttering and I just wished a hole would open up and I could go right through it.

These days the fast bowlers have increased their repertoire and many of them have a very useful slower ball. It wasn't something that happened a lot in my day apart from the Australian Neil Hawke who bowled a beautiful slow ball. When I played for South Australia I was able to watch him at close hand and he had Rohan Kanhai caught at least twice in the covers off that slower delivery. He hid it so well and even if you watched him carefully a hundred times you would struggle to pick it because the disguise was so clever. I understand he developed it from his baseball playing days, basing it on a pitch called the knuckle ball.

In my county days, I heard on the circuit that the West Indian Franklyn Stephenson had a good slower ball, perhaps the best. The batsmen I spoke to about it said that they saw the ball coming at their head and would duck only to find it suddenly dipping gently towards the base of the stumps.

Stephenson was not just a good bowler, he was an underrated cricketer. He talks about his achievements as an all-rounder but he hasn't got a lot to back it up other than county matches because unfortunately he never played at Test level. That was not his fault. He regularly used to do the double of 1,000 runs and 100 wickets in the county championship – and that was not something that was done very often – but the selectors consistently overlooked him.

The spin bowlers also had a slower ball in those days. Bishen Bedi was very clever, a magnificent left-arm spinner who used all his guile. He took the weight off the ball nicely; he also had a useful straight one plus a quicker one. He used the full width of the crease and flight variation, which made him fascinating to play against because you had to be very careful and watchful, wait and see and hope you were good enough to cope with it. He was a top-class bowler. In his day, there was no one better.

Charlie Palmer of Leicester bowled what he called a donkey drop, a ball that was tossed high and gently in the air for it to steeple lazily down towards the wickets. It was very effective, as West Indian Nyron Asgarali would testify. He once watched and watched the dropping ball until he stepped right back on to his stumps. Frank Worrell laughed at him from the non-strike end – and was then out in exactly the same fashion.

But of all the English bowlers my favourite personality was the inimitable Freddie Trueman, a larger than life character and great cricketer. In this case I use 'great' in the true sense of the world. I know he certainly believes it and tells anyone who listens that he was. It upsets him these days when he hears the amount of money some of the modern bowlers are earning for the sort of stuff they bowl. I find it hard to argue with the man. Most of them cannot hold a candle to Freddie; he was such a good bowler, accurate, fast and with a big heart. Bowl him on any wicket and he would do it without complaint, or at least not to his captain. There were always plenty of words for the batsman who played and missed, and for any fielder whom he thought had let him down.

When Richard Hutton was playing for Yorkshire he used to listen to the great man telling how he had bowled this one or had that one caught.

'Here, Fred,' Richard asked him one day, 'did thee ever bowl one that didn't swing?'

'Yes,' said Fred, 'and it was a f****** full toss.'

It's true. Listen to Fred and every ball he bowled did something. He never bowled a straight ball according to him.

He and I always got on well together. In 1960 at the Kensington Oval, the West Indies were in trouble facing a big England total when Frank Worrell and I put on 399. I scored 226 and Frank was 197 not out. During the innings, Fred bowled me a bouncer. I didn't even hit it, I just flicked it, and it ended up hitting the top of the roof of the stand still on its way up. Fred came down the wicket and I prepared myself for a typical verbal volley but instead he said, 'Good f****** shot, laddie – but it wasn't that short you know!' He didn't bowl me another bouncer for the rest of that tour, but he had a memory lapse a few years later. In my first year playing for Notts, we met Yorkshire at Sheffield. He bowled me a bouncer, I hooked him for six again and he followed through, saying, 'Eh lad, you mustn't do that to me. We're two old ones. Do that to the youngsters.'

'Well, Fred,' I retorted, 'then don't bowl the bouncer at me.'

We had a lot of fun and I had so much admiration for him. For England, he worked so well in tandem with Lancashire's Brian Statham. The difference between them was that Brian was too accurate; once you had set your stall, you knew exactly where the ball was going to pitch, and if you were an intelligent player you could move into position before he began to deliver. Brian had to get the good batsmen out early or he could bowl them into form. With Fred in the early days, there would be one here and one there and then one under your nose. Later, he could move the ball both ways and had good variation.

I spent a lot of time with Fred off the pitch. We both liked a drink and we could both tell a story. One year, he and I spoke at around 14 functions together, and he started off by telling everyone that I was his rabbit. He had claimed my wicket on a few occasions and he was the first to get me for a duck in Test cricket when he had me caught by Kenny Barrington at the Queen's Park Oval in Port-of-Spain in 1960. Eventually, I got fed up with it and stuck the knife in first. When I spoke I said that Fred would tell them that I was his rabbit but that what he wouldn't say was that in the same series he also took my wicket for 198 and 226. That's how much of a rabbit I was. He soon stopped using that line because he knew I would get him back sometime down the way.

When he started to do his after-dinner speeches and comedy turns it was not easy to take because of his heavy use of Anglo-Saxon, but with experience he was able to tell what sort of audience he was facing and change his speech and his act accordingly. He was always good to listen to and I enjoyed working with him and being with him. Whenever I was in Yorkshire we used to meet and he would entertain everyone with his stories.

He gets a bit carried away sometimes with the modern bowlers and the wickets they take. He may pour scorn on the batsmen they were bowling to and complain that when he played against the West Indies he would have to bowl to Rohan Kanhai, Everton Weekes, Frank Worrell, Clyde Walcott and Garry Sobers. He can't shake himself out of the habit and stay quiet. But most people like Fred anyway; they understand his little idiosyncrasies and go along with them.

We agree that the game has changed and isn't what it used to be, but you have to look at it from both sides and give credit. Bowlers now have to bowl from the full 22 yards instead of from halfway down the wicket because of the change in the no-ball law. Fred had a drag that would take his front foot over the batting crease. He wasn't the worst. Gordon Rourke in Australia would not be able to bowl at all today because he dropped that far behind the crease. When he delivered the ball, his back foot used to be past the batting crease and his front foot used to be a mile up the wicket. Colin Cowdrey joked that he had to play off the back foot because if he didn't, Rourke would be so far down the wicket that his front foot would have landed on Colin's toes.

Ray Lindwall was another big dragger. There weren't many fast bowlers in those days who didn't use the crease to their advantage, and who could blame them when it was within the laws. These days, you cannot put your foot over the line at all so they are bowling a yard slower than they were. I admire the modern bowlers. The batsmen now have more time and a lower trajectory to deal with. When you were being bowled at from halfway down the wicket, the ball climbed sharply.

In Fred's day, a good quick bowler could run in against a batsman and maybe frighten him, but these days you don't run them so easily because they have their protection. Bowlers are up against batsmen wearing helmets, chest pads, thigh pads, arm pads and all the rest of the paraphernalia. A good quickie can hit them easier but they are well covered. Young players regard the protection as an ordinary part of their equipment, just the same as pads and gloves. They know nothing else. I once asked Imran Khan why a batsman as good as he was found it necessary to wear a helmet and chest pad. He replied that it was his profession and he wanted to remain fit and well enough to earn his living. I don't know where that left the likes of me, or Viv Richards, who refused to wear a helmet when they were in common use. I feared that a helmet would stifle me, particularly those with a grill. Somewhere along the line there must be blind spots and it must affect your vision. But, as in all walks of life, you have to accept that nothing stays the same, everything changes.

I have watched the changes in the West Indian bowling since I retired. We didn't realise how lucky we were. As well as the four-pronged pace attack, there were three others who could have walked into any other team – Sylvester Clarke was the quickest of the lot; Wayne Daniel, when he put it all together, was as quick as anyone; and Colin Croft left the Test arena too early.

I don't think you could find a better attack than Michael Holding,

Andy Roberts, Colin Croft and Joel Garner. We were extremely fortunate to have Malcolm Marshall, Curtly Ambrose and Courtney Walsh arriving on the scene after them. Walsh was third or fourth choice at one time and it is amazing what he has done since then. His figures, and his world-record wicket haul, are staggering because there were times when he wasn't picked at all.

He carried a huge workload in his later years after competing with Marshall and Ambrose, who were strike bowlers of great quality. Kapil Dev had one or two spinners, but he had no quickies at the other end of any real quality, unlike Walsh who was always competing for the ball and the wickets. Walsh and Ambrose with almost 700 wickets between them carried the West Indies during the years when they slumped.

Walsh was helped in his record-breaking haul by the change in the number of Test matches played every year. Freddie Trueman, for example, was lucky to play a maximum of 10 a year, and it was less if he had been a naughty boy and upset the selectors. If you play 15 Test matches a year and you are in your prime, you are going to take a lot of wickets and maintain that standard a lot longer. You are comparing someone who played 60 Test matches in 10 years with someone who has played 140 in the same time.

I have said for years that current records and those from the past should not be regarded in the same category because it's a different game now. It would be fairer if, instead of totals, the records were done by percentage, but even then it would not be a true guide because the game has changed so much.

I would love to see Holding, Gilchrist or Roberts run in and bowl the modern batsmen five bouncers an over with two men in their hip pocket and another behind, and without the helmet, arm pad and chest pad to hide behind. It's just a different era.

CHAPTER SEVENTEEN

On fielding

It used to be said that the only thing I didn't do was keep wicket to my own bowling. Wicket-keeping is a job they can keep! I have tried it. When I first competed as a youngster, I would sometimes keep wicket in between bowling spells. On one occasion at the YMPC (Young Men's Progressive Club) ground, the batsman played forward to an off-spinner and had everything covered. The next thing, the ball came through and hit the bail, which hit me in the mouth. I swore then that I would never again keep wicket.

Nevertheless, I did the job on the odd occasion in the old Sunday Cavaliers cricket to the likes of Sonny Ramadhin, Cec Pepper, Roy Gilchrist and even Wes Hall. We had enough bowlers so I kept wicket, but not on a regular basis, and I was left in no doubt at all that it is a specialist job.

The flamboyant Godfrey Evans of Kent was one of the best of the English wicket-keepers. Keith Andrew was probably as good behind the stumps but he could not bat and Godfrey could. Keith was a much better wicket-keeper than John Murray or Jim Parks who were both given international precedence over him because they could bat. Keith was a very safe wicket-keeper, handling spin and the quicks equally well. You can always tell a good wicket-keeper by watching how they retrieve the ball and how they get into position.

Alan Knott was excellent although I reckon that Bob Taylor was better. Alan got the nod more often, again because he was a better bat. There wasn't a lot to choose between them but if selection had been purely on wicket-keeping skills, Bob would almost certainly have been picked. A similar thing happened years later when England turned opening bat Alec Stewart into a full-time wicket-keeper at the expense of Jack Russell.

I never saw a lot of Godfrey Evans. He was keeping wicket when I played in that one Test in Jamaica in 1954. I did not come across him again until three years later and that was the last series he played in. He was on his way out but he was still a very good wicket-keeper. He was classed among the greats, including Australia's Don Saggers and Don Tallon.

They have always seemed to find top-class keepers down under. Gil Langley was one. I saw him at first hand in June 1955 in the West Indies when he was magnificent. I remember one catch he took after being out all the night before in Kingston with our opening bat J.K. Holt. Frank Worrell glided a Ray Lindwall ball down the leg side and Langley just walked round and picked it up in his left hand like it was nothing. Others would have been diving and scrambling for it. That shows the incredible judgement the top wicket-keepers have. They know where the ball is going and they are there early enough to take the catch.

Unfortunately, he was nearing retirement although he was still very good, very confident and safe to spin. Keeping to fast bowling is fairly straightforward, it's just a matter of how you move, but when you have a good spinner in action, that's when a really competent wicket-keeper earns his money.

Another fine Australian wicket-keeper was Wally Grout. I played against him in Tests and in state games. Wes Hall, who played in the state team alongside Wally, spoke very highly of him, and he undoubt-edly had tremendous class. Barry Jarman wasn't a bad wicket-keeper either.

The West Indies had some useful wicket-keepers, too. Trinidadian Deryck Murray, Barbadian David Allan and Jamaican Jeffrey Dujon were all very competent with the pace attack. Before them, Gerry Alexander from Jamaica was excellent, but in my estimation the best wicket-keeper we had was Jamaican Jackie Hendriks. He may not have been beautiful to watch, he didn't just pick one bail off or a single stump, he would clatter down all three, but he handled both spin and pace equally well.

David Allan was very unfortunate when he went to England as number one in 1963. He was keeping really well but he took ill and Deryck Murray stepped in and set records. He took 22 catches, mainly off Wes Hall and Charlie Griffith, and made a couple of stumpings.

As a batsman, I never let the wicket-keeper influence me, partly because I never left my crease. I think I left it once or twice when I was young and got myself stumped, and I rarely ventured out of my ground after that. They talk about good batsmen going down the wicket to spin bowlers but I have always looked at it from the other point of view – there are so many different ways of getting out, why increase them by leaving the little safe haven that belongs to you? Why go all the way down there when you can play it off the back foot with more time and have a bigger area into which to hit the ball with the whole of leg side at your mercy? When you go down the wicket you narrow the angle and if you are not a good reader of the leg-spinner, he will lead you on so that you don't have a chance of getting back.

I was stumped once in my entire senior cricket career and that was against England at Bourda in 1960, by Roy Swetman off David Allen – but not before I had reached 145.

Early in my career, I played against a spin bowler in Barbados named Eddie Perkins. He really used to throw the ball in the air and at times he turned it bigger than Shane Warne. I went down the wicket to him and misread his googly. Fortunately, so did the wicket-keeper and we both went down the same side. He was relying on me knowing which way Perkins was spinning the ball. It went through the off side for four byes and I escaped when I was on 10. I remember it well because I came back the next day and took my score to 202! They remind the wicket-keeper of that miss all the time, even to this day.

I spent so much time at the crease that I used to get to know the wicket-keepers well; I used to talk to them all the time. I never used to worry about them although some of them worried about me because I used to play back so close to the wicket. When I played a ball outside the leg stump I would swing right round and they had to watch their heads or I might have scalped one of them.

Fielding is altogether a specialist job. It has always been an important part of cricket although some people may not have realised just how important until one-day cricket demanded that teams become fitter, move quicker and throw the ball better. There has to be a result so there is no sense in fielding the ball casually. Fielders move in with the bowler, pick up the ball and move it pretty quick. Before the advent of the one-day game, picking up the ball was enough to stop the batsmen running. Now every run counts. It is not how many wickets you lose, it is how many runs you make. You might as well be 60 all out as 60 for no wicket. Fielding has been taken to a new level by the one-day game, with sliding stops and throws over the wicket from off the floor.

You can pick out the good fielders. Jonty Rhodes from South Africa is outstanding, as are Ricky Ponting, Mark Waugh and Mark Taylor of Australia. Taylor is not only a fine fielder, so quick that no one takes chances with him because he hits the stumps from anywhere, but also a very good aggressive batsman.

The Caribbean has produced some top-class fielders. I'm thinking of Clive Lloyd, Viv Richards, with his three run-outs in the World Cup final, and Gus Logie. But perhaps the best I ever saw was Colin Bland. South Africans are always making comparisons between him and Jonty Rhodes. That is a difficult shout. Colin could run and pick up on the boundary, spin in midair and throw in, all in one flowing movement. I never saw Jonty do that, but he was always closer to the wicket. Colin could hit the stumps from anywhere. At an exhibition at The Oval, Colin hit the stumps five times out of six. Ken Barrington told the story of when Bland ran him out at The Oval by throwing the ball through his legs.

Slip fielding is another specialist position. Australia's Bobby Simpson and England's Phil Sharpe were brilliant slip fielders. From the West Indies, Phil Simmons, Carl Hooper, Gordon Greenidge and Viv Richards were all good. Joel Garner was unusual because it was not often that you saw fast bowlers fielding close to the wicket apart from Freddie Trueman who liked to field around the corner at backward short leg. Garner and Michael Holding were exceptional, as is Shane Warne who has hands like buckets.

We had to have very good slip fielders in our West Indies sides because that was where we won most of our matches. It is all very well having three or four pacemen bowling at 90 miles per hour but you still have to take the catches. If we did not have the quality slip fielders we would not have won as many matches.

I would go to the slip machine to practise day after day, and bounce balls off walls and off the ground to sharpen my reflexes. When I was a youngster, I'd throw stones at mangoes and catch them before they burst on the floor. I also played a lot of table tennis, which was brilliant for sharpening-up. In one exercise, I'd hit a table-tennis ball against a wall close to, over and over again.

Good fielding puts batsmen under pressure by cutting off runs. When they can't score runs, they make mistakes in trying to force matters and by taking chances. During my career, at every net session, time was allotted to fielding. Every player should practise this aspect of the game or he could give away more runs than he makes, and in that case he would not be worth his place in the side.

Apart from slip, I used to enjoy fielding around the corner where Tony Lock, Mike Smith and Fred Trueman were recognised as experts for England and their counties, Surrey, Warwickshire and Yorkshire respectively. In that position, you need to know what you are doing.

It's like third slip or gully. A newcomer might want to watch the bowler instead of watching the edge. The man at first slip has the luxury of watching the bowler but those at second and third slip watch the edge, and the man in the gully watches the shape of the shot. You have to have an idea of where the batsman is trying to hit it. Good fielders cut off shots because, from the batsman's shape, they have a fair idea of where the ball is going to go, and they are on the move instead of being caught flat-footed.

Slip fielders have to stay down for as long as they can because it is easier to get up rather than get back down. Good slip fielders stay down and take the low ones comfortably, but it only comes with practice.

I liked being in the slips to Wes Hall and Charlie Griffith among others because I felt that the ball was going to come my way at any time. Most of all, I enjoyed fielding at leg slip to Lance Gibbs, again because I felt that I was involved with every ball. I always felt that something was about to happen when he bowled. Also, I could move around. As soon as Lance bowled, I would move up and sometimes take the ball off the face of the bat. Sometimes I would watch Lance turn and from the way he ran up, I knew exactly what he was going to do. I also knew the batsmen and how they would shape up. From this and the flight of the ball, I could quickly work out whether it was going to go fine or square. It all came with experience and studying the game. It kept me involved and it kept my concentration going.

It is when you relax and stand up that you do something silly because your reflexes are not there. You have to concentrate with every ball. It's tiring and a big strain but you have to be trained for that or you shouldn't be playing at that level. There is no excuse. Certainly it is never an excuse to say nothing had been happening and so you relaxed.

I was only ever hit once fielding close in and that was when Lance was bowling to Ian Chappell. Lance tossed one up, Ian went forward and I started to move in when suddenly Ian changed his mind and played a lap shot. It turned into a full-blooded sweep and I had nowhere to go, nowhere to hide. It hit me, I clutched at my chest and

215

was amazed to find that the ball was there. Ian could not believe it. He said, 'Sobey, you bastard,' and stumped off. He has never allowed me to forget it. The ball caught me rather than me catching it.

I also liked being in the outfield unless nothing happened for over after over. I liked the covers where you could run in, pick up and throw. I suppose I'm the schoolboy who never grew up. I want to be in the action all the time. That's what you're there for. If you're standing doing nothing, in my opinion, you should be somewhere else. If the ball was being hit regularly to the same area, I would ask to field there.

When I was captain, if a situation called for someone to be in a dangerous position, I would put myself there. I wouldn't send anyone else to field in a position I wasn't prepared to take up myself. I never wore any protection when I was fielding, no matter how close to the bat I positioned myself. I think it is ridiculous that close-in fielders wear helmets, body armour and even pads to protect themselves. Fielders will soon look like American footballers if this trend continues. The worst thing is that youngsters coming through now think it is normal.

Part of the game was the batsman trying to move the close-in fielders, frightening them off by hitting them on the foot or the legs. Now it hits them on the pads and they feel nothing, and the next time there is a leading edge the catch is taken. If you are going to field there, it should be under your own steam and with confidence that the bowler is good enough. If he isn't, you shouldn't be there to start with. A good bowler will protect his close-in fielder.

There has, of course, been the occasional injury. Alan Jones of Glamorgan was struck when fielding close to the wicket and almost died as a result. That hastened the introduction of helmets. In England, youngsters have to wear a helmet to bat unless they have a letter from their parents saying they needn't do so. It is good that youngsters are protected but it makes cricket an expensive sport with bats costing so much along with gloves, pads and the now compulsory helmet. It's cheaper to kit yourself out for golf than for cricket. A set of golf clubs costs $200 to $300. A cricket bat costs well over $100 and by the time you add the rest of the gear, it is over $700. They will all need replacing in a couple of years while the golf clubs will last a life-time, if you wish. What's more, the gear you wear to play golf can be worn anywhere, but that's not the case with whites. Cricket, suddenly, is very expensive. The players are making so much money they can afford it but the youngsters and their parents also have to pay out. At least it costs nothing to field!

There were, of course, no helmets in my day and I don't think I would have worn one anyway; not that I blame young batsmen for wearing them because it is now part of the uniform. The helmet is part of their kit, along with bats, pads and all the rest.

I never even used a thigh pad because it felt too ungainly. When I was growing up, the pads were very thin with canes inside and the gloves were green pimpled rubber. I reckoned that if a bowler hit me on the leg it was my fault and on those thin pads it would hurt a great deal against someone as fast as Hall or Charlie Griffith. That is why I used the bat and was rarely hit on the pad.

I had some of my early kit given to me by the Barbados Cricket Association and when I played for the West Indies they gave me two bats of my own choice, pads, gloves, creams and a blazer. Then in 1958, I signed for Slazenger and I used go to the factory to select my own bats, tailor-made for me. My first bat provided by them was a Gradidge and that was the one with which I made 365.

Sometimes teams can become besotted with fitness and with train-ing. This big running is all very well at the start of the season to sharpen up the wind, stretch the muscles and build up stamina, but after that with the amount of cricket the top cricketers play, they should keep sharp without it. I believe that many teams over-train these days, and how often do you hear of an injury picked up while the players were playing soccer after a day's cricket. I cannot understand for the life of me why, at the end of a hard day's play, teams are running and jumping around. That should be when they are resting. Once you are match fit, you are match fit. You go in the nets, you field, bowl and bat and that should be it.

Once the season was under way, I felt I was match fit and I'd rest at the end of play rather than overstress the muscles by doing too much. I don't think anyone could ever accuse me of not being fit enough during the season.

CHAPTER EIGHTEEN

The
all-rounders

The role of the all-rounder is crucial in the balance of any cricket team but, over the years, the position has been a victim of fashion. Fast-medium bowlers dominated for a while but sometimes it's been a spin bowler who can bat. Even wicket-keepers such as Alec Stewart of England and Adam Gilchrist of Australia have been classed as all-rounders. Since I retired in 1974, the best all-rounders seem to have been bowlers of the quicker variety who can hit the ball hard, such as New Zealand's Chris Cairns. Perhaps that's the influence of one-day cricket.

There are others who call themselves all-rounders but surely the criterion must be that an all-rounder is worth his place in his side both as a batsman and as a bowler, or as a batsman and as a wicket-keeper. The fact that he can do both to a high degree is a bonus.

Back when I started, two Australians were dominant in the all-rounder department – Keith Miller, who was coming towards the end of his illustrious career when I played against him in 1955, and Alan

Davidson. I would nominate those two as the top all-rounders I saw during my career.

The mercurial Miller was still a magnificent bowler when I played against him, a wonderful cricketer in every sense of the word. There was someone who was undoubtedly worth his place in the Australian side for both batting and bowling while his fielding was also of the highest calibre. With Ray Lindwall he formed the best opening fast-bowling partnership of their era. Keith, with his height, bowled a wicked bouncer. He could move the new ball in the air, and even when the ball was old he was dangerously unpredictable. He bristled with hostility and intent whenever he ran in. He scored runs and took wickets in the West Indies and was outstanding.

Alan Davidson must be ranked among the best. He had good movement and control with the ball and was a very good lower-order batsman, as he proved in the tied Test. If he hadn't been run out, we would surely have lost that match. I doubt whether we would have taken another wicket. He was a tremendous fielder close to the bat, hence his nickname, 'The Claw'. Earlier in his career he was noted for his outfielding and his ability to hit the stumps on the run. He was a fine new-ball bowler, perhaps the best in the world for a period of about five years, while he was a magnificent hitter coming in late on when he would destroy tiring bowlers.

Richie Benaud was another good Australian all-rounder although better known as a leg-break and googly bowler. He was, however, an excellent attacking batsman, maybe not as good defensively in terms of technique as he might have been, but he could accumulate quick runs.

Englishman Trevor Bailey of Essex was another recognised all-rounder. He was a good bowler who could take the new ball or come on later, but how can you talk about his batting? He opened the innings for England on occasions and sometimes went down the order, stopping a collapse, holding up an end, more often than not just pushing the ball around. He was a penetrating opening bowler, a sharp fielder and an excellent student of the game but his batting at times did not seem to be there. He could take forever to make 50 or, worse, 100.

It could lull you to sleep. He wasn't called 'Barnacle Bailey' for nothing. I played against him in the 1957 series and in county games against Essex in the autumn years of his career. He was a reasonable all-rounder but, because of that slow batting, not rated with the greats.

When I finished, probably the best all-rounder was England's South African-born Tony Greig. Like most South Africans, he was a consummate competitor and was capable of producing a match-winning innings. On occasions, he could win the game with the ball as well. I remember him taking 13 wickets for 156 runs on a good wicket in Port-of-Spain, Trinidad in the 1973–74 series, bowling off-cutters against a very strong West Indian batting side. He achieved considerable bounce off the wicket because of his height, but I rarely saw him bowl in that style again. He reverted to medium-paced bowling in England and Australia where he was just another bowler. Had he developed his off-cutters, he might well have been an outstanding all-rounder.

Unfortunately, I never played with or against Imran Khan or Kapil Dev. I did, however, play in a little friendly match against Ian Botham, to see him at first hand. He could have been head and shoulders above them all if he had put a little bit more application into his batting. He was certainly a magnificent bowler, the kind of bowler you want on your side. He was always trying something different and he would work himself into the ground for the team. As a fielder, he had a beautiful pair of hands wherever he played, taking spectacular catches either close in or in the outfield.

As a batsman, he could go in and change a game in the blink of an eye but you never knew when he it was going to happen. He rarely built an innings in the way other top-class batsmen would, by going in, pushing it around and then taking the bowling apart. He went in and simply threw the bat at the ball from the start. If it came off all well and good, and if it didn't there was always someone ready to make excuses for him.

Great players should not need others to make excuses on their behalf. I have always believed that a top batsman makes things happen. He doesn't collect runs by taking chances and relying on good luck. Ian allowed his reputation for being a big hitter control him. It's sad because, as good as he was, he had the genuine talent to be even better, one of the greatest all-rounders in the history of the game.

Sure he made runs, but the way he scored them was reckless, hit and miss. He was much better than that, but take away that side of him and we may have had a different, less dynamic personality. Who can ever forget that match-winning innings against the Australians in 1981 when all seemed lost? He also had the priceless asset of being able to bring spectators back to the game whenever he played. People would pay to go and watch him. The happy-go-lucky style extended beyond the pitch and that did not help, nor did the back problems that forced him to alter his bowling style as he became older and less fit.

While Botham was the brightest star in English cricket, there is little doubt that Imran Khan was Pakistan's superstar of the post-war era. I appreciated the way he could score runs when it really mattered, and he could generate a great deal of pace when he warmed up, although his confessions of ball tampering did little to enhance his reputation.

He captained a difficult side, showing his depth of knowledge of the game and his ability to bring a group of individuals together as a team. He was adored by his players and the fans alike. His best performances for his country came as captain, even though he was not afforded that honour until he was almost 30. He always raised his performance against the better Test sides. He had an abundance of natural ability and kept himself remarkably fit, which enabled him to overcome a damaging shin injury when his powers as a quick bowler were at their height.

When Kapil Dev was playing, India were not as strong as England or Pakistan. He played against some high-quality bowlers, particularly in the West Indies when they were at their fast-bowling pinnacle, and he still made many runs and always took wickets. In fact, he took more wickets and scored more runs than Ian Botham or Imran Khan – but then he played a lot more Tests. He felt that he was more a bowler than a batsman. He was capable of the same late outswing as Botham, but he was an exciting batsman who gathered his runs quickly.

His greatest achievement was to lead India to victory in the 1983 World Cup final against the West Indies who were the bookmakers' and the experts' strong favourites. Statistically, his contribution was not that strong, just Andy Roberts' wicket, but we took just 21 runs off his 11 overs while he scored 15 crucial runs in a low-scoring match. It was his leadership that singled him out. Earlier in the competition he played what can truly be called a captain's innings when he came in against unfancied Zimbabwe with the Indian score standing at 17 for 5 on a nasty, damp pitch at Tunbridge Wells. He went on to score 175!

It is very difficult to separate the three of them, but if I was forced to give an edge, I would give it to Botham because he had that ability to tear bowling apart and you could usually rely on him for quick runs. Imran would knock the ball around but I always felt that good bowlers could tie him down, much more so than Kapil Dev or Ian.

Two others who come close to these three are Sir Richard Hadlee of New Zealand and the late Malcolm Marshall of the West Indies. Malcolm's bowling was outstanding but his batting wasn't in the same class as the others. He was certainly one of the West Indies' best all-rounders.

Richard Hadlee was not blessed with the same natural talent as the other three but he worked hard on what he had to become one of the most probing of bowlers, a man who could put the ball exactly on a spot, disguising which way it was going to move.

He started as a tearaway, an erratic opening bowler, but he cut down his speed and used his brains. By the time he went to play professionally for Nottinghamshire, he had learned and he became one of the best medium-pacers of all time, able to work on a batsman's weaknesses and get him out almost to order. What's more, he took the majority of his wickets away from his own grassy New Zealand tracks. His batting also developed late. He was not a noted batsman until he went to play in World Series Cricket for Kerry Packer. A clean hitter of the ball, he could change the course of a match in the twinkling of an eye. You could argue that he should be ranked with the other three because of the quality of the opposition he played against throughout his entire career.

Nowadays, there does appear to be a dearth of top-quality all-rounders. Cricket tends to go in cycles so perhaps it's due to that. It could also be that in addition to ability, there needs to be dedication. The older players worked very hard at all aspects of their game; it's possible that the modern players tend to specialise too early.

They are a different breed, the all-rounders, but I guess we have one thing in common and that is that we have more fun than most because we are always in the game.

CHAPTER NINETEEN

Out of Africa

The worst period of my cricketing life came in 1970 when I accepted an invitation to play in a double-wicket competition in Rhodesia, as Zimbabwe was then known. I was there for 36 hours but it caused massive repercussions that threatened my reputation and my international cricket career.

It all began when I was leading the Rest of the World against England. One of my team, South African Eddie Barlow, suggested I took part in a double-wicket tournament in Rhodesia. I asked for a couple of days to think it over but after delving into the matter I thought that, as a professional cricketer, there was little or nothing to stop me earning my living in what was a fun competition. I was well aware of the politics. We were playing England as replacements for South Africa who had been excluded from international cricket because of their government's apartheid policies. I asked around among players and other people who had been there, and was told that apartheid was not a problem in Rhodesia. Their national football team were all black and there was no discrimination in the selection of their sporting teams.

Add to that the fact that I had four white South Africans in my multi-racial World XI, and this was a team selected by those bastions of good taste and all that is politically correct, the MCC. Given all this, I thought there was nothing wrong in travelling out to Salisbury, the capital of the former British territory that had made the headlines by declaring unilateral independence. How wrong could I be!

I went back to Eddie and told him I accepted. I was to partner Dr Ali Bacher, the South African captain who went on to restore South African cricket internationally after the apartheid ban. A very healthy £600 was the fee for what amounted to two days' work.

I was living in England at the time and was unaware of attitudes to Rhodesia in the Caribbean. My decision to play was applauded by the British press while in Barbados Peter Short, Secretary of the West Indian Board of Control, issued a statement saying that it was my decision and had nothing to do with the Board. I did not have to consult the Board – they did not run my life – but, even so, they gave others the assurance that Rhodesia did not have the apartheid problem of South Africa. I thought I had no worries.

However, Frank Walcott, general secretary of the Barbados Workers' Union, was extremely critical and in a statement said that I should be disqualified from captaining the West Indies. It gave him the sort of national and international platform he had never before experienced. His statement, which went round the world, said:

Mr Sobers is an international personality and represents the heart and soul of millions of people in the West Indies who see their national identity manifested in cricket and their symbol of pride and equality with nations in Gary Sobers. He cannot lapse into any area which is an offence to the dignity and character of West Indians.

I was stunned. I had no concept of the repercussions and had certainly not intended to upset anyone, far from it. Although I was going to play cricket and earn money, I thought that I would be aiding the cause of multi-racial sport in Africa. Frank Walcott's statement took me totally by surprise.

No one told me I should not go or, indeed, not to go. It was a country where black and white mixed, unlike South Africa. To me it seemed little different from other places in the world where the white people usually seemed to have better living conditions than their black counterparts. It was certainly not a replica of South Africa with separate pavements, buses, schools and other obscene things like that.

I was not even that successful at the cricket, hardly surprising as I stepped off the plane and played after just a couple of hours' rest.

During the cricket and afterwards I talked to a lot of people, both black and white. The real problem arose after I had lunch with the Rhodesian Premier, Ian Smith. When I was interviewed later, I described him as a great man to talk to. It was a personal opinion and had nothing to do with me playing cricket in Rhodesia, nor was it an opinion on his politics or his role as a leader.

Smith wasn't a popular man, especially among the neighbouring African countries, including Gambia. By coincidence, one of our West Indian prime ministers was in Gambia talking to their leader and telling him how we were blood brothers, when the news item came across that I was having lunch with Ian Smith. The Gambian leader reacted by saying, 'How can we be blood brothers when one of your greatest ambassadors is having tea with Ian Smith and telling the world how good he is?'

I arrived back in Barbados a few days later to be met at the airport and promptly told that I would not be welcomed in various of our islands.

Dr Eric Williams, the prime minister of Trinidad, which had a large Indian population, realised the magnitude of what was happening when Mrs Indira Ghandi said she would not let the Indian team tour unless the matter was sorted out. The entire affair had escalated out of all control and was headlines across the Caribbean.

Forbes Burnham, the prime minister of Guyana, made a statement saying that I would no longer be welcome in his country unless I recanted and apologised for my foolish and ill-advised stand. The president of the Guyana Cricket Board of Control, Kenny Wishart, also demanded an apology. Peter Short said simply that there was no reason to apologise and Cameron Tudor, the deputy prime minister of Barbados, described the attack on me as an affront to the people of Barbados.

It was getting silly as more and more politicians jumped on the bandwagon. Michael Manley, cricket historian and leader of the opposition party in Jamaica, demanded an apology, adding that I would 'not be welcomed anywhere by people who believe that justice is bigger than sport'. The ruling party in Jamaica trumped that by demanding that I resign as captain of the West Indies.

Dr Williams sent Wes Hall to ask me what was happening and to explain his position. Wes said, 'Have you hit Forbes Burnham? If you have, you would have to apologise, but you hit nobody and you do not have to apologise to anybody.

'We all knew you were going there and if we didn't want you to go, we should have called you and told you not to go. But seeing that the West Indians love their cricket and want the series against India go on, get someone to write something that sounds like an apology and I'm sure that Mr Burnham will accept it.'

My prime minister, Errol Barrow, was in America at the time and when he heard about the growing furore he cut short his trip to return home. He asked me what was going on and I told him exactly what had happened. He agreed that I didn't have to apologise and said that he would write the letter to the president of the Guyana Board of Control. It read:

Dear Mr President,

When I accepted an invitation to take part in a two-day, double-wicket competition in Rhodesia I was assured that there was no segregation in sport in that country but I was not made aware of the deep feelings of the West Indies people. I have since learnt of this feeling and the wider international issues involved.

I am naturally deeply distressed by and concerned over the tremendous controversy and bitterness which have arisen after my return from Salisbury. As I was not aware of the serious repercussions I may have expressed myself in such a way as to create the impression of indifference to these issues.

Mr President, I wish to inform you in all sincerity that this is far from my true feelings as the prestige of West Indian cricket and the unity and dignity of the West Indians and African people are interests I have always served.

I therefore wish to convey to you and the members of the Board my sincere regrets for any embarrassment which my actions may have caused and assure you of my unqualified dedication whenever I may be called upon to represent my country, the West Indies, and my people.

I signed it G. St A. Sobers. It was widely publicised and immediately accepted. It appeared others were keener to extricate themselves from this mess than I was! For two and a half months it was front page news, back page news and the main topic for radio phone-ins and as far as I was concerned it could have carried on because I did not feel that it warranted an apology from me. The letter was a happy compromise for everyone.

The Indians came to the West Indies and I played in Guyana where Mr Burnham sent his car to meet me as he usually did, to take me to his party. When I arrived I said to him, 'What was all this nonsense you were talking about?'

'Let's forget about it,' he replied, 'and go and have a drink.'

It was the same in Jamaica with the soon to be prime minister Michael Manley, who had said that I wouldn't be welcome in his country. He asked some friends of his to arrange a party for me but not to tell me that he would be present. I knew he would be there and when we met he said that he was so sorry and that he had to do it because although he looked on me as one of his sons, the other party were making gain from the situation so he had to use it too. That was politics. I told him that I held no malice against him or anyone else over the matter. He had done what he thought he had to do and that was the end of it, and it was soon all forgotten.

It has been suggested that I was deeply hurt. It is simply not true. I went to Rhodesia as a professional cricketer to play my sport, and not to fraternise with or support any political party. In those days that £600 was a lot of money to me. I was playing with and against the people I had played with and against all my life. Bacher, my partner, was the only one among them whom I did not know. I could not for the life of me see what all the fuss was about. I thought that I was on pretty good ground. I didn't know that Forbes Burnham was in the next country or that it would become an international incident.

All I did was say that I enjoyed the company of Ian Smith, which I did. I talked to him about these same things. He said that he didn't mind criticism from anybody as long as it was constructive, and that too many of the critics were people who had never been to his country and did not know him. I have to say that he was a very pleasant man. He sat down normally with me and we talked like men. He didn't try to overpower me, look at me in a funny way or try to change my opinions. He was as relaxed as anyone can be when meeting someone for the first time.

Over the years I had received several invitations to play in South Africa but I refused them all. It never bothered me that I didn't play there. I knew I never would because of the way it was, so I never gave it a thought.

As a cricketer, it was a disappointment that we didn't have the opportunity to play South Africa anywhere else when they had that great team, on neutral ground in England or somewhere. It would have been a tremendous match. They had some outstanding players – Barry Richards, Graeme and Peter Pollock, Mike Procter and Eddie Barlow, who could have been one of the great all-rounders, to name just a few. Unfortunately, these players could never be given full world-class status because they didn't play enough Test cricket. They didn't have the opportunity to play at any length because of their government's vile policies.

Regardless of what the records do or do not say, Barry Richards must be considered one of the best batsmen ever as far as technique goes, and the way he played so easy and relaxed. Graeme Pollock played a lot more than Barry and he showed his class at that level but it is still difficult to judge him on so few Test matches. Quite often a player comes in and his first two or three series go very well but then the wheels fall off, as they did for the Australian Norman O'Neill. To confirm class, a player has to be judged over a long period.

I feel very sorry for anyone who was involved in sport in South Africa during that period, not just cricket but athletics, tennis and rugby. It was a rough time for all of them and a great pity for those people, black and white, who never had the opportunity of performing on the world stage. They must look back on it with great sadness. I remember Barry Richards being interviewed in England, and being asked about how many runs he had made. He said, 'I would rather have made more friends and fewer runs.' I'm sure he was talking about being denied the chance of touring in the West Indies, India and Pakistan.

However, it has all come to a good conclusion. The banning of the South Africans from all sport had some kind of bearing and helped to force the hands of the politicians. You have to hand it to President de Klerk – he stuck to his guns with one man one vote despite serious opposition. If he had not told everyone to stop this nonsense and get on with life, life might still have been the same. It was de Klerk who paved the way for Nelson Mandela to take the whole thing forward.

Now here was a truly great man. To go through the years of imprisonment the way he did and then not even mention it when he came from captivity to run the country was very humbling. He never looked as though he had gone through so much pain and punishment. He took over the country that punished him and never seemed to give it another thought.

I had the privilege of meeting him when the authorities were trying to bring South Africa back into the fold of international cricket. The ICC wanted either Sir Donald Bradman or myself to go there and assess the situation. Sir Donald wasn't doing a lot of travelling then so they asked me. They knew that, as a cricketer, I would say that they should come back into the sport. There was talk of bringing them back into the fold gradually over three years, but I said that they should come back in immediately and that is exactly what happened. Colin Cowdrey, who was president of the MCC at the time, personally asked me to go because he knew that we both felt the same way.

It is simplistic to say that politics is politics and should not be mixed with sport. They go hand in hand and always will although at times we try to separate the two. In every country, sport looks to the government for help; it happened even in those days. I believe that while governments should help, sport should maintain its independence.

My meeting with President Mandela in 1991 was brief. I was on the trip with West Indies' highly regarded cricket commentator Tony Cozier and a few others who were promoting the return of South Africa to the international fold. We were in Soweto taking a look at some young cricketers who were being coached by men and women, hundreds of kids, black and white. We watched them, talked to them, and the next day it was arranged for us to see the great man.

We went to his house and he came down to greet us in his robe. He talked to us for about 45 minutes. He knew a lot about cricket and said that his two favourites were the Don and me. He said how glad he was to meet me and how pleased he was that I had come to South Africa. We talked a little about his life and times. He was a fascinating man with a great presence.

To be so upright, to stand for justice and not criticise or harm the people who had imprisoned him I always thought was remarkable. He stands out because of what he has achieved after all he has gone through. He has never once mentioned revenge and I'm sure that's how he truly feels. It's not something he puts on. Although I met him for only a brief period, I felt I knew the man; I could feel the sincerity that was coming from deep inside him. I looked at him and wondered how he could do all that he had done. I was asking myself what made this man tick. How did he work the way he did? That's why he is accepted so well around the world. He has been a gracious, serene man. There is no one to compare with him, and of all the people I have met in my lifetime, I have to put him in a class apart.

We were due to meet de Klerk the next day but he was out of the country. It was a pity because I was also a great admirer of his and of all that he had done for South Africa.

I liked what I saw in South Africa and I have been back since. It is a fine country and I particularly liked Johannesburg when I first went there. It's a shame that things have changed a lot and that there is now so much needless violence. It was such a nice city. I have also been to Port Elizabeth and Cape Town, which is a beautiful city.

I was, of course, asked many times for my thoughts on the rebel tours to South Africa during the later stages of their isolation. It was and remains my view that every man must look to himself and live with what he sees in the mirror. These men were professionals and some of them were never going to play for the West Indies; others were on the way out and this was an opportunity to better themselves financially.

There was always the hope, which one would want to believe, that by going over there they were smoothing the path for the future. If they went with that in mind, maybe there was nothing wrong with it. Change had to begin somewhere and maybe, just maybe, those tours by the West Indians and the Sri Lankans helped to break some of the barriers down. South Africans who had not seen a lot of the blacks or coloureds play cricket had an opportunity to watch the likes of Lawrence Rowe, Franklyn Stephenson, Ezra Moseley, Alvin Greenidge and Collis King. White people, indoctrinated with the government policy of apartheid, could see that black people were not bad. These players, by their talent and demeanour, could show them that black people possessed the same potential and ability as white people. Much depended on how those rebel players deported themselves, on whether they were really trying to promote what was good and help the oppressed black people in South Africa. If, because of their visits, they achieved some or part of that, maybe the tours were worthwhile.

But at the time, many people were against it and the players knew what the consequences would be – unlike me with my unfortunate visit to Rhodesia! They made their beds and had to lie on them. They knew of the risks of being banned well before they went and they had no one to blame but themselves.

However, the question has to be asked why, when things changed, were some selected to play for the West Indies while others were left out? That was a problem and if there was a whiff of hypocrisy about, it was on both sides of the fence. No one has been able to tell me the reason for, or even explain the thinking behind, Ezra Moseley later being selected for the West Indies while Franklyn Stephenson was steadfastly ignored.

Stephenson could have been a force in the later years because he was certainly the best all-rounder the West Indies had produced for a long time. He was overlooked after going to South Africa with the rebel team and then, afterwards, they just seemed to forget all about him. Others were brought back but he was cold-shouldered by the selectors.

It was a great pity but what can anyone do about it? I am afraid the answer is nothing. That's what happens when you mix politics and sport. The end product is more often than not a great deal of hypocrisy.

CHAPTER TWENTY

Strictly personal

I have always been a free spirit and maybe not always the conventional professional cricketer. I like to gamble, I certainly enjoy a drink and I never objected to a late night out and the company of a pretty lady. I was lucky. I was never one who needed eight hours or more of sleep – four or five hours and I would wake up totally refreshed. If I went to bed too early, I couldn't sleep, and if I had energy to burn, I would burn it.

My philosophy was simple. As long as my social life did not interfere with or damage my cricket, I was doing nothing wrong and in many ways this spurred me on to even greater efforts, particularly the day after the night before!

A classic example occurred in 1973, when I was coming to the end of my career, and playing my last Test match in England at Lord's. It was the first day of the Third and final Test in late August. We had piled on the runs with Rohan Kanhai, also making his last appearance at headquarters, turning back the clock with an energetic 157. Roy Fredericks had weighed in with 51 and Clive Lloyd 63. The stage was set for me on the following day. I always loved playing at Lord's and with us one up in the series and with runs on the board, I was very relaxed, so when Clive Lloyd suggested a night out, I was up for it.

We visited some of his Guyanese friends in London for a meal and later I met up with an old friend, Reg Scarlett, just as I was leaving a nightclub and heading back to my hotel. The former Jamaican and West Indian off-spin bowler was living in London at the time. I was pleased to see him and abandoned the idea of returning to the hotel in favour of a drink with him. We ended the evening at a club where we enjoyed the dancing and drinking, and come four o'clock we politely offered to escort our dancing partners home before I returned to my hotel for a quick sleep. We waited for the ladies to collect their coats but they failed to turn up. I realised I had long gone past the need to sleep.

'I have so much liquor in my head,' I said to Reg, 'that if I go home to the hotel and go to bed, I'm not going to wake up.'

He asked me what I wanted to do and I suggested that we go back to the Clarendon Court, where the team were staying, for a few more drinks and a little reminiscing about the good old days, and that's exactly what we did. As morning dawned, I had a cold shower to wake me up, and joined the rest of the team for the short journey to the ground.

There was no chance of a rest in the massage room this time because I was 31 not out overnight, batting with Rohan, and due to take the first over against England's quick opening bowler Bob Willis. This was a vital day and I thought I should change my approach – I played forward and missed the first five balls. Willis was glaring at me down the pitch as though he could throttle me. I imagined I could hear the fellows up on the balcony laughing because they knew that I had not been to bed and had a fair idea of exactly what was happening out there in the middle.

The sixth ball hit the middle of the bat and I began to settle, but when I reached the 70s the alcohol stated to work on me and I desperately wanted to go to the toilet. However, it was going so well and I did not want to break my concentration, so I decided to hold on. When I reached 132 I gave up, and told the umpire Charlie Elliott that I had to leave the wicket. He asked me what for because he hadn't seen anything go wrong for me while I scored my century. I explained that I had been in agony for 25 minutes. I couldn't hold on any longer and if he didn't let me go there would be a nasty accident. He said, 'Go,' but I was already on my way.

'I don't care what you say, I'm gone anyway,' I shouted back.

When I reached the dressing room, Rohan Kanhai, who was captain of the side, was waiting.

'Captain,' he said — he still called me that out of habit — 'what's wrong with you?'

'Skipper,' I replied, 'boy, my stomach is giving me hell. The only thing that'll help me now is a port and brandy mixed.'

He called for the drink and I swallowed it quickly. He took one look at me and shouted, 'Bring the captain another brandy and port — but make it a big one this time.' I liked the idea.

'No problem,' I said, and drank that down as well.

Suddenly my stomach felt good and I didn't even need to find the toilet. By this time Bernard Julien and Keith Boyce were batting and when Boycey was caught by Dennis Amiss off Tony Greig, I went back out. I am told that John Arlott, who was commentating at the time, observed, 'West Indies six hundred and four for seven — and Sobers still to come.' Thanks to the medicine, I went on to score 150 not out. Bernard Julien and I added 155 in less than two hours before I'd gone off and in the end Rohan declared the innings closed at 652 for 8.

That was my last innings in England. It was a memorable match for me at the age of 37. The Lord's crowd gave me several great ovations as I trotted backwards and forwards to the wicket over those two days. I read afterwards that I showed great maturity in playing myself in steadily before proceeding with grace and power. Little did they know! I did not take any wickets but made my contribution in the field as I managed six catches.

I wouldn't recommend that sort of preparation to anyone else but it certainly seemed to work for me, just as it did in Australia in 1968 when I was playing for the West Indies against Western Australia in Perth. Night seeped into dawn on that occasion, too, and I arrived back at the hotel just as the team were leaving. I was batting at six and decided to catch up with my sleep. I padded up to be ready when the call came, and nodded off. It wasn't long before I was shaken awake and told that I was in and that a bowler named Sam Gannon had taken a few wickets and had us in trouble. I had never heard of him and hadn't seen him bowl a single ball until I went out to the middle. But Gannon, Graham McKenzie, Laurie Mayne and Tony Lock all went the same way as I hit 132 in 113 minutes. When I was out, I resumed my seat and went straight back to sleep.

I even managed to celebrate in Kanpur one Christmas when we found some rich friends with a supply of good Scotch. Team manager Berkeley Gaskin saw me creep home in the early hours of the morning but decided not to say anything until after my innings. There was not a lot he could complain about then because I scored 198 before being run out while batting with Joe Solomon.

Former Warwickshire and West Indian fast bowler Dr Rudi Webster, a sports psychologist, interviewed me for a book he was writing called *Winning Ways*. He began by asking me what was my motivation. I answered late nights. He looked at me as though I were mad and said, 'How do you work that one out? That's a strange way to motivate yourself.'

'When I was out late at night,' I told him, 'I had to make runs the next morning. Late nights relax me and if I go out I relax, and when I get back to my bed I sleep properly. The whole point is to relax. A few drinks and a late night out did the job for me. I wake up feeling fresh and ready to take care of the job in hand. To maintain my lifestyle, I had to perform that day, the next, and the next. It was not harming my cricket and, in fact, it gave me the motivation I needed. It was not the only thing that motivated me, but I had to let you know that.

'What really motivated me was to look at the scoreboard and see what West Indies needed. If we needed a hundred and fifty, I knew that I had to stay there and make sixty, seventy or even a hundred. The position of the team motivated me more than anything else.'

I admit that I was a law unto myself, but everything I did, I did for West Indies. If I had to bowl all day for them I would and did; if I had to stand under the bat to take catches I would and did. West Indies cricket did a great deal for me and the only way I could give something back was by performing to the best of my ability, not for me but for the team. That was my way of showing my gratitude. I knew that if I performed, it would benefit me too, but West Indies were always first and I was second.

There is, by nature, a lot of free time in cricket, not just on the rainy days during an English summer but away from the square in strange towns and foreign lands with little to do to pass the time. Having a bet often filled that space and I admit I liked gambling and still do. I especially liked the casinos but I also enjoyed playing poker and betting on the horses. I could stay all night in a casino, playing roulette and blackjack; I'd have a few drinks, talk to people, make new friends, have a rest from the tables, walk around and then start again.

I still like a bet on the horses and occasionally on the dogs, but I'm not one for the casinos any more. I changed my opinion when I was on the same table as a lady in her 80s who followed the same numbers every spin of the wheel. She had lots of chips and was so busy, betting on so many numbers, that I had no opportunity to place my own modest bets before she had covered most of the board. I asked myself what she was doing there on her own at that age. She looked sad and lonely and it put me off.

Prior to that, when I lived in England, I used to go to a little casino in Manchester run by a friend of mine. Apart from the gambling, they had a bar and dancing. I would play blackjack until dawn. It was just killing time but I used to enjoy it.

The last time I went regularly to casinos was 20 years ago in Sri Lanka. I was coaching their national team. Apart from a couple of weeks when my children visited me, I had little or nothing to do and I knew few people, so I would go and sit in the casino until two or three in the morning and then go back to my hotel.

I still pop into a casino now and again with friends if they want to have a little flutter but I find it difficult to play.

I didn't gamble solely to win; I gambled because I enjoyed it. It relieved boredom, especially in the days when I was playing league and county cricket in England. I began to use the bookmakers regularly when I lived in Radcliffe. The first year I knew little or nothing about it but, again, I was left with a lot of time on my hands during the week. The instinct was there. Even as a little boy I was attracted to the horses, and in my early teens I regularly visited the atmospheric Garrison Savannah for the race meetings. I would buy a ticket and watch the horses run. It was a way of passing time as well as spending money.

Eventually, I looked forward to having a bet every day and at times I spent more than I could afford, betting when I knew I had some money coming in to cover the losses. I suspect that I became a little addicted.

On tours there were a few of us who liked a bet and we even bought a little television set on the 1966 trip to England so that we could watch the races. There were no complaints and it was no problem – I was the captain! I had a runner to go and put a bet on for me when I couldn't leave the ground.

Wes Hall, Seymour Nurse and lots of the boys liked the horses and so did the English and Australian players. I have heard stories of Keith Miller having someone signal him, when he was in the field, and tell him what was happening. He would make an excuse and go off or, if he was batting, get out the next ball.

I stopped going to the races because usually, when I went to a track, I'd meet friends, maybe Josh Gifford or Terry Biddlecombe, and they would want to drink and chat in the bar. I found myself rushing out to put on a bet without studying form or looking at the horses. When I woke up next morning, I'd discover I'd lost £100 without knowing exactly where it had gone.

Fortunately, gambling hasn't done any great lasting or permanent harm to me as, sadly, it has done to some others. My wife Pru was always against it, but if something went wrong I would just say to hell with it and back I went. At the time, I had nothing to replace it.

When I returned to live in Barbados, I used to go to the Garrison Savannah regularly until I started playing golf. After that, I would probably have a bet on the English races in the morning and then go and play golf. That was a much better balance.

I still enjoy a flutter. It always seems to be a challenge, trying to beat the book – not necessarily trying to win a lot of money, although it makes me happy when I do. More often than not when I do have a win, I succumb to the challenge of finding more winners by reading form, and give it all back. When they come in, it's still a big thrill. After all, it has been a part of me for a long time.

The gambling and the rest are all very well when you are footloose and fancy free but not so easy when marriage and a family come along. The responsibilities tend to bring about changes.

I have the great fortune to have two sons, Matthew and Daniel, who were both born in England, and a daughter, Genevieve, whom we adopted when she was two days old. Genevieve is from Bogotá in Colombia. Pru told her she was adopted when she was old enough to understand; she also knows how much we love her and how much a part of the family she is. She is a tremendous girl, the perfect sister to Matthew and Daniel. I am lucky. They are three terrific kids and I couldn't ask for better.

As a father, I have followed the ideals and principles from my own family life. My mother brought up six of us and never had any problems. It's the same with my children. They go their own way and use their judgement. I can trust them with anything, to go anywhere, do anything and not get into trouble.

Matthew, born in 1971, went to school in Australia and then to St Michaels, a public school in Barbados. He did his degree in accounting in Barbados. After that, he went back to Australia to study for a Masters, but he changed tack and took a three-month course in computing instead, and returned to Barbados to work and live. Now he is back in Australia working with his stepfather. He is a director of the company, and planning to bring it to Barbados when he is sure it will work.

Daniel wasn't as brilliant academically as Matthew but he was very good with his hands, especially at drawing, painting and making things. When he sat his exams with 200 other children, going for the 90 available university places, I admit that Pru and I were a bit concerned, but he made it comfortably. Four years later he had a degree in graphic arts. He grew up in Australia, coming to Barbados for his secondary education, but once he earned his degree in Australia, he came to work in Barbados where he is very successful.

Both boys were very sporting with good hand-eye coordination. I was not at home too often but when I was, I took them to the indoor cricket centre. They were never keen to follow me professionally and I never tried to force them. I have watched sons of famous fathers and listened to them talk, and I was careful not to let my boys become just their father's sons, denying them their own development and personalities.

I remember Ron Headley getting very fed up because wherever he went he was introduced as George Headley's son. After a while, Ron stopped being polite and started to tell people that he had a name – many people never knew it – and that while he loved his dad dearly, he was a person in his own right. Richard Hutton had a similar experience. Folk would say, 'Meet Sir Len's son.' Don Bradman's son had to change his name to get on in the world and be his own person.

I didn't want my boys to be branded like that as Sobey's sons. They were both blessed with ability. Daniel, who was born in 1974 and was smaller than Matthew, had good coordination and might have done well if he had been interested in making a career in sport. Matthew bowled well and could have been an excellent cricketer. When I came out of cricket he was about 17 and I had him bowl at me in the nets. I was impressed. He was pretty quick and could bowl a quick leg-spin and a googly. I felt he was very talented.

Rather than concentrate on a single sport, both boys took advantage of the sports-mad Australian way of life. They took up judo, Australian rules, cricket, football, tennis and played as many sports as they could. They were both very athletic and Matthew has developed a fluent, rhythmic golf swing.

Genevieve is now past 21 and living in Barbados. We decided to adopt her after Pru said that she wanted a girl and didn't want to keep producing boys until we had enough for a cricket team. She had some friends who had been to Bogotá to adopt and she went to investigate. The Colombian authorities were very thorough, even keeping pictures of us in a bid to match us up as well as possible. They eventually called to say they thought they had found a suitable baby and all four of us went to South America. The country backs the system because it brings in visitors and much-needed dollars. Normally it took about a week to complete the formalities but we were there for longer. I had to go back to Australia after two weeks because of my contract, but Pru and the boys stayed on and brought Genevieve home.

There was a long time when I didn't see her because she was growing up in Australia and I was back in Barbados. The only time she had been to Barbados was as a baby when she passed through with Pru and the boys on the way to join me in Australia. Her mother thought it time she found out more about the place and spent some time with her father. Getting her Barbados residency was a little more difficult than expected because she was born in Colombia and we had to obtain all her documents from their embassy. It took an eternity and was very complex.

My daughter is not much of a sporting person. She is an intelligent girl and she will decide on the direction her career will take. I am so happy that Daniel and Genevieve are also living in Barbados now. What delights me most is that the people of Barbados love them all.

I met Pru, an Australian, in England in 1968 when she was working for a company called Admona on public relations for the Australian canned fruit industry. Her job was to arrange interviews around the country with prominent people who had been to Australia, to promote tourism and sell the canned fruit. That was how we met. She interviewed me in Nottingham, and afterwards I invited her out for dinner. She disappeared off on her work and we met now and again when our itineraries coincided or when she was in Nottingham where I was captaining the county side.

She gave me her address and telephone numbers in Melbourne and when I went to Australia with the West Indies I went to meet her parents, Mr and Mrs Kirby. Pru was still in England at the time and then travelling home by boat. She was very surprised to find me waiting with her father when she arrived in Sydney.

However, far from being the great romance, things were not too good. She wasn't sure about the long-term relationship I wanted and I felt that things were falling apart. I was captaining the West Indies and went off to Queensland to play, sensing we had reached an impasse. I shrugged my shoulders and was philosophical about it, although more than a little sad. Some you win and some you lose and it looked as though I had lost this one even though I cared for her and loved her very much.

A week later she called me in Brisbane to say that she had talked to her sister who had told her that if she loved me we should get together and she should forget all the nonsense and get on with it. She said that she would see me when I came to Melbourne, but not to discuss marriage.

It was when we were dancing on New Year's Eve that Pru, apparently, made her decision, and after that we became engaged and decided that we would tie the knot in England. We were married on 11 September 1969, as soon as the season had ended, and spent our honeymoon travelling through the English countryside.

We divided our time between Barbados and England, and it was not until Kerry Packer started his world series in 1976–77 that we lived for any length of time in Australia. We were there again the following year. The year after that, when the series was cancelled, I was playing for North Melbourne. It was then that Pru decided there was no better time to move back to her home country, and we lived there from 1978 to 1983. I returned to Barbados in 1984.

I had always said that I planned to spend some time in Australia but it was understood that I would not be living there permanently, as much as I loved the country and the people. In the event, we were there for five or six years. During that time Pru settled back into the Australian way with her Australian friends, and she thought that my gambling was getting on top of me. She didn't like it and I wasn't doing anything about it. When I was finally ready to return to Barbados, Pru wasn't.

'Look, my dear,' I said, 'it's time for me to go home.'

I had been going to Barbados for five and a half months a year from 1980 to work with the Tourism Agency and I was ready to go full time with them, but she wasn't prepared to accompany me. The marriage, a very happy one as far as I was concerned, lasted for 15 years; we married in 1969, broke up in 1984 and the divorce came through in 1990 and that was it.

We are still very good friends. When I'm in Australia, I visit and we go out for dinner. The kids see her, of course, and she calls regularly. She was, and still is, a beautiful and intelligent person and a lovely mother to our kids. She has written books on health and diets including two or three best-sellers. She makes her own jams and sells them into Safeway's supermarkets and she had a radio phone-in programme at one stage. She's a very busy and creative lady.

It's never easy when you break up but I suppose it helped that we were so far apart. There was no malice or envy and the children hardly realised that we had broken up with me having been away travelling so much anyway. But it's funny how children know and understand what's going on, and how well they adapt. Their grandmother was always there and they always had comfort and love, and they came to stay with me.

Being a professional cricketer, and especially a Test player, is not the ideal job around which to build a marriage. I never envisaged being married while I was playing and travelling the world up and down. It was even worse then than it is now because we were not allowed to take our wives with us and if we did we had to sleep in separate hotels. Even if a player did want to take his wife, it was usually out of the range of his pocket. I couldn't afford a decent meal for two never mind hotel rooms.

Hotel food was always a problem, anyway, with or without your spouse. To West Indians, it was always bland. When we were in England, we would occasionally buy a Chinese takeaway, or go to a Chinese or Indian restaurant, or round to Guyanese or Trinidadian friends for a good curry, or Bajan friends for a nice rice and stew.

Chinese and Indian food have always been my favourites rather than French or Italian, which are a bit rich for my palate. I eventually became accustomed to English food. The traditional Sunday lunch of roast beef and Yorkshire pudding, beef stew and plaice and chips were the favourites. These days I have to watch what I eat. I still like a nice steak or a piece of beef with béarnaise sauce but I limit myself to having these treats two or three times a year.

My drinking habits have changed, too. I have cut down on spirits, giving my stomach a long-deserved rest from the short stuff. A glass of wine or a bottle of lager does me now. I never drank beer in England because I didn't think it had much taste and was often warm. I preferred lagers, Tuborg or Carlsberg.

I was lucky with injuries when I played – I didn't have many – but they must have been lurking there, waiting for me to pack up. I have flirted with death several times since my retirement. The worst occasion was in the early nineties and involved the knees, which had gradually disintegrated under the constant wear of thousands of overs and days in the field and running between wickets. I'd had an operation in Barbados, one of half a dozen on the left knee alone, and it didn't seem to work too well. Later, in England, I was taken ill with it. It was so bad that I could hardly walk. The knee was red and puffy and I was full of fever. I never paid much attention to injury or illness, usually waiting for it to clear up and go away as it had always done in the past rather than going to a doctor or a specialist. But this was different. I knew things were bad and I went to see a doctor in London who immediately referred me to an orthopaedic surgeon at the

Wellington Hospital near Lord's. He took a look and told me that if I was thinking of going home to Barbados to forget about it for some time. He pushed a needle into my knee and when he pulled it out I could tell by his expression that he was shocked. The knee was seriously infected and he put me into surgery the same night. It was bad with septicaemia and the inflammation was working its way into the blood. He went back into the knee and drew off what he could and two days later he had to go back in again and took out the lining.

Every day he would come along and remind me that I was a very sick boy. I was lying there for two weeks with a drip feed and all the usual paraphernalia, taking more than a dozen tablets a day. It was not until later that friends told me how close to death I had been.

I was told that I had to drink a lot of water, something I was not used to. I never drank water because I preferred soda in my Scotch and Coke in my brandy. It tasted like poison but I had to drink it.

The oddity was that I never really felt ill. Gradually, I began to improve and move around a little. Vince Nurse, a friend of long standing, used to come in almost every day to sit with me and often he would smuggle in some Chinese takeaway. He was great company; he would talk to me and bring me anything I wanted.

I had to work really hard on the knee when I started to walk. They were all so good to me at that hospital, the doctors, the nurses, the surgeons and the physiotherapists.

The entire incident was kept quiet from the media because we didn't want any fuss but BBC radio commentator Brian Johnston found out about it and came to visit me, as did Tim Lamb from the ECB. Very few other people got to know about it. I heard later that, after visiting me, Brian collapsed as he climbed into a taxicab, suffering a near fatal heart attack. I must have looked worse than I thought.

I was in hospital for four weeks and even then the doctor was reluctant to release me. I'd had enough by then and all I wanted to know when I checked out was whether it would come back again. That was more than 10 years ago now and, touch wood, it has not returned. I presume everything is all right.

I had a problem with cataracts, having suffered with iritis in my eye for some time. I didn't know anything about the retina or the eye in general and used to have treatment to correct it without giving it much thought. One day I saw a dark spot and assumed that it was the iritis getting worse. I didn't bother mentioning it to the doctor, even when it got so bad that I could scarcely see out of that eye. Then it started to affect my beloved golf and when I was in Jamaica playing in Montego Bay, I finally found the time to see another eye specialist. I remember him well because his name was Garfield. He informed me that the iritis had cleared up but when I told him about the black spot he checked the back of the eye and said, 'Oh my dear, you have a very bad torn and detached retina.'

I didn't know what that meant, but I knew it was serious when he immediately telephoned a specialist in Miami and tried to arrange an appointment straightaway. Unfortunately, it was Sunday and I couldn't get an appointment until the Monday. It was a long and nerve-racking wait because of the urgency, and things did not improve when the American specialist took a look and said that it was very bad with only a 50-50 chance of saving the eye. Worse was to come as he discovered that the other eye was slightly affected, too.

They operated and when I came out of the theatre I had to lie on my face for over two weeks with a weight on the back of my head to keep the retina down. Finally, he said that they were unable to do anything more to help me. He told me that they had lasered the other eye as well while I was under the anaesthetic. It also had a hole and the retina had started to come off.

Since then, I've had a lot more laser treatment both in Barbados and England. I still have black spots and when the iritis flares up I cannot see out of that eye. I have to use drops for anything between four and six weeks until it clears up and it is very frightening to think that I could lose my sight altogether. There are always reminders. When I went to Australia in 2000 for the tied Test match reunion, it flared up badly again and I had to see yet another specialist. He prescribed me some drops and I immediately returned home.

All grown up now, Matthew (left), Daniel (right), and Genevieve with Dad at his special honours gala thrown by the Barbados Tourism Authority in April 2001

Below Sir Garry and fiancée Jackie White share a moment

Overleaf You never lose it! A bit of beach cricket in Barbados in April 1990

Arise Sir Garfield. Honoured by the Queen in Barbados in 1975

On being made a National Hero of Barbados in 1998

Above Two all-rounders together – with England's exciting Ian Botham during a Rest of the World match in Barbados

Right Handing over my world record to compatriot Brian Lara in Antigua in 1994

Pink pads! Whatever next? The influence of the Packer era as I pad up for a net session in Sydney in 1979

Posing for a painting by the late Sarah Raphael at Lord's during England's Test match against Pakistan in 1992

Right Batting in my final tour of England in 1973

Far right Bowling at Edgbaston in the same game

PATRICK EAGAR

PATRICK EAGAR

Raising a glass at the headquarters of cricket, Lord's, after my final Test appearance in England

PATRICK EAGAR

Showing the way to my Rest of the World team in England in 1970

End of a day's play and the youngsters come running for autographs at Lord's during the tour that replaced the visit by banned South Africa

With wife Pru and baby Matthew

At home in Barbados and loving it

The vision in my left eye is blurred and I have to keep a careful check on the right eye. Fortunately, the latest check-up revealed that it was better than it had been for years. The doctor said that he could see right into the back of the eye and there were no more holes developing.

They say you have to get hit or have a bad jolt to suffer a detached retina and I have no clue when it happened. The annoying thing is that if I had mentioned it when I first saw the little black spot, something could have been done. I also saw tiny flashes of light and, incredibly, I dismissed those as fireflies when, in fact, they were another warning sign of what was happening. It was going on for a long time and they were both clear indications, but I didn't know that. My advice to everyone is that if you see a little black spot and it's not moving, or you see flashes that look like fireflies darting around – go to the hospital straightaway.

It was unfortunate but plenty of people around the world are a lot worse off than I am and I have to be grateful that it didn't happen to me during my 20 years of playing top-class cricket.

I can still see reasonably but when I play golf I have depth deception – everything seems to be closer than it really is and when I land in bunkers I find it difficult to get out. Once the club is off the ground, I don't know how high or how close it is or where to get the club back in behind the ball. I either blade it or take too much sand and leave it in the bunker. That's the only problem and it isn't really a big one. When the sand is hard and flat I have no problem at all but when it's soft the club goes right down and I usually hit the top of the bunker or go right across to the other side of the green.

The only other physical ailment I suffer from is a bit of arthritis but every sportsman has that after a lifetime of battering the joints with piston-like movements, the running, jarring and jumping. I have lost the fluid out of most of the joints and they rub together and are painful unless I remember to take my anti-inflammatory tablets.

The first time I had a problem with my knees was when I was playing league cricket in England with Radcliffe and it did not flare up seriously again until I was playing county cricket with Nottinghamshire. I was sent to see a specialist. He took one look and said, 'How you are still playing cricket on this knee I will never know. I have never seen a knee so chewed up and destroyed like this one. All the bones are flaked, rubbing together and breaking off. You won't be able to do much on that knee for a long while.'

I ignored his well-meant advice, went back to Trent Bridge and played on it for another four years. They have been telling me that I need a replacement for the last 14 but I doubt whether I will ever have one now; it's like an old friend.

I use a cart to go round the golf course and it's only when I have been sitting down for a long time that I really feel it. However, I find it difficult to play golf in the morning because although I wake up, my body doesn't! I have to wait for it to catch up, and then I can move around, particularly when I feel that warm Caribbean sun.

Back home in Barbados, after the last operation in England, I used to meet my old West Indies team-mate Cammie Smith at six every morning, and we'd go for a long swim, which left me feeling good. Once I started on my travels again, the early morning swim went by the board, but sun and seawater are good healers.

Over the years you discover what is good for you and what suits your body. Walking is fine but jogging jars too much. No one will ever convince me that running on a hard road is good for you. Running on the sand, which gives a little, is a lot better.

Fortunately, my injuries and illnesses have not slowed me down too much since I stopped playing cricket. There has been plenty to keep me busy with lots of travelling to my old haunts in Australia and England.

When I finally came home in 1984 to work for the Barbados Tourism Authority as a sports consultant, the government of the day, the BLP, laid on a motorcade. My job was to help organise sports sponsorship and attract more tourists through the medium of sport. England was always going to be one of the main areas in this work because that was where I played most of my cricket and that is where most of the holidaymakers and cricket teams come from. English travel agent Don Gooding, a friend of mine, suggested setting up a tournament called the Sir Garfield Sobers International Schoolboys Tournament, and he brought some of his travel agent friends, cricket mates and school teachers to look at the facilities. The tournament was set up as a result of that visit and I travelled to England every summer to promote it and the island, showing slides and talking to pupils and parents, convincing them that everything works and the boys would be safe. I explained that it would be a tournament from which the youngsters would benefit – they would enjoy the cricket and would be well looked after.

In the first tournament, we had a dozen visiting teams competing, eight of them from England, two from Trinidad and two from Canada, plus our own Barbados sides. It went reasonably well. We suffered the inevitable teething problems but we worked on it so that it improved year by year. The masters who came from England passed the word on to other schools. It was organised originally for the English schools because that was where the nucleus was. The kids came for three weeks at the beginning of the school holidays. Their parents joined them for the second and third weeks, after they had settled in. We still adopt the same system.

Trinidad was also a good source of teams and gradually the whole concept began to grow with other Caribbean islands including Dominica, St Kitts, Antigua, Grenada, and St Vincent sending over teams. One of the purposes behind organising the tournament, apart from attracting tourists to Barbados, was to give the youngsters from England and other countries an opportunity to play in our conditions, and also to help strengthen cricket in the Caribbean. We now have teams coming from South Africa and we are in negotiations with Australia, India, Pakistan, Dubai and New Zealand. We have been expecting teams from India for the past few years but the first has yet to arrive. We have had a team from Jamaica but Guyana simply cannot find the finances to send a team.

Airfares and accommodation are paid for by the teams while we organise all the transfers, transport, grounds, lunches, two functions, one at the beginning and one at the end, and the final at the Kensington Oval. We supply the brochures and have souvenirs and trophies for every school that competes.

It has certainly improved cricket in the Caribbean, not only in Barbados but overall. The tournament is very competitive rather than 'friendly' cricket. A lot of youngsters who have taken part have used the tournament as a stepping-stone to a higher level – Lara, Dhanraj and Rhamnarine, for instance, and from Barbados Roland Holder, Adrian Griffith, Hendy Bryan, Sherwin Campbell and Courtney Browne, along with Chris Adams from England and one or two South Africans. Nearly all of the Barbados players who play for West Indies played in our tournament, as did many English players who went on to play county cricket. It has been good for the country and good for the game. We celebrated the tournament's 15th year in 2001.

We have just been able to purchase covers, due to Virgin Holidays' generous sponsorship, and we have persuaded the Barbados Cricket Association to adopt them for senior competitions. Ours are probably the oldest grounds in the world not to have covers, and contrary to popular opinion we do have rain in the Caribbean! I believe that the best cricket is played on covered wickets. I had to ask myself what we were doing playing on uncovered wickets when everyone else had covers. What were we training the youngsters for?

Our wickets are unlike English wickets, which often play better when wet than when dry. You have to be brought up on our wickets to know how to play them. When the top comes off, the ball doesn't just hit and come through, it stands right up and looks at you. You have to acquire the technique to deal with it, leaving the English boys at a disadvantage. Our boys stand up and play off the back foot. They wait for it and pull it all over the place while the English boys still try to play off the front foot.

When the covers were introduced in 2001 we lost very little playing time, and some good scores were made by most of the teams. It is a happy change of circumstances and has brought satisfaction about the quality of wickets throughout the tournament. We now lose very few fixtures to rain and are able to make sure every team plays eight or nine games and a practice game.

I am very happy that the Sir Garfield Sobers International Schoolboys Tournament has been able to lead the way in introducing covers to Barbados. All of the senior BCA clubs are now using them for the first division and knock-out tournaments.

As a young man, playing at Kensington Oval was the highlight of my career and so it is for the youngsters and their parents when they come over to Barbados. The tournament is played while we have our great Crop Over Festival and the boys have the added opportunity of visiting the entertainment tents and listening to the calypso music, giving them time to relax after the tough competition.

Apart from England, I also visit Canada and the United States promoting Barbados. We don't have the facilities for American football and baseball, but the Sir Garfield Sobers gymnasium, which caters for something like 14 sports disciplines, has volleyball and basketball courts. In addition, we now have three good golf courses.

Americans are also playing a lot more cricket than you may imagine. People will be amazed to know that there are over 200 teams in New York alone in addition to the hotbeds of Miami, Philadelphia, San Francisco, Los Angeles, Boston and Connecticut among other centres. America and Canada enter teams in the one-day series in the Caribbean, so it means we have a wider scope to promote the island and its sports in North America.

I love promoting Barbados because I am a great lover of my country, and Barbados has so much to offer. The climate lends itself to doing so many things the year round. The job gave me a great opportunity to come home, but promoting my country was nothing new because I did it all the time when I played cricket, spreading the news wherever I went. I was always being asked to tell people what Barbados was like and I was only too happy to oblige. Now I am paid to do it. I can be sincere and honest, not like a salesman who is selling a product he doesn't believe in. I don't have to be a salesman to sell my country. I will do it as long as I am able.

I have had plenty of offers from various places to commentate on cricket. I resisted for many years because I couldn't see myself sitting down all day talking into a microphone. I was finally persuaded to do it but I found it very boring. I'd spend seven hours at the ground in order to do two hours of commentary because of the rotation system. I'm not a good watcher of cricket, I never was. It wasted my time when I could have been at the golf club.

Then the station I worked for stopped doing commentary and required me to do a 15-minute summary. That was even worse. I don't think I will be doing it again. When I go to cricket, I like to go for an hour or two, watch a little, meet some friends and then go and play golf. If I don't feel like playing golf, I might stay for a couple of hours in the afternoon to meet friends I don't see very often from all over the Caribbean. It is always nice to renew old acquaintants.

Over the years since my retirement, I have been given a number of great honours, of which I am so proud. The knighthood, of course, caps them all because I believe it was given not only for my success at cricket but also for fulfilling my obligations as a person and an ambassador. Two other awards I am fortunate to have received are National Hero of Barbados and the Order of the Caribbean Community. I am the only living 'hero' and just two or three of us have the latter award. They are magnificent tributes, given not just for my cricket but for the way in which I have conducted myself all these years. People say that I have been a role model, an icon even, for the way I have behaved. I have always been happy to carry the flag for my country and for my sport. I am sure that people like me are awarded honours such as these to show how the general public feel about you. The world is full of cricketers who have achieved all sorts of records but have never been honoured in this way. It makes me extremely proud.

I can honestly say that I never expected to be named a National Hero of Barbados. I suppose our government are showing the young-sters that you don't have to go to war or be a revolutionary to be a hero. It takes all sorts of people to form a country and if you have been a successful sportsman and achieved things in your life, it is just as important for you to carry your country's flag and fly it to the highest standard. I am lucky because I have walked with giants and have been called a legend in my own lifetime by people whose opinions I respect.

I have never found those descriptions or titles a burden to carry. The praise and the honours that have been bestowed on me have come my way because of the way I am and the person I am, not because I have put on any airs or graces or deliberately gone out of my way to achieve fame. What people see with Sir Garfield St Aubrun Sobers is what they get. I live the way I have always lived. Therefore it is not a burden. I can walk barefoot down the road or go to the bookmakers in my slippers because people have always seen me that way. Those honours were given to me for what I was then, so why would I change now?

I like to think that I have conducted myself in an orderly and well-mannered way. It makes me proud that those I have played with and against have described me as one of the most honest and gentlemanly people in cricket. This was me, not someone I tried to be, but me. I was born that way. No one will be allowed to take away my common touch; I achieved everything as a common man and the friends I had when I was growing up are still the friends I have today. I can mix with the people at the top of the hill but I was never going to forget those elsewhere. I choose my own friends and that is my reward from life.

That is not to say that I haven't enjoyed rubbing shoulders with the good and the gracious, and especially sportsmen and women I admire from other sports. Jack Nicklaus, for example, was my golfing idol and I was delighted to meet him and Gary Player. I also got to know Sir Bobby Charlton and a lot of footballers whom I am happy to call my friends. I watched and met Cassius Clay when he first started boxing and again when he was Muhammad Ali. And there were others from outside the sporting arena whom I admired when I was a child, Nat King Cole and Ella Fitzgerald, for instance.

You always think of those people as famous, not yourself, and this was brought home to me when I was inducted into the Black Hall of Fame in the United States many years ago. The comedian and television star Bill Cosby wanted to perform the ceremony, claiming that he used to fly to Jamaica when I was playing and then fly home once I was out. He picked the right place to watch me because I always seemed to do well at Sabina Park. The induction was an experience to remember and I sat next to former world heavyweight boxing champion Jersey Joe Walcott while I awaited my turn.

I have been fortunate to meet people some of whom think of me in the way I think of them, and discover they wanted to meet me as much as I wanted to meet them. Famous people always want to meet famous people. It is part of what makes your life so interesting, especially for an ordinary little boy from a humble background. I am grateful to the game of cricket and to the West Indies for giving me the opportunity.

But my real hero is not a sportsman, nor an entertainer. It remains the former South African president, Nelson Mandela. Now there is a real hero and a legend.

Of course, I will never forget the joy and the pride of my investiture in Barbados at the Garrison Savannah racecourse, which everyone thought was very appropriate – not just for me, I hasten to add, but for the Queen, too, who loves horses, as does the Duke of Edinburgh, the Queen Mother and Princess Anne. I was thrilled that the knighthood was conferred upon me on my own island rather than in London. I have been to Buckingham Palace and Clarence House and whenever the royal family come to Barbados I see them at Government House. I am flattered that they remember me and want to talk. More often than not, the topic with the Queen is horses and the Duke chats about cricket. I am always impressed that they seem to have a keen interest in everything that is going on. They know exactly who is going to be present and whom they are going to meet. They are marvellous people who have always struck me as down to earth and very pleasant.

My acquaintance with the royal family was used to lure me into an appearance on 'This Your Life' in 1975. That was a big surprise. I had just been knighted and was attending my first function in England since that memorable day in February, and I was told that Princess Margaret was going to be there and my presence was something of a royal command. I remember driving past the Barbados Board of Tourism in London and Pru looking up to the windows and signalling to someone inside. I didn't have a clue what that was all about but, it transpired, it was a pre-arranged signal to say that they were not ready for me. I was told that the princess had not arrived and protocol insisted that we had to wait until she did.

We went to the Hilton Hotel in Hyde Park and sat and waited for 20 minutes before we were told that they were ready for us, and we strolled down to the function at another nearby hotel. Good fortune was with us that day for no more than half an hour later a terrorist bomb went off exactly where we had been sitting at the Hilton.

We arrived at the party, and I couldn't see Princess Margaret anywhere, but I did see Eamonn Andrews and I knew instantly that I'd been had. He walked over, produced the red book and uttered those words – 'Sir Garry Sobers – this is your life.'

It amazed me that I could live with Pru and not know what was going on. She was continually popping off to see people without telling me who and I asked no questions, but I wondered without ever coming near to an answer.

The arrival of my mother Thelma was the most amazing part of the show because she had never travelled abroad before. She revelled in the new experience. Not only did she stay for two weeks in England but when she got home she immediately flew off to spend some time with my sister Elise in America.

There are only so many things that can happen in one's life and it seems that they have all happened to me. I am grateful for the honours, and that I am still around to appreciate and accept them on my island in the sun. Now there is some discussion about a life-sized statue to be placed at the roundabout near the gymnasium.

I have always been grateful to God for giving me the ability, the strength, the knowledge and the will to fulfil all these things. Without him I know I could not have done it. Don't get me wrong. I am not overly religious, a born-again Christian or anything like that. I went to church every Sunday when I was a child but rarely as an adult. Like many people, I go to the occasional funeral and wedding these days but that doesn't stop me believing that there is a God, and I try to do the right things by him. I don't think you have to go to church to worship if you are sincere about it. Belief in God has been one of the most important cornerstones of my life.

CHAPTER TWENTY-ONE

The modern game

One of my regrets is that I never had the opportunity to play a lot of international one-day cricket. In fact, my one-day international career was limited to just the one game and not a run to show for it!

The development of the one-day game came at the wrong end of my career. Although I was selected to play in the very first World Cup finals in England, won by the West Indies in 1975, I picked up an injury towards the end of the season with league side Littleborough and that was my chance gone. I could have played with the slight groin strain but with all the fuss over the Australian tour when they didn't play me, I didn't want them to put the team in jeopardy by saying I was all right when I wasn't. They had to name their squad and wouldn't have been able to change it.

Rohan Kanhai was brought in and he did very well in the final against Australia. Clive Lloyd justly received a lot of praise for his hundred but Rohan was well into his 30s and although he didn't score as many runs (55), he stood up well to the pace of Dennis Lillee and

Jeff Thomson, helping Clive put on 149. Rohan once again showed that he was a very good player and the West Indies deserved their narrow win.

I'm certain that I would have enjoyed playing one-day cricket and I don't think it would have changed my game. After all, I played in the same way whether it was league, county or Test cricket. I have always tried to play in an attractive manner.

My whole game was based on attack whether as a batsman, bowler or captain. My declaration against England in Trinidad, which turned so many critics against me, proves the point. When I captained Nottinghamshire, I made a lot of similar declarations and won most of them. Opening batsman Brian Bolus used to come up to me and say, 'I see you gave them the old one-two again.' My attitude was that the game had to be played so that everyone could enjoy it, not only the players but the spectators as well. That's why so many fans turn up to watch one-day cricket – they know they will see attractive cricket and a result. How many turn up for four-day county matches?

For me, the pioneer of one-day international cricket was the Australian television magnate Kerry Packer but his 1977 breakaway series was not all that good for cricket in general. Sure, it was good for the players who went to Australia to compete in front of Packer's cameras for excellent money, but his personal battle with the ABC had a damaging effect, particularly on cricket in Australia. During the Packer series, something like 50 Aussies were banned from domestic cricket and this is one of the reasons why their cricket was pushed so far back. It meant that the youngsters did not have the opportunity to emulate, watch or play with or against the very top players. There's no doubt that good players bring on the youngsters; against second-raters, they can only remain at that level. It proved to be a watershed in Australian cricket and the game there suffered serious repercussions.

But the Packer series had a dramatic effect on the one-day game. Not only that, I'm sure that if he hadn't come along when he did and paid good wages, modern-day cricketers would not be earning anything near their current salaries. Those many players who criticised him and complained that he did great harm to the game should kneel down and kiss his feet for getting them what they have now.

He also improved the lot of the armchair cricket fan. The increased number of television cameras at grounds means that the game can be looked at from every possible angle.

But mainly, he improved the game. Many of the decisions he and his people made all those years ago are a regular part of the one-day game, from the coloured clothing to the sensible rule that four men should be in the inner circle at all times. Pre-Packer, the one-day game was becoming very boring. As soon as a team needed 10 runs to win off the last over, the entire fielding team spread around the boundary with even the wicket-keeper dropping back. Cricket did not need that; it needed excitement and Packer gave it to them. He must be given great credit for his innovations whether you like the man or not.

While Packer and his rebels were busy developing new ideas, including floodlit cricket, the Australian Test team went backwards. When they came to the West Indies in 1977–78, our players were able to come back and play while Packer's Australians were banned. The veteran Bobby Simpson led the touring side after being out for 10 years. That was how far back their cricket had gone.

We won the first two Test matches in less than three days and then when some of the West Indies players pulled out over a row in Guyana, Australia were able to come back at us and nearly won the series. That served to show how strong the West Indies were at that top level and how weak they were underneath, just like the Australians.

It took the Aussies a long time to rebuild but now they are a great team again, the best in the world. They took stock and made the changes that transformed their game with the start of their successful Cricket Academy.

The rebel cricket was beautiful to watch and certainly not the sort of festival cricket that I had played on a Sunday in England. Packer made sure that it was competitive because he based the prize money on winning, and if he saw any of the players slacking or wanting to make it a friendly affair, he made sure they knew that he knew what they were up to. After the West Indies had won their first series easily, they coasted. Packer called them in during the second series. He told them to look at the big iron bird in the sky and to remember that they would be on it, on their way home to the Caribbean, without a penny in their pockets if they didn't play properly. They took his meaning and went out there and played hard.

In fact, Packer did more for West Indies cricket than he did for any other country because he succeeded in bringing the players together. He made them realise what they could achieve if they played as a team. They understood that if they wanted to win the top bucks, they had to play as a team, regardless of politics or island favours, in order to win the series. This was a chance to earn good money and better themselves. Clive Lloyd took it from there. When they came back into West Indies cricket, they brought that attitude with them. When they asked for improved wages, they knew they had to perform to earn the increase, and were thus more likely to get it. That was all down to Packer and World Series Cricket.

The Packer West Indians missed just one series, against India, but we could have been in a similar situation to Australia if all our players had been banned. Instead we came back better and stronger with some of the best fast bowlers in the world.

One-day cricket has helped a lot of players. It has certainly helped the overall standard of fielding, which is now quite fantastic worldwide, and the running between wickets is so much better. Fitness has had to improve.

If I'm being honest, there are things about it that irritate me. I like the system whereby teams have two good attacking players with sound technique to accumulate as many runs as possible before the field is allowed to spread out. The top order can bat normally – but if you bat down at five or six, more often than not you have to throw the bat around and the batsmen gain no benefit or learning from it. That, to me, is where one-day cricket falls down.

Another area that irritates me is this nonsense about opening the face of the bat. It has become so commonplace that you see players trying to do it in Test matches, opening the face to run the ball down through slips. The bat is made to play with the full face and every time you open the face you are taking a risk.

For all its merits, the one-day game is not a true breeding ground for Test players. A handful move smoothly from one to the other. Samuels from Jamaica has come through that arena. He is a good, strong player and can switch, but there are many young players who cannot make the change. They should be held back until they mature. It is my oft-repeated opinion that one-day cricket should be restricted to experienced players. Although some aspiring players can adapt, it does not help with development of sound techniques. Equally, some older players are not suited to the one-day game. It requires a combination of knowledge and understanding. Good bowlers of all types are likely to succeed.

The one-day game probably saved professional cricket in England with the money it brought in, but it did some harm in encouraging the development of so many medium-pace bowlers. Spinners and the real quickies seemed to disappear. Only now is it being realised how important spinners are in Test cricket, and England trail a long way behind the rest of the world. In my opinion, England simply picked too many ordinary all-rounders to the detriment of good spinners and have, accordingly, paid the price ever since.

Cricket is serious and you have to bowl seriously at every batsman. I have always been against the rule of two bouncers an over. No one should tell a bowler how he should bowl. Can you imagine an umpire telling me after I hit Malcolm Nash for six sixes in an over that I wasn't allowed to hit any more boundaries because it was unfair to the bowler!

If I have a weapon, I use it. Certainly ban the beamers, which are the really dangerous balls, but if you are not good enough to face bouncers, you shouldn't be playing at Test level. Real fast bowlers depend on pace rather than swing so when you take away the bouncer, the batsman has no fear. It changes the balance of power. It also robs the spectator of the excitement of a batsman hooking a bumper for six.

When England tailenders Murray, Higgs and Snow put on their

stands, they weren't bowlers, they were batsmen. Do you bowl bouncers when that happens? Of course you do. They were getting behind the ball and getting in line. I'm not saying bowl to hit them, but shake them up, or try to persuade them to hook.

When Keith Stackpole came over to the West Indies in 1973, we had a chap from Jamaica called Uton Dowe who thought he was another Roy Gilchrist, but he didn't have Gillie's pace and accuracy. He tried to bounce everyone out but Stackpole hit him for a couple of sixes and a couple of boundaries before one wag in the crowd shouted out, 'Remember the eleventh commandment.' We all wondered what he meant until he added in a loud voice, 'Dowe shalt not bowl.'

No one told Stackpole not to hit this fellow. Personally, I would have been bloody well annoyed had anyone stopped pacemen bowling bouncers at me. I always thought they were bad balls that you couldn't set a field to, even though it was easier then because they could have as many fielders behind square leg as they wanted. Now there can be two only, and a batsman has to be unlucky to hole out to one of those.

That rule doesn't help the inswing bowler who has to start the ball outside the off stump. It is hardly fair that he should have just two behind the wicket when the outswing bowler can have five slips and a couple of gullies if he wants. Why rob the good left-arm bowler of his main weapon by telling him he cannot have more than two men behind square? That's a ball that can give a good batsman a lot of trouble because it comes into his blind spot. What's wrong with two leg slips and a leg gully? Two leg slips and two back made it very difficult to penetrate down the leg side but now if you have two in close, it's a free hit.

The inswing bowler was helped, however, with the new lbw law, which allowed the umpire to give a batsman out for a ball starting outside the off stump if there was no shot played. But the laws these days seem to help the batsmen more than the bowlers.

Modern technology and aggressive players have changed the lives of umpires all over the world. It is no longer a friendly, pleasant way to earn a living or pass the time. Umpires must now live in fear. With television cameras perched on their shoulders and former Test players ready to jump on their case whenever they make a mistake, umpires seem to be afraid to make decisions for themselves.

The way players appeal does not make the umpire's life any easier. I worked on a video as vice president of the Umpires' Association. One of the cameos was of four or five players rushing at the umpire, constantly appealing, with their mouths wide open, putting the official under severe pressure. How is an umpire supposed to cope with that sort of behaviour? It did not happen in my day, all these high fives and fielders running in from deep third man to congratulate the bowler even before a decision has been made. When the wicket-keeper and bowler appeal, everyone appeals with them whether it is for a catch or even an lbw! How can anyone tell whether a batsman is out from square leg or fielding on the boundary? The new rules that have been brought in should, I hope, curtail this aggressive, intimidating appealing.

Technology is massively advanced but much of it is to the detriment of the umpire. One thing I am sure of is that you cannot have someone judging from a screen. Umpires should be the sole judges of what is right and what is fair. Judgement cannot be made without consulting the umpires. It is wrong to ban someone just like that without the umpires' consent. The umpires have always been the policemen of the game. Once you start sitting someone in the stand to look at actions and give them the power to ban people, you have to wonder what the umpires are doing out there at all. I understand that there is even a 'throwing committee' whose sole job is to look at suspect actions on television and administer bans.

It is all very well using slow-motion replays and all the rest to identify a bad decision, but that can only happen after watching it several times. I don't know of any umpire who can see through a pair of pads, or who is able to watch a ball over and over again; nor does he have a line drawn from stump to stump so that he can see exactly where the ball is dropping. These commentary aids are all well and good to educate the viewing public, but they generate what I believe is largely unfair criticism. There are unreasonable people who expect umpires to be perfect and get all their decisions right, especially when they are umpiring in their home country. The technology is a new toy for the television people to play with but is it fair on the umpire? I think not.

I agree with the introduction of the third umpire. Who knows how many of us were run out many years ago with direct hits and were not given out. It is amazing how many direct hits are out but impossible to judge with the naked eye. At least now the umpire has the opportunity of help if he is unsighted or unsure. It is also used for some catches to see whether the ball has carried, but there are limits to its use. I don't think it should be introduced for lbw decisions, even though television shows them. If they do that, they might as well give the umpires a television monitor. Can you imagine umpires standing there and saying, 'Hold on a moment, let me have a look at this.' It would take everything away from the game, and games would have to start at eight o'clock in the morning to allow enough time for umpires to check every appeal. The third umpire is fine for run-outs, stumpings, close catches to the ground and boundaries when the umpire cannot see clearly, especially with the sliding stop where the body or the legs can easily go over the line.

It's reckoned that some places around the world give hometown decisions but it is difficult to judge whether that's from bias or just poor decision-making. It is not often it becomes actual cheating. Fortunately, that sort of thing is extremely rare.

Most umpires who do not have enough international exposure or enough high-profile matches are liable to make genuine mistakes. They are amateurs and don't always know what they are looking for. As with most things, umpires get better with practice.

I must say I found the umpires in Australia to be very good. I find it difficult to believe that they would do anything unsporting in that part of the world. I can only believe that contentious decisions were genuine mistakes.

Obviously, the best umpires are those who stand regularly in first-class cricket, seven days a week, throughout the season, but that only happens in England. The umpires there are consummate professionals, standing most days for five and a half months of the year. For the umpires in other countries, it is either Saturday afternoon cricket or competitions such as the Sheffield Shield, the Curry Cup or the Ranjit Trophy in India, with the occasional Test match thrown in. It does not give them the exposure the English umpires have week after week. That's why England has produced a number of world-class umpires including Sid Buller, Charlie Elliott, Alex Skelton and Dai Davies, who were all reliable, honest and very good. Charlie Elliott was outstanding as was Dickie Bird. I also liked David Constant and was surprised when I heard that Pakistan objected to him standing in 1987.

Skelton was funny. He would give you out if you played a bad shot. If you played down the line and missed it, that was fine, but if you played across it he would say, 'That's a bad shot and you're out.' I had a good rapport with Charlie Elliott. We often used to travel together as he lived near Nottingham. We got on like a house on fire. Sid Buller was much quieter and you couldn't ruffle him at all.

I always reckoned that the Australian umpire Colin Egar was one of the best. I had a lot of dealings with him in Sheffield Shield matches, Test matches and club cricket. He was an outstanding umpire. He would give you out for a duck and wasn't afraid to come and have a drink and a laugh with you afterwards. Some umpires wouldn't come near you when they had given you out cheaply, even when they were right. Colin was the same whether you scored 0 or 100. He would just tell you not to get your foot in front.

The umpires in the West Indies have been fairly good. Cortez Jordan was excellent and Clyde Walcott's uncle, Harold, was also of a high standard. A lot of the umpires in the Caribbean were influenced by English diplomacy and at times there were little things that went England's way when they might have gone our way. While we abused our umpires, the English would tell them and the world how good they were.

I got on with most umpires. I respected them and their decisions. But perhaps the most difficult umpires were in the Leagues. If the professional was hit on the pads in front of the home umpire, there was only one decision. At least it taught the players to play with the bat and not their pads!

Colin Cowdrey and I asked about the possibility of neutral umpires for all Tests, back in the seventies. We suggested that a panel of Test captains and managers pick the best, and then they couldn't blame anyone but themselves if anything went wrong. Colin proposed neutral umpires for Test matches while I offered up the idea of a panel of top officials from whom to select the umpires for specific matches. We are heading in that direction now and the sooner the better as far as I am concerned – but who would want to take the abuse and suffer the ridicule that come the umpires' way nowadays?

It used to be a gentleman's game but now good manners seem to play little part. Referees and umpires have to report players who misbehave and either suspend or fine them. Who walks now when they get a touch behind the wicket? How many catches are claimed when the fielder knows the ball has touched the ground first?

Of course, these things happened going back to the days of W.G. Grace but they were always the exceptions that proved the rule. One time in England, Basil d'Oliveira hit the ball to Conrad Hunte who caught it. Basil did not move so I asked Conrad if it was a clean catch and he told me that it was. The umpire gave it not out but I knew that if Conrad had said it was good it was, because he was into this moral rearmament business and had renounced all the wrong things he had done in life in public. He was so upright. But d'Oliveira stood his ground and I said to him, 'Basil, as far as I'm concerned I believe Conrad, and if I were you I would have walked.'

Personally, it's not something I would do. If I hit the ball and was sure it was caught, I was off back to the pavilion. I didn't wait for the umpire's finger to tell me to go. However, perhaps he felt it had not carried, and as the umpire also was not sure he was able to continue. In cricket, some players wait for the umpire's decision, some walk.

It was the same with catches. Fielding close up to the wicket, whether you managed to scoop your fingertips under the ball before it touched the grass was often a matter of a fraction of an inch. Only you knew for sure so you were beholden to be honest and not claim the catch if it had touched down. Several times in my career I have told an umpire it was not out when I have caught the ball on the half-volley.

There have always been some who cheat and sadly that number seems to be growing. Over the years, players have been known to claim 'catches' when they knew the ball had touched the ground first. I don't see the sense in cheating a batsman out. It's the same with walking. If I was on 10 and did not walk when I knew I was out and then went on to score a century, I would not feel that I warranted that hundred on my record.

On one occasion when I was playing for South Australia against Queensland, I walked after the faintest of tickles. Australian wicket-keeper Wally Grout asked me what I was doing. He hadn't seen or heard the snick and he hadn't appealed but I knew that I had touched it and I was on my way even though the umpire would not have given me out. It was something Wally never forgot. He told me he would never have appealed but I felt the touch. I have always done that, taking my gloves off and putting my bat under my arm and heading off to the pavilion. I have never, ever stayed at the wicket when I have known I was out. Had I done so, it would have destroyed everything that had gone before, everything that I stood for in cricket.

I am aware that there have been batsmen who wouldn't walk when they were on a low score but when they'd reached three figures they would go. That's not the way; in many ways it's worse. You should not walk ever if you are not a walker. They say that Colin Cowdrey was a little like that. I remember him playing against us, waiting and walking around until the umpire lifted his finger. They say Colin was a good walker when he passed 100 but that, to me, is defeating the object. All it does is put more pressure on umpires.

Ian Chappell was the opposite. He never walked and made sure that everyone knew about it. That was fair enough. He declared his hand early, claiming that the decisions evened themselves up over a season, especially when put against lbw decisions. It is true that a batsman often knows whether he is in front of his stumps and out. But Ian was wrong to use that as an example because two wrongs do not make a right. Yet again, it makes the game more difficult for the umpires.

Players are becoming more aggressive. There is nothing wrong with aggression in fast bowlers but if it gets nasty, it needs to be controlled. In my opinion, when a fast bowler starts to give it mouth as well as the old-fashioned stare, that is going a stage too far. You can see on television when the bowler has said something by the batsman's face. When a bowler is taking wickets he's happy, but when he's getting some stick he seems to feel that he can say what he likes. If a bowler is slogging his heart out and something goes wrong, it's easy for him to say something on the spur of the moment to the batsman or even the umpire. It's normal, but when the complaints, remarks and moans are pre-planned, personal or racist, that's going too far. It is difficult to digest.

When players came back into the dressing room after being given out, complaining that bowlers and fielders were giving them verbal abuse, my advice was always the same – keep quiet and let the bat do the talking. That was what I did and eventually they would stop. If you hit them hard enough, they don't want to know you at all. They will be careful not to rile you because they know you will cut them to ribbons. If you answer back, they know they are getting to you and will do it all the more.

There has always been sledging but not as bad as it is today. There has also always been gamesmanship to unsettle the batsman. When the batsman replies it can escalate and cause friction. Today what happens on the field seems to go on and on whereas when I played, whatever happened on the field was forgotten when you returned to the dressing room and you all had a few beers together.

These days players don't bother to hang around after a game. As soon as stumps are drawn they are off. I suppose in my day we did not earn enough money to rush off for dinner. Sitting around in the dressing room having a chat and a beer was a cheap and delightful form of entertainment. That's not a consideration any more and most dressing rooms are empty 10 minutes after the finish of a match.

I was watching a Test match in India one time, and after the game decided to go to the dressing rooms to say hello to the two teams. By the time I had worked my way around from the stand through the crowds, the dressing-room attendant told me that the teams had left 15 minutes earlier. They hadn't even changed out of their whites. The attendant told me that it was quite normal, nothing like our day when even the attendants would stay and enjoy listening to us talk cricket into the night.

I understand that it is now a business and the players are working 10 months a year, but it is still a sport, and the camaraderie between the two teams plays an important part.

As for ball tampering, I used to see bowlers using hair cream, lipsalve and Vaseline to keep the shine on the ball, but in the main it used to be perspiration or saliva. I used to rub it on my flannels and it left a big red streak on my whites. You rarely see that now. There was the odd player who lifted the seam with a fingernail but then some started using bottle tops and real nails. Now it's so bad that the ball has to be given to the umpire between overs because players cannot be trusted to leave it alone. They brought that on themselves.

An old trick was to use lipsalve. When rubbed on one side of the ball, it made that side shiny and heavy, and it would make the ball swing late. Ted Dexter once thought he'd observed a player doing this, talked about it and thereafter the bowler stopped doing it and became far less effective.

I enjoyed the game most when it was being played hard and tough but fair. Most of the people I played against were friendly and found time to chat, even when I was making a lot of runs against them. I suppose that was down to me. I enjoyed what I was doing and always liked to communicate with others whether I was batting, bowling or fielding. When you are batting for a long time, you have to relieve the concentration sometime. Why not break it when the ball goes for four and have a chat with the keeper rather than wait until the bowler is running up to start thinking about something else?

In a long innings, a batsman always has to find ways and means of keeping his concentration. We all had different ways of doing it. Ian Chappell would pull at his pad, fiddle with his hat and kick his bat, others would walk off to square leg, and others would just go down the wicket and pat down an imaginary divot even though there was nothing there. If a fielder tries to break that concentration by saying something as the bowler embarks on his run up, something is seriously wrong.

It has nothing to do with professionalism – we were professional as well. Cricket was our main source of income. That didn't mean we tried to take unfair advantage or, much worse, to make money out of the game illegally by bending results or throwing matches. The lack of good wages has been raised as a reason why the bribery scandal has raised its ugly head. I might have believed that 40 years ago when we got very little for playing, but I really can't understand it now when the players are being so well looked after. Greed is a hell of a thing and the bookmakers and whoever else is involved can see that, with so much money available, the opportunity is there to entice players into these situations.

I still find it hard to believe that a chap like the former South African captain Hansie Cronje would take a bribe. I never played with him but I have met him on a few occasions and I have watched the man and how he carried himself. He looked and sounded like the most upstanding cricketer in the world with all that dignity and pride. I thought the entire thing was impossible when the story first broke. Looks can be deceiving and he certainly deceived me.

The bribery scandal is awful for cricket and its future, and has done a tremendous amount of damage. Whenever something like that happens, people look around to see what else might be wrong. There will be niggling doubts for years to come. I sincerely hope that the ICC and the authorities get to the bottom of the problem, root out all the culprits and put a stop to it so that it never comes back again because there is no room in our game for anything like that. If they come up with any more big names it will push the game even further back – but better that than letting these people get away with it.

When I read the stories, it seems that most of the names being bandied around are international captains or players who are close to them. I can see the logic and it is a great worry to me. They are, of course, the ones who can influence results most. If you are going to find someone to manipulate the game, it is the captain you need because he can do all sorts of things with his batting order, his instructions, his field placings and his use of the bowlers. Outside the umpires, they can affect a game most of all.

The authorities are doing the only thing they can do in banning the transgressors from Test cricket. If they are allowed to play and are not selected even though they are performing well enough, they may have legal claims over restraint of trade. But if they are banned, they can have no complaints.

If they want to play in club cricket or friendly cricket, let them because they cannot do anyone any damage at that level. It's up to the teams if they want to pick them and play with them, particularly if they are young. Those who are on the way out don't matter anyway. As a team member, I wouldn't want to play in the same side as a match fixer but I would have no problems playing against them.

There was never a hint of anything like that happening in my day simply because there was no money in it, and there was no betting to speak of. Backing your team to win can only be an added incentive and I don't see anything wrong with it, but doing it the other way around repulses me. How anyone can do that I do not know. To go against your team-mates and the country that has given you the opportunity to see the world is beyond my comprehension. To let them all down by taking bribes when they have given you a decent living, allowed you to meet people and better yourself, is appalling. How can anyone do it and still want to carry on playing at that level?

I couldn't commit treason against the West Indies in the first place so there is no way I can put myself in a bribe-taker's shoes to see how he feels. I could never have done that. I like to think that my reputation and the way I was brought up would have dissuaded anyone from trying to bribe me but Hansie Cronje had a good Christian upbringing, was paid very well and married into money. I understand that Cronje said that he was addicted to money. People are addicted to all sorts of things, cigarettes, drugs, alcohol. It is an illness, but where it is wrong is when it is allowed to corrupt others. We can never truly know what goes inside someone else's head.

It sent shivers through me when Brian Lara and Gus Logie were mentioned in the police reports from the subcontinent. But Brian and Gus turned away the advances, told them they were not interested and to get lost. That was confirmed as true. Brian was under scrutiny until he left Australia and I hoped and prayed that nothing would be found against him. I am delighted that no West Indian appears to be involved. That is the trouble when it happens to someone like Hansie Cronje – it shakes your faith and you begin to wonder about everyone.

It would be good if people could sit back, treat it all as a bad dream and get the game back on its feet, back to what it used to be. But after the scandal there will be stricter rules and regulations. We all hope that the players will not be tempted to court the shame and bad publicity. That's why the punishments are important. Let the guilty ones escape and others may think they can get away with it as well. I don't see how they can escape punishment, not just from the cricketing authorities but also in a court of law. The bookmakers and others involved should also be severely punished.

I enjoyed all of the sports I played. I also enjoyed a modest gamble, but while winning is good I never believed in winning at all costs. The first approach is always to win but you mustn't go out of the way to win, running out batsmen unfairly without a warning, for instance, or snicking a ball and waiting for the umpire to make a decision, or catching the ball first hop when you know it was grounded. Cricket is first and foremost a sport and I like to believe that there are still some gentlemen out there. The game and the way it is played is more important than winning.

CHAPTER TWENTY-TWO

Over to Lara

I was fortunate to watch Brian Lara grow up as a cricketer. From a shy schoolboy who could hardly hit the ball off the square, he developed into the player who broke my world record, hitting the ball not just off the square but out of the Recreation Ground at St John's in Antigua. I was delighted to be there that day in April 1994. I went into the dressing room during a break when his score was around 240 and told him to get his head down and the record would be his.

It was an innings after my own heart. Brian came to the crease when the West Indies were in trouble, having lost the wickets of Phil Simmons and Stuart Williams for just 12 runs. When he was last man out, caught by wicket-keeper Jack Russell off the bowling of Andrew Caddick, the score was 593 for 5 declared and he had dominated partnerships of 179 with Keith Arthurton, 183 with Jimmy Adams and 219 with Shivnarine Chanderpaul. When he passed my record, I walked on to the square to shake the young master's hand.

And it didn't end there. Lara left after that Fifth Test to start his county career with Warwickshire at Edgbaston and scored 147 in his very first innings against Glamorgan, followed it with two centuries in the match against Leicester and 136 off 94 balls against Somerset. His run ended when he was out for 26 at Lord's against Middlesex, but it was nothing more than a blip – he scored 140 in the second innings.

All that was simply the prelude to his next innings, against Durham, when he broke Hanif Mohammad's world record of 499. His score of 501 also gave him the records for the highest individual score for the county; the highest score by a West Indian in England and the highest individual score in English cricket and, of course, it was his own highest total. He brought up the 500 with his 72nd boundary from 427 balls. He had reached his 1,000 runs in seven innings and he went on to score over 2,000 runs for the season with Warwickshire, winning three trophies.

I was in Antigua as a guest of the Prime Minister, Vere Bird, and attended that entire Test match against England as part of the anniversary celebrations for my 40 years in cricket. I was thrilled to witness the record broken and equally delighted for Brian who batted so very well. My only sorrow is that since that fantastic season he hasn't done as well as he should have done, not half as well.

I have known Brian since 1987 when he came to Barbados from Trinidad for the first Sir Garry Sobers International Schoolboys competition. He was a promising young cricketer brought over by Charlie Davis, who scored 100 for the West Indies at Lord's. Charlie was convinced that Brian was going to make it. Aware that I lived only 200 or 300 yards from where the cricket was being played, Charlie sent someone to tell me I had to come and have a look at this young Trinidadian batsman. I trusted Charlie's opinion and made my way down the road. Charlie introduced me to the youngster and when I shook hands, Brian could scarcely speak. He just kept repeating, 'You're Sir Sobers, you're Sir Sobers.'

Then he went out to bat and when I looked at him I could see all the technique and all the ability. He could hardly knock the ball off the square but they couldn't get him out and eventually he accumulated his 50.

He came back the following year and was a far different player, pushing the ball around and penetrating the field. Boy, did he play well! It was no surprise that he was soon playing inter-island cricket for Trinidad and Tobago and I became his biggest advocate, pushing for him to be selected for the West Indies team long before he was eventually picked. He was so naturally talented, an exciting stroke player, the kind to bring in people to watch the game. He was a real West Indian batsman in the time-honoured tradition, an attacking, attractive, beautiful player. He was also a student of the game and when he was on the field he stood out from the others. He had class.

He went on a tour of England under Sir Viv Richards but didn't play in a Test. It was ridiculous. The selectors were saying he had to wait his turn. Wait his turn? I thought it was about ability not about queuing up. I thought if you were good enough, you played. What use was sitting around for three years waiting to be told that it was now your turn? I kept asking the West Indies Board why he wasn't being picked and told them that their policy was nonsense. My point was proved when he was finally selected and immediately scored runs. He should have been captain long before he was given the task.

I was genuinely pleased when he broke the record. It established him as a premier world cricketer of all time. It also helped him financially. He was given all sorts of rewards, including airline travel, land and even a house by his government. I know all this because the Trinidadians asked me to travel from Antigua to Port of Spain for his welcome home and I heard for myself the Prime Minister promising him this and that. When I set my world record all those years before, I received the key to Kingston and a ride home from the airport in a motorcade, both of which I was very pleased to have. Times have changed and good luck to the boy for making the best of it. I doubt that the thoughts of reward ever came into his mind during that innings.

We stayed at the same hotel and that evening he telephoned my room to ask me if I would travel in the motorcade the next day but I declined. I told him that it was his show, not mine.

After that we became close and he would often telephone me to ask how he was batting. I was able to tell him little things and offer advice when, for example, he was getting too far over to the off stump or he wasn't moving his feet enough. He would call back and ask if I had watched him again and was that better now that he had put it right. The calls became less frequent as he matured and stood on his own two feet, but we have remained friends and chat from time to time.

If I have a criticism it is that sometimes he doesn't think as much as he should. This happens with players with that kind of ability because after a while everything becomes so easy for them; they think they can destroy every ball that comes down. It is the mentality of great players and it is something that great players can often do, but there is always the odd one that you have to respect. If you don't, it will get you. There are certain times in your innings when every ball bowled at you looks like a half-volley even when it is not.

It's a lonely place at the top of that pedestal. When things go wrong, the critics look for a scapegoat, the higher up the better. The media pry into everything that goes on, peering into every corner of your private life. Depending on your make-up, this sort of thing can sometimes help, making you focus on what really matters, if you are a person who is accustomed to a certain sort of life as you grow up. I know this from personal experience.

Brian, in his teens, was probably a little sheltered. He was close to his father and when he died it left a gap. He didn't have the kind of exposure I had when I was a youngster. But he came into cricket early and that can change a person's outlook. A lot of players who come into the game in their early 20s are less outgoing than Brian. When you are in the limelight early, it gives you the opportunity to become a more outgoing person. You travel and meet people, important people want to talk to you and invite you out, and therefore your outlook on life is going to be a lot different from the player who comes in later and misses that part of his cricket education. Brian played for Trinidad when he was 17 and that is the sort of exposure a lot of teenagers simply don't get. When you are a cricketer of his ability in the West

Indies, and popular with it, everyone wants to be with you, do everything for you. It provides an easy lead into life. Let's not be naïve. If you are better than another fellow, you have more opportunities whether it is with the girls or business contacts. Brian, like myself, had that opportunity very early on. It gave him an idea of what life is about and he clearly enjoys it. It is probably helping him more than his critics think and it is when he is not in that environment that he suffers and does not do so well.

I believe I can put myself in his shoes and think the way he does. He needs to take his mind away from the game now and again, and concentrate when the time comes. Some of us need to be away from the game completely at times and not think, eat and dream about the game morning, noon and night as some critics and so-called coaches believe should happen. I don't. In fact, the theory is a complete joke. It's all right when you are growing up and are desperate to make it. As a youngster you do eat, sleep, drink and live cricket until you reach the top, but you cannot sustain that pressure forever. You need to break the cycle and relax.

Even with ability, you have to think about your game while you're playing, and not take everything for granted. That's what turns a great player into a genius. Without that, you can achieve only so much. It is the thinking and analysing that keeps you above the rest. I have watched Brian when he gets in. He is on top, he is destroying the bowling but he doesn't tell himself that it is not time to go yet. Even when you are on top, you have to be careful and not let that little lapse in concentration spoil things.

I have heard all the stories about him missing aeroplanes, not turning up for team meetings and carrying a mobile telephone out on to the pitch. Any cricketer who takes anything out other than a handkerchief in his pocket isn't thinking right. How anyone can take a telephone on to the pitch is beyond me. As for missing flights, these things happen, I know, and often it depends on circumstances. Flying from London's Heathrow to Paris or New York is not the same as catching a flight in the laid-back atmosphere of the Caribbean, as countless holidaymakers will tell you. I remember flying back to England with Brian when he was captain of Warwickshire. He missed a county game because of a mix-up over his tickets in Port of Spain that meant he did not catch his connection in Barbados. The press in England never mentioned that. They slaughtered him.

But as a professional cricketer it must be your obligation to be there on time. Everything else comes second. You owe it to your profession to put yourself in a position to be on time except under exceptional circumstances such as an illness in the family, or when an act of God, such as extreme weather conditions, prevents you.

Another reason why he has not wholly fulfilled that enormous potential is that he was playing in a West Indies side that was in decline and the weight of expectancy weighed heavily on his shoulders. I have not been close enough to the West Indies team to know the inside story but it is abundantly clear that West Indies cricket relies very heavily on Brian. There is no doubting his enormous ability or that the other players look to him every time they play.

I don't think playing county cricket at his age was conducive to his Test career flourishing. He helped Warwickshire to all sorts of cups and titles, carrying the burden of great expectation, especially after his monumental 501. A great deal of forgiving went on at Edgbaston because of what he achieved for them. I don't fully agree with that but there should be some leniency when someone is performing so well. The complaints started when he did not perform. That is when the finger can be pointed.

At Warwickshire he set a lot of good examples that weren't followed by other players. He gave the county service that no one has ever given, before or since. He told me it worried him that he was setting a bad example in certain respects but I told him to pay no attention because he was delivering the goods. It is no use pointing out the faults if you don't point out the good things. Which is the best example to follow?

There were players in that Warwickshire team who made allegations about him, such as that he left the field when there was nothing wrong with him. They also complained about how much money he was getting, but he was earning it by winning games and trophies for them. He put Warwickshire in a position that they, nor any other county come to that, had ever been in before. I told him, 'Brian, don't worry about that. Let them say what they want. You are performing. The day you stop performing, then you have to start worrying and look at other things.'

I found the attitude at Warwickshire very silly. There is often jealousy, people in the team who are envious of the slightest thing you do. They will try to make a mountain of things, and encourage other people see it their way just for spite. I know because the same sorts of criticisms were aimed at me, and the majority of them were totally unfounded. They never bothered me. Once I was performing, doing my job and giving 100 per cent, it didn't matter to me what anyone said. That was their business and they could say what they wanted. When I did not do well, I would take the stick and listen to what was being said and try to do something about it. But when I was doing well for my team and myself, what I did was my business.

The fact that it was a West Indian who took my record was a pleasant coincidence. I would have been thrilled for whoever it was because cricket is cricket. All the same, it was nice to know that it was one of my own. I would like to see the West Indies win every match but I am not going to walk around when they are not playing well and pretend they are the best. Too many people have been doing that in recent years and look where it has taken us!

CHAPTER TWENTY-THREE

Whither Windies?

It was sad for me to see West Indies cricket in the state it was in as we moved into a new century, but I have to confess that it was no surprise. It has been coming for years and my old Barbados and West Indies team-mate Wes Hall faces a serious problem in sorting it out now that he has been named the president of the West Indies Cricket Board.

Since my retirement, I have been regularly asked why I have not become involved in helping to right the wrongs, and used my experience to help put Caribbean cricket back where it belongs. The answer is simple – they haven't asked me.

I had been popping backwards and forwards from Australia to Barbados for several years, and when I returned permanently in 1984 I was informally approached to see if I would be prepared to accept the position of coach to the West Indies team. I would have loved to accept but I had to say no because I had been away for six years and didn't really know who was doing what and who were the good youngsters coming through. It was the wrong time, and it would have been totally unfair for me to jump ahead of all those coaches who had worked their fingers to the bone for the good of the game. Former top Test players Everton Weekes and Seymour Nurse in Barbados, and others around the Caribbean islands, had earned the honour ahead of me.

I asked for two years to pick up the pieces and see what was going on. I told them that if they still thought I was good enough and equipped to do such a job, then I would be very interested and, indeed, honoured. I felt that by making that decision and waiting a suitable time, no one could accuse me of being given the job on the back of my reputation and fame. Who was I to come back and jump on top of them when I didn't know one player from another? How could I take a West Indies team somewhere when I didn't know who could do what? But I would have been happy to do it if they were still in a hole a couple of years later – I'm still waiting. No one ever came back.

In times of strife, and there have been plenty of those in recent years, the critics start putting up their favourites and when they all fail, my name invariably comes up again. 'What about Sir Garry Sobers?' they ask, but there is never an answer. It was not up to me to go back and tell them that I wanted a job. That's not and never has been my style.

When I was first approached, the team was experienced and established and with so many senior players around they might well have wondered what I could offer that they did not know already. It would have been something of an ordeal. I suggested that the time might be ripe for me if Brian Lara took over with a younger team and I could be used as manager or coach if they thought I was the man for the job.

It had been taken for granted around the world that when I finished playing I would be involved in helping to develop the West Indies team. When asked why I haven't done so, I can only reply that maybe they didn't think that I was good enough or the right person to do it.

It's not as if I have been shy and retiring. I could see from the teams being selected that it was going the wrong way and said so in interviews in the newspapers and on radio and television. I said that there had been mistakes and they should have been rebuilding instead of recycling. I don't think they liked those strong opinions very much.

I could see what they were doing and where they were heading. I even predicted what was going to happen in the future. They needed to experiment in order to rebuild, instead of carrying on losing with experienced players who had no future, many of whom didn't even have a present. The promising young players should have come in and stayed in even if they had failed initially. All I wanted to do was help. It hurt me to keep predicting that they would lose in tournaments and lose series. I did it because I knew what I was talking about, not because I was having a go at them. I would have been happy to talk to the players I criticised and would have tried to help them. But no one came and the same mistakes are repeated.

I cannot help feeling that there are still some officials who don't know what they are doing. They came into the sport thinking they knew more than those who have been there before and have the experience. I don't have a lot of time for some of them and what they do. I just hope and pray that the appointment of Wes Hall makes the difference we have been looking for.

Despite what is said and written, there are some good young players coming through. They just need the right helping hand and the correct guidance. The trouble is that I'm not sure we have the right people to do that. If they can find the right personnel to help Wes Hall, then in four or five years' time we could see a revival of West Indies cricket – but I fear the worst.

Some of the team selections in recent years show that we are in need of someone who knows what he's doing in respect of rebuilding the team. We have to get away from the insularity that has crept back in to West Indies cricket. The players, wherever they are from, should be given the chance when they deserve it. I have seen for myself talented young players with all the right qualities who are not being nurtured because their faces don't fit.

Coaching can be as tedious a job for the coach as it is for the players unless it is gone about in the right way. There are coaches and coaches. The good ones look at players and try to develop the talent they have.

They help the youngsters with potential to become better players, utilising their natural ability. They don't try to take the skill away and turn them into robots, or try to make them the mirror image of someone else. That, I'm afraid, is what happens when you have the other types of coaches, those with certificates who know one way of coaching only and treat everyone the same when they should be looking at players' individuality, trying to tighten up the little flaws in their technique. If youngsters find that difficult to cope with or boring, it's up to the coaches to try to find a different way to help them rather than just discarding them, as happens now.

At present, they seem to be looking at promising young players and telling them they are better suited to the one-day game, or they should concentrate on five-day Test match cricket. I don't know how people arrive at that opinion yet cricket authorities are doing it all over the world. They pigeon-hole players by describing them as one-day cricketers only. We have players in the West Indies who are categorised like that and ignored when it comes to selection for Test matches and tours when, to me, they are better than those picked. It seems to me that when coaches find it difficult to help certain players because of their natural talent, and worry that the players aren't inclined to pay attention to them, the coaches dismiss them as one-day cricketers.

What they should be doing is finding a way to get through to them, helping them to channel their ability and talent. A good coach can get results from any player by studying his technique and using different methods and ideas to bring out the best in him. It is going to happen that sometimes the youngsters don't understand what the coach is trying to tell them, but rather than give up on them, a different approach should be adopted until you do have their attention.

From my own experience, a coach should also be a psychologist. That's one of the facets that a top international player can bring back to the game. I don't mean that they should run off to university and study the subject but rather use their experience to help tackle the mental attitudes of the players. A good coach can help a player think through difficult situations, such as what to eliminate from his game and what risks are worth taking. Once a player gets an understanding of that, it will help him to stop playing rash shots. The coach can help the aggressive batsman to eliminate certain shots in certain situations and teach him when to take risks.

The coach should explain to the player that if he wants to reach the top, he has to learn to buckle down and sometimes play within limitations. Coaches shouldn't just talk technicalities. Let him know he has the ability to do it and give him the opportunity.

Psychology is something the selectors do not always use. The young Jamaican Ricardo Powell, who was selected to go to New Zealand a while ago, provides a classic example. He is a shot player and very aggressive with it. He top scored with 32 when the West Indies were bowled out for 70. So the team failed, but did he as an individual? I would have thought not as he scored almost half his side's runs in one innings. He has not played in another Test match since then. They immediately branded him as a one-day cricketer, not a Test player. Here is a boy bubbling over with ability. All he needs is guidance and the right handling and he would be the answer to many of the West Indies problems.

Another Jamaican, Marlon Samuels, is also a naturally talented player and I just hope that the coaches don't grab hold of him and try to change his game and make him what they think he should be. He should be allowed to play the way he does. He may have faults but he has talent and that should be the overriding factor.

I listen to the call-in programmes on the radio and I have been interested to hear comments about the new West Indies Cricket Academy in Grenada, and the comparisons with the Australian model, which has produced so many good Test players. The academy has helped to make the Aussies the undisputed, if unofficial, world champions. The main argument in the Caribbean seems to be over education. I thought the idea was to produce cricketers, not doctors or high court judges. Surely the academy is for those with natural cricketing ability. When they are attuned to working at their game and playing cricket and once they are developing their skills, then other subjects can be introduced. The main object should be cricket first and foremost and that is what they should be learning. I could understand it if they were youngsters without any education but these are boys of 18 and over. I thought that the idea was to produce future Test players, not academics. The academy is there to help the youngsters play better cricket; the studies should be an important extra.

There have been some suggestions that former Test players such as Viv Richards and I could help out but, just as before, it is mentioned and then forgotten. Antigua is close to Grenada and that should ensure that Viv plays some part. A player of his quality is very important to its development. The trouble is that Viv, like me, does not have a certificate to say that he knows his cricket and is a qualified coach, but everyone knows that he is the type of former player who is needed.

I won't hold my breath. They have already let him down once when they appointed him for a short trip to New Zealand and then got rid of him because he didn't have the right piece of paper. It is very difficult for a person like Viv to apply for the job and that is something he should never have done. In my estimation, a man with his ability, class and prestige in the world should never have to apply for a job in the West Indies. It should be automatic. You don't achieve what he has achieved without considerable knowledge of the game. Once he applied, they should have snapped him up but then they introduced the business about the coaching certificate and Viv, of course, didn't have nor need one.

He went out of the door and so did West Indies cricket, as far as I was concerned. I would have loved to see Viv in that job. He might not be the best technical coach but the respect he would have won from that team and the attention he would have had from those players would have been invaluable.

What people don't understand is that Viv has a special talent, an ability you cannot teach people. Great players such as Viv and Everton Weekes and certain others can do things with a cricket ball that the average or even good cricketer cannot do. Viv, for example, would take the ball outside the off stump and hit it past square leg, but he could have hit the same ball through the covers if there was no fielder there. Therein lies the difference, for the coaches with their pieces of paper would encourage the batsman to hit the ball into the covers whether there was a run there or not.

That doesn't mean that Viv would teach others to play the way he did, but at least he could pass on ideas and opinions after they have learned all the basic techniques. He could tell them how to look for areas to score runs, where they can do it and how they can do it. Now that's what I call advanced coaching. He was also a winning captain and learned a lot about what it takes to be successful at the highest level.

I could understand the attitude in a university for academics, for the potential lawyer or doctor, because you don't pick up those things naturally, you have to learn them. But when it comes to cricket and football, there are people who know their subjects backwards but would never bother to go and work for a certificate to tell them that they understand the game. They have a lot more knowledge than their examiners.

There is no substitute for greatness. Class is permanent; form is temporary. Viv has class and you cannot substitute that.

It is not just Viv and me – although I believe that we both have something to offer. They have not bothered to use Everton Weekes either, and he was one of the world's great batsmen. At least we practise what we preach in Barbados where Everton was one of our first professional coaches along with Seymour Nurse and Charlie Griffith who joined him in developing our youth. I think that Seymour might even have had one of those certificates but neither he nor the others ever had a look-in outside Barbados.

It is very difficult to rebuild a young team with young coaches because there is no respect. I don't think that the youngsters put in charge have the knowledge of how to pull the team together and motivate them. Because of the different islands and different cultures it is not an easy job, especially when the team is not winning. A lot of insularity seems to have filtered back, not only in the cricket but also at the top and in the administration.

If you have the right people at the top, those who know about cricket and are willing to give something to the game, you will always have a chance, but for God's sake keep people who know nothing about cricket away from the game.

We have had problems for a long time and we should have started rebuilding when we lost Viv Richards, Joel Garner, Michael Holding, Gordon Greenidge, Des Haynes, Jeffrey Dujon and a number of others in the space of four or five years. It was then that the Board should have taken stock. But no, they thought they could keep the fires burning by bringing back all kinds of players, including some who weren't good enough in the first place. They were playing them because they had been around and were experienced, and hoping that they would win.

When we did win Tests, they were just scrambling through, not winning with any confidence or authority. We weren't showing any strength, especially when the tailenders were scoring the runs that were winning those occasional matches.

It appears from the outside that no one in authority in West Indies cricket ever sat down and looked at how or why we were winning. We were bowling out teams in a one-off way for a low score, and they were thinking we were good. I watched South Africa when they needed 70 odd runs in a day with seven wickets in hand. The Springboks pushed and prodded away until the bowlers got on top. But it was their deficiencies not our strengths that cost them what should have been a comfortable victory. It was nothing to crow about.

It was the same with India. We bowled them out for 121 and won but that was due to our tailenders scoring runs. A couple of wins and some think that everything is all right without taking everything into consideration.

I am told that you shouldn't change a winning team. How can you not change a winning team when there are obvious weak links? They kept playing the weak links even though it must have been known that they simply weren't good enough. If you keep players in the side while they are failing, they will not improve. If they are dropped and they are good enough, and really have West Indies cricket at heart, they will fight to get back in the side and will return as better players. If they are picked whatever their form, they have no reason to work on and improve their game.

When the older players were on the way out, that was the time to bring in youngsters and try them out while the team was still winning and playing with a bit of confidence. When that strength was gone, all that was left were the weak links who were now suddenly seen as the best players. No wonder we struggled. Instead of rebuilding and taking a few defeats, the selectors just kept on recycling the same players so that the side never improved; it just got progressively worse.

I predicted in the early nineties that this is what West Indies cricket would come to but no one took any notice. Now they are starting to rebuild and I hope that with the grace of the Lord we do not mess up the promising youngsters because that is what we have been doing, messing them up with all sorts of nonsense.

Certificate coaching is a complete and utter joke. Many of the people who hold the certificates are well educated rather than having a true cricket background. They can read a manual, listen to a clinic and pass exams. That earns them their piece of white paper rather than proving they can do the practical work. A lot of those who should be doing the coaching are not, because they do not want to be classed in the same category. No certificate can make you a better coach any more than having been a great cricketer automatically makes you a good coach. The good coaches are the ones who are respected and can pass on their knowledge in a sensible and understandable manner.

Ironically, I was offered a certificate but I didn't want to be with those people who tell players to push up and down the line. You don't get the practical experience, or learn how to help people to think by sitting an exam. All those things you learn from your own playing days, along with the technical aspects of the game. There are little things that you can pass on that the coaches who did not have international experience will never know.

Perhaps we should be coaching the coaches. That's what I was asked to do when I was out in Australia. Thirty or 40 coaches used to come at a time to listen to what I had to say and my ideas on the game. Jackie Burkinshaw used to say that he heard things from me that he had never heard from any other coach, and because most of it was pure common sense, he reckoned that had he still been playing he would have put it to good use and made many more runs than he did. Jackie went on to coach Leicestershire in the English county championship.

At times I used to make jokes about the English coaching manual, things like pointing your toe in the direction in which you were playing your shot. I used to ask whether they had seen anyone point their toe towards midwicket. They would have looked like Charlie Chaplin. I was very straightforward and blunt. I was there to do a job and I was going to do it, and if they thought I was talking nonsense they would have told me. They are like that in Australia.

I once attended a little clinic with some English coaches in Trinidad. I watched them coaching and then I went to listen to what they had to say in the evening. I said nothing until someone asked me to pass an opinion. That was my opportunity and I blew my top. I told them that they had been telling the kids a lot of nonsense. As it was their clinic I didn't want to jump in, but now that they had asked, I was ready to give them the answer, if not the one they wanted to hear.

'I can tell you right now that I heard you telling the kids to lead with their heads. That', I told them, 'has to be the biggest joke I have heard in cricket. Lead with the head? That is the biggest part of the body, how can you lead with it? That's what makes batsmen off balance when their head is pushed too far forward.'

I asked them if they had ever seen a man walking and leading with his head? Of course not. You lead with your feet. You move your foot and your head follows. It's the same with batting. You push your front foot forward and your head will come. Lead with your head and you might well fall over.

They tried to pretend that they did not mean it that way and after I had told them what I thought, they didn't want much to do with me. When I went home I told a few players what they had been saying and it became a big joke on the island to lead with your head.

The foot is the first thing that has to move because it is your feet that have to take you into position, not your head. When you go back and across you don't put your head there first.

The other joke was sticking the front foot down the line and playing around it. Cricket is not meant to be played in that way. They use that theory in England because of the ball moving off the wickets against the little medium-paced bowlers. They talked about narrowing the angle, which I could understand, but they didn't tell you how close you must be to the ball to do it. If the ball is five feet away and moving, it is going to move just enough to find the edge. If it is two feet away and you get there, that is narrowing the angle. None of that was explained.

I could explain, and do it. I could explain what is right and what is wrong. That was what I could have offered West Indian cricket.

I could also explain the mental approach, how to read a cricket match and what to do in certain circumstances – what shots should be eliminated and which ones should be played. You do not read that in books.

Since my retirement, I have enjoyed watching the batting of the likes of Viv Richards, Clive Lloyd and Brian Lara and the quick bowling of Michael Holding, Malcolm Marshall, and Joel Garner with his different bounce. But while the world watched in admiration, Australia developed their team so that they could compete with us. We sat back and did nothing, relying on the conveyor belt to keep churning out world-class players without any help at all. It didn't work and we have left Wes Hall to shoulder a massive burden and responsibility.

I feel now exactly as I did back in the early nineties. The West Indies waited far too long to introduce new and younger players to the team. Had the youngsters been introduced then, they would now be at the top of their game.

It did not help when the English counties limited their overseas players to one per side, and those seem to be mainly Australians. The West Indies have no top league of their own so it denied the top players experience at that very important level.

The current dearth of fast bowlers is another result of these two factors and only time will tell whether the West Indies can recover. Even if they do, it will take much longer than if they had brought the young players in at the right time. There was a time when the West Indies would have – and, indeed, did – provide half of the world's best 11. Now only Brian Lara would be considered.

CHAPTER TWENTY-FOUR

Greener grass

If I had my life again I would be a professional golfer rather than a cricketer. That may surprise many people considering I have had so much from cricket. Don't get me wrong. Cricket is a wonderful sport and it opened many doors for me. I loved playing all over the world and enjoyed every minute of a long and exciting career.

But there were also disadvantages. When you start ageing, for instance, and are not performing quite as well as you used to, or more to the point as others are used to, the cricket media tear into you and rip you to pieces. You may bowl well all day but not take a wicket and immediately the critics are at your throat saying that you are finished, over the hill and should retire. They forget the catches that have been dropped and the chances that didn't go to hand. They just look at the result and think of their headlines.

In golf it's all so different. Look at Jack Nicklaus, Greg Norman, Arnold Palmer and other veteran players. They still go out and play and the galleries follow them round to watch them for what they have been. Nobody dares to write them off. Everyone is glad to see them and if they don't play well, the critics and the public just shrug. They may have had their day but they are still enjoying their golf and giving so many people pleasure. The older players who have given the game so much receive tremendous ovations and have the respect of their fellow professionals, the crowd and even the media.

Players such as Nicklaus are revered and quite rightly so. At the British Open at St Andrews he received an incredible ovation, and he's an American, not even playing in front of his own audience.

You don't see many cricketers being received like that at the end of their careers unless, like Courtney Walsh, you have broken some record or other. Maybe he was the wise one, getting out while he was still on top, like Mike Atherton who slipped quietly away at the end of the Ashes series against Australia in August 2001.

In cricket, the reporters do not make any allowances. They just look at your figures and assume the worst. It's the same with batting as it is with bowling. There is a fine line between success and failure. You can be batting well, hit a magnificent shot and suddenly from nowhere a fielder dives, sticks a hand out and takes a terrific catch and you are on your way back to the pavilion. The next batsman might come in, lob up a simple catch and the same fielder drops it. They don't write that you were unlucky with the brilliant catch. No, they write that you are past it and should give up the game.

I'm not just talking about myself here. It happens to a lot of players who have given so much and played so well before being jumped on and banished behind the boundary. Some of those critics are just waiting for something to go wrong. There is no sympathy in cricket, certainly not the sort of understanding that sportsmen receive in individual sports. They have a go at us when we are part of a team and rely on other people, not just on our own ability.

Much the same thing happened to Wes Hall. The media said that he was finished and the selectors listened and wanted to axe him from the team. When he went to Australia in 1968–69 he bowled really well but slip catches went down and when he returned all they noticed was that he had taken so few wickets.

If I had to live my life again, I would do something where the press weren't always waiting to criticise and write you off, not just the West Indian press but globally.

Unfortunately, I didn't have the choice between golf and cricket because there were no outlets for golf when I was growing up. I never even saw it until I went abroad and I didn't pick up a club until I was 25. I didn't know what par, a birdie or a bogey were because I knew nothing about the game.

Sonny Ramadhin tried to persuade me to play for four or five years before I finally took him up on his offer while we were playing in Australia in 1960–61. Up until then, I didn't have the time or the inclination to try it. It seemed an alien sport.

Sonny was a very keen golfer and, in fact, was a caddy in the Caribbean before he became a cricketer. He was a brilliant spin bowler, spotted as an unknown in the north of Trinidad. When they brought him south no one could read him; they couldn't tell which way the ball was going. He quickly made the West Indian team but he continued with his golf and eventually I played a lot with him.

Towards the end of the tour, he persuaded me and fellow Barbadians Peter Lashley, Seymour Nurse and Wes Hall to play at the nearby Royal Canberra course on a free day, for a bit of fun. Sonny had warned us that even though it was a stationary ball, we wouldn't hit it cleanly no matter how much cricketing ability we thought we had. We thought he was joking but he was right. I missed the ball by yards. Wes swung at the ball and took out a huge chunk of earth because he thought that was the only way he wasn't going to miss it after watching our efforts.

Much like my cricket, I was never coached and never received a lesson. I watched and learned all I could about the game and practised whenever I could. I felt I was making good progress until I went to England to play county cricket for Nottinghamshire in 1968. Then I lost it. I thought I would be able to play every Sunday but guess what happened – they brought in the John Player League and there went my Sundays and my golf. I was playing cricket for something like 20 days before I had a three-day break and then, rather than play golf, I felt that I needed the rest. Occasionally, I used to go down to the local course but only to knock the ball around without playing properly. For those seven years on the English county circuit, I was not able to play much serious golf. I didn't know anyone who played and just had the odd round.

It was only when I came home to Barbados in 1974–75 that I became deeply involved in the game. The only two courses on the island at the time were Sandy Lane and Rockley and it was there that I put in the hours you need to spend on such a technical sport. Eventually I played off scratch, which I did for a long time, and then off two.

When I first went to Australia to live I played quite a lot, although not as much as I would have liked, but then I lost the game and drifted away again. It took another return to Barbados to get me back into the sport in a serious way. I had more time to play and I took advantage and enjoyed it immensely.

For someone who travels the world a lot, golf, particularly if you play it well, is the ideal social sport. You can generally find someone with whom to go round. Otherwise you can play against the course. All you need is a good caddy and a set of clubs. There is no other game in the world where you can do that. There is terrific satisfaction in shooting a below-par score, even if you are playing on your own and just taking on the course. If you are good, the word quickly gets around and soon there are people who want to play. You make friends and your holiday is a success. That was what made me realise what a wonderful game golf is.

It's a sport that brings out the true character in a person. I can always tell what a person is like when I play them at golf. Michael Simmons comes to mind. He was a very good friend who had never played golf but came to watch me playing with another friend, Dennis Bailey. Dennis hit a terrible shot and let loose with a volley of abusive language. Michael had a go at him and told him how unnecessary the bad language was. A year later Michael took up the game and his language was as bad when he played a bad shot. I reminded him and he admitted that he never realised how the game could get to you.

Others say, 'Golf – that silly game. I'm not old enough to take that up yet.' All of a sudden they take it up and tell you that they never realised what a good game it was. They admit that they left it too late. So did I.

I wish I had started earlier, but I was in the prime of my cricket career. I had something fulfilling and I wasn't searching for another sport at the time. I was doing well and didn't need a substitute.

The moral is never criticise another man's sport until you have tried it. Top sportsmen in every sport admire and respect other sportsmen and women who are on top of their game because they understand.

Personally I think the American basketball player Michael Jordan is a genius. He is the greatest basketball player I have ever seen and I loved to watch him play. I also admire him for the way he has carried himself in life. I don't think there has been a better role model and he commands respect as both a person and a player. You can always tell the great players in any sport because they rise to the top when the going is tough. Whenever the Chicago Bulls were in trouble they gave the ball to Michael and more often than not he would do it for them. He was dedicated to his team and even when he was ill he would go out there, play his heart out and help them to win. I would watch him as often as I could and when he quit the sport I stopped watching until he came out of retirement.

I am very flattered when people come up to me and say that they stopped watching cricket when I stopped playing. I suppose I was special to them in the way that Michael Jordan was to me.

Despite starting so late, I played golf to a decent standard, captaining Barbados in the Hoeman Cup, the Caribbean's own inter-island golf tournament. I played in that for six or seven years against the best the Caribbean had to offer with everyone playing off scratch. My best finish was third place, which was very satisfying. Even more satisfying was when my son Matthew qualified for the team in July 2001, playing the difficult course at St Croix.

Initially, the tournament was between six islands – they have since increased it to 10 – Barbados, Jamaica, Santo Domingo, Trinidad, Puerto Rico and the Bahamas. Each team had six players and the best four scores counted every day and were finally totalled up.

It's a big event held at different venues around the Caribbean every year. The standard is very high with all the top players and any number of professionals. Stephen Ames is the only one who made it on the international circuit. During the tournament, he would be out hitting balls for an hour and a half before his round and when he finished he would be hitting balls for two hours.

He had the ability and the dedication. Too many West Indians in most sports are very keen when they are young, put everything into it and look very good but when they reach a certain age and a certain standard, it just goes and I often wonder why. Well, I suppose I know why. Even now, with all that sport has to offer, I see youngsters of 14 and 15 looking good but all of a sudden they get to know about life and find out about girls. By the time they are 16, those distractions make it difficult to hold and maintain their interest in sport. They want to find out about other things and all that ability and talent go out of the window.

Wherever you go these days, there are wonderful courses to play. I loved playing golf in Australia, especially at the Royal Melbourne. Between the late eighties and early nineties I played some of the top courses in America around Miami, Carolina, Los Angeles and Philadelphia. But the majority of my golf outside Barbados has been played in the United Kingdom and especially at Sunningdale where I have played many times with Ted Dexter, a wonderful golfer and one of my closest friends. Scotland's courses are a tremendous challenge and I find the links courses tough. My favourite course there is Rosemount, Blairgowrie, an inland course lined with trees.

I like the difficult courses better than playing into big, wide-open fairways because they help you concentrate your mind. La Romana in Santo Domingo, known as 'the teeth of the dog', is one of the hardest golf courses I have ever played with the problems of an almost constant wind and extreme length. When I played in the 1968 Caribbean championships, a pair was selected from among the competitors to play in the world amateur championships at this famous course. I was picked along with my partner Rodney Jones to play at 'the teeth of the dog' against players from all over the world.

The players still talk about the events at the par three. They have since made it a lot easier but in those days the approach was all bunker and sea. I used to hit the ball a very long way with a one-iron but few were prepared to take it on. Rodney, also a long hitter, would have had to use a one-wood to reach it. He declined and took a three-wood, hit it up on the right side and then chipped down to the green. My pride wouldn't let me take a wood for a par three. It was hard but I made it. They had some holes on that course the like of which I have never seen. It was a real difficult challenge.

Another difficult course is Frigate Bay at St Kitts in the Caribbean. They have 13 water holes and although the water does not come into play in every one of those holes, you have to hit the ball properly otherwise you are in trouble. It's frightening, especially when the wind blows, which is more often than not. It's a lovely golf course but long and windy, and only compensated for by the delightful people.

One of my favourite rounds of golf was with Peter Alliss. He was recording a video with a different celebrity on a different course for each of 18 holes. He asked me to go to South Africa to a vineyard that had been turned into a gorgeous hotel and golf course. We didn't just talk about the golf but about the country and how beautiful it was and how visitors should go there.

While in South Africa I met Gary Player. We sat down, had a drink and talked. I played golf in his presence and felt as though I had known him for years. Later, in a pro-am tournament in Australia, he asked to be paired with me but on the morning of the match they told me that it was not possible. The draw had already been made and I was playing with the outstanding American Hubert Green. I went to watch the professionals practising and Gary asked if we were playing together.

When I told him we were not, he responded, 'That's okay with me if you want to travel second-class.'

Unfortunately, I never had the chance to play with him although I have had the good fortune to play with the likes of Ben Crenshaw, Lee Trevino and others from the top level of the professional game.

For the sportsman golf offers a great life with rich rewards, good company and the respect of those involved on both sides of the fence. I loved playing for Barbados from the time I made my debut around 1970 until I stopped playing for them in 1984.

Although cricket dominated my professional life, it did not take up every waking moment and as a child and a young man growing up on the beautiful island of Barbados, I enjoyed a lot of other sports. When I was 16, I played in goal for Barbados at football, despite being so small. I began as a left-wing for Notre Dame, our top team. I didn't play in goal because we had a brilliant goalkeeper named Harcourt Wilkinson. He had a reputation for stopping every penalty until Graham Wilkes, a Scotsman who played for Hearts, toppled his castle. Wilkes, for some strange reason known as 'the Limey', cut a comic figure in his three-quarter length shorts, but the laughing stopped when he took a free kick or a penalty. When his team won a penalty against us we all expected Harcourt to save it as usual, but Wilkes took a run of about 100 yards and thumped the ball as hard as I have ever seen it hit. The ball whistled over our goalkeeper's head and he made the mistake of trying to maintain his record by getting both hands to it. The ball hardly checked its flight on its way into the net and Wilkinson had broken bones in both of his hands.

I had started to keep goal in practice matches and when Harcourt was injured, I was picked for the first team. In training one day, a ball was gently rolled towards me but on its way it hit a bump in the pitch, bounced through my arms, between my legs and into the goal. The other players must have wondered what they had been given as a replacement. I played a lot of basketball at the time and had no problem catching the ball so Everton Weekes, who was watching, shouted, 'You may be able to catch them in the air but you need to keep your legs closed on the ground!' They never let me live it down.

I was in the Barbados team that beat Guyana 4–1, but soon afterwards the cricket association asked me to stop playing football because of the danger of injury. The Barbados Cricket Association thought I was more valuable for them at cricket than I was at football, and the Barbados Football Association agreed. In those days, cricket was by far and away the dominant sport. The only international football played was the Inter Colonial Cup between the islands. Unlike today, there was no future in the game as a professional because it was so low profile. The closest we came to top-quality football was when a team came over from Martinique or an English club such as Southampton paid a visit at the end of their season for a little rest and recreation.

When I was in England in 1960 playing league cricket, I was friendly with Frank Taylor, a football writer for the *Daily Mirror* who had survived the Munich air disaster a couple of years before. We used to meet in a club in Manchester owned by Paddy McGrath. I liked to go there to listen to Danny Blanchflower's wife sing, as well as a crooner named Gerry Dorsey who later became somewhat better known as Engelbert Humperdinck. One night I happened to mention to Frank that I had kept goal for Barbados. His ears immediately pricked up and before I knew it Everton invited me for a trial at Goodison Park. Frank had spotted a good story in the making but I said, 'Frank, how could you? Me, in England in the winter! You have to be joking. I have trouble coping with the summer, never mind wearing a pair of shorts in the winter on Merseyside! What's more, I hope I will be going with the West Indies to play a series in Australia.' There was no point in even going for the trial. I was not going to leave a certainty for an uncertainty.

Another sport I excelled at was basketball. Gerry and I used to play for the same boys club. We had a decent team and I went on to play for Barbados at that as well. I had an opportunity to play table tennis for my country but I turned it down. The Barbados team were short of a man for an international in Trinidad when they asked me, but I hadn't played for nearly two years and I feared that they wanted me to make up the numbers. I was going nowhere unless I had a chance of winning, or at least of putting up a good performance. So I never did become an international table-tennis player but, much later, I represented the island at golf, making me an international in four sports.

Goalie Cumberbatch taught me to play dominoes when I was around 12 and by the time I was 15 I was as good as anyone on the island. I loved it and would play morning, noon and night, when I wasn't playing cricket. During the holidays we would sometimes play from Saturday through to Monday with no sleep, eating while we played.

It can be a noisy game in the Caribbean because you slam the dominoes down when you play them. I stopped playing for a while but I started back and I still love it if it is played properly. Now there is too much coding with players on the same team working out a series of signals to let the other player know what they hold or what they want the other one to do. I cannot play that way. In the days when I played, there were only two signals – if you wanted the game blocked you put your dominoes down and if you didn't you kept them up. Everyone knew that. But then people started to create their own codes to let their partner know what they had in their hands. I stopped playing then. I played in a competition once where it was happening and although I won it, Goalie said afterwards, 'This signing thing is not for you.' I never played competitively again. It has not changed, either. I managed a Barbados dominoes team on a tour of England in the late summer of 2001, but they were coding there, too. It's no fun playing that way. It does not interest me because the joy of the game is to use your brains and read the dominoes from what the other fellow plays.

I occasionally played for money with a variation called cut-throat, putting a penny or a dollar into the kitty every time you passed. That wasn't too bad because you couldn't lose a lot and if you were a good player you usually finished on top.

Later, I took up bridge. They used to call me a poker bridge player because I used to bid with six points; I didn't want to be dummy all the time. Cricket played its part in that because I used to play with Everton Weekes, Jackie Hendriks, Gerry Alexander and Peter Lashley.

Yes, I have enjoyed all the sports I've taken part in, including, of course, my life as a professional cricketer. But, if I were starting over and the opportunities presented themselves again, maybe I would have gone for life as a touring professional golfer. Don't they say that the grass is always greener on the other side?

APPENDIX

Garry Sobers

A CAREER RECORD

Compiled by BILL FRINDALL

FIRST-CLASS CAREER

BATTING SUMMARY

Season	Venue	M	I	NO	HS	Runs	Avge	100	50
1952-53	WI	1	1	1	7*	7	–	–	–
1953-54	WI	2	4	1	46	113	37.66	–	–
1954-55	WI	7	13	3	104*	435	43.50	1	2
1955-56	NZ	7	9	1	53	212	26.50	–	1
	WI	1	1	–	71	71	71.00	–	1
1956-57	WI	2	3	1	77	119	59.50	–	1
1957	E	25	44	6	291*	1644	43.26	3	8
1957-58	WI	6	10	3	365*	1007	143.85	4	3
1958	E	3	5	–	75	252	50.40	–	3
1958-59	I	12	18	4	198	1162	83.00	5	3
	P	5	8	1	75	257	36.71	–	2
1959	E	1	2	–	74	119	59.50	–	1
1959-60	WI	6	9	1	226	863	107.87	4	1
1960-61	A	12	22	–	168	805	36.59	3	3
1961	E	3	5	1	103	210	52.50	1	1
1961-62	A	7	13	–	251	573	44.07	1	2
	WI	6	8	1	153	451	64.42	2	1
1962	E	1	2	–	28	38	19.00	–	–
1962-63	A	10	18	2	196	1006	62.87	3	6
1963	E	24	34	6	112	1333	47.60	4	6
1963-64	WI	2	4	1	107	261	87.00	1	2
	A	9	14	–	195	1128	80.57	6	2
	I	1	2	1	123	130	130.00	1	–
1964	E	3	4	2	44	104	52.00	–	–
1964-65	I	1	2	–	102	185	92.50	1	1
	WI	8	14	2	183*	734	61.16	2	3
1965	E	1	2	–	5	5	2.50	–	–
1965-66	WI	5	4	1	204	410	136.66	2	1
1966	E	18	25	3	174	1349	61.31	4	3
1966-67	I	5	7	2	95	426	85.20	–	5
	C	1	1	–	115	115	115.00	1	–
	WI	5	8	1	165	424	60.57	1	1
1967	E	2	2	–	26	50	25.00	–	–
1967-68	WI	6	11	3	152	638	79.75	2	3
1968	E	27	44	7	105	1590	42.97	2	13

Season	Venue	M	I	NO	HS	Runs	Avge	100	50
1968-69	A	10	17	2	132	1011	67.40	5	3
	NZ	4	7	–	54	155	22.14	–	1
1969	E	20	26	2	104	1023	42.62	2	6
1969-70	WI	2	3	1	116*	159	79.50	1	–
1970	E	19	32	9	183	1742	75.73	7	7
1970-71	P	1	2	–	25	25	12.50	–	–
1970-71	WI	9	15	3	178*	889	74.08	4	2
1971	E	23	38	6	151*	1485	46.40	3	8
1971-72	A	9	14	4	254	562	56.20	2	–
1971-72	WI	5	8	1	142	253	36.14	1	–
1972	E	6	9	1	71	222	27.75	–	1
1972-73	WI	1	2	–	23	43	21.50	–	–
1973	E	18	29	5	150*	1215	50.62	3	6
1973-74	WI	6	7	–	57	195	27.85	–	2
1974	E	15	27	4	132*	1110	48.26	4	6
TOTALS		**383**	**609**	**93**	**365***	**28315**	**54.87**	**86**	**121**

FIRST-CLASS CAREER

BOWLING AND FIELDING SUMMARY

Season	Venue	O	M	R	W	Avge	Best	5wI	10wM	Ct
1952-53	WI	89	40	142	7	20.28	4-50	–	–	–
1953-54	WI	82.5	24	220	6	36.66	4-75	–	–	–
1954-55	WI	180	62	376	11	34.18	3-20	–	–	4
1955-56	NZ	103.5	50	169	4	42.25	1-3	–	–	6
	WI	67.1	22	134	6	22.33	3-49	–	–	–
1956-57	WI	91	41	146	5	29.20	4-24	–	–	–
1957	E	476.3	146	1172	37	31.67	5-39	1	–	26
1957-58	WI	213.3	75	425	6	70.83	2-39	–	–	2
1958	E	28	8	60	1	60.00	1-13	–	–	4
1958-59	I	194.2	48	514	18	28.55	5-31	1	–	11
	P	79	40	126	2	63.00	1-1	–	–	5
1959	E	5	–	36	–	–	–	–	–	1
1959-60	WI	155	23	471	9	52.33	3-59	–	–	8
1960-61‡	A	356	45	1209	34	35.55	5-63	2	–	23
1961	E	78	19	214	13	16.46	4-69	–	–	1
1961-62‡	A	210.2	19	770	35	22.00	6-72	2	–	8
	WI	246.5	70	521	27	19.29	5-63	1	–	11

Season	Venue	O	M	R	W	Avge	Best	5wI	10wM	Ct
1962	E	50	10	164	2	82.00	2-69	–	–	1
1962-63‡	A	384.3	49	1355	51	26.56	7-110	4	–	2
1963	E	758.3	182	1844	82	22.48	5-35	3	–	29
1963-64	WI	65	5	270	10	27.00	4-86	–	–	1
‡	A	411.4	50	1441	51	28.25	6-71	2	–	16
	I	46	9	141	9	15.66	6-63	1	–	–
1964	E	93	14	336	10	33.60	4-59	–	–	3
1964-65	I	39	4	167	4	41.75	4-94	–	–	1
	WI	282.1	72	757	22	34.40	3-41	–	–	10
1965	E	17	4	45	1	45.00	1-45	–	–	–
1965-66	WI	141.3	31	414	16	25.87	6-56	1	–	6
1966	E	557.2	158	1235	60	20.58	9-49	3	–	23
1966-67	I	217.4	68	546	23	23.73	6-83	1	–	12
	C	18	4	56	–	–	–	–	–	1
	WI	146	40	346	11	31.45	2-22	–	–	7
1967	E	75.5	16	195	11	17.72	4-46	–	–	3
1967-68	WI	252.5	80	562	13	43.23	3-33	–	–	5
1968	E	798.4	229	1964	84	23.38	7-69	5	1	25
1968-69‡	A	310.1	49	1120	36	31.11	6-73	2	–	13
‡	NZ	120	24	390	9	43.33	3-70	–	–	5
1969	E	532.2	155	1319	54	24.42	5-42	2	–	19
1969-70	WI	91	22	269	4	67.25	1-32	–	–	4
1970	E	676.1	193	1540	64	24.06	6-21	2	–	20
1970-71	P	20.3	4	62	2	31.00	–	–	–	3
1970-71	WI	331.3	110	625	25	25.00	5-44	1	–	5
1971	E	660.4	190	1641	53	30.96	5-11	2	–	29
1971-72‡	A	128.6	7	528	14	37.71	3-67	–	–	7
1971-72	WI	181	56	332	10	33.20	4-64	–	–	2
1972	E	157	45	351	15	23.40	3-37	–	–	4
1972-73	WI	16	4	40	–	–	–	–	–	–
1973	E	326.1	98	788	32	24.62	4-64	–	–	22
1973-74	WI	243.2	98	469	15	31.26	3-54	–	–	2
1974	E	350.4	82	925	29	31.89	4-84	–	–	17
TOTALS		**9234.5**	**2651**	**28942**	**1043**	**27.74**	**9-49**	**36**	**1**	**407**
		‡1921	**243**							

‡ Eight-ball overs

FIRST-CLASS CAREER

TEAM SUMMARY

BATTING

Team	M	I	NO	HS	Runs	Avge	100	50
Barbados	30	40	9	204	2355	75.96	8	8
Cavaliers	1	2	–	35	43	21.50	–	–
Commonwealth XI	4	8	–	102	456	57.00	1	4
A.E.R.Gilligan's XI	2	3	–	75	194	64.66	–	2
C.C.Hunte's XI	1	2	–	107	118	59.00	1	–
Jamaica XI	2	3	–	129	267	89.00	2	–
MCC	3	5	1	103	154	38.50	1	–
Nottinghamshire	107	174	30	160	7041	48.89	18	38
Rest of the World XI	19	31	5	254	1250	48.07	4	4
South Australia	26	45	2	251	2707	62.95	10	10
E.W.Swanton's XI	1	2	1	123	130	130.00	1	–
WEST INDIES	93	160	21	365*	8032	57.78	26	30
West Indians	91	130	22	219*	5464	50.59	14	25
Sir Frank Worrell's XI	3	4	2	44	104	52.00	–	–
TOTALS	**383**	**609**	**93**	**365***	**28315**	**54.87**	**86**	**121**

BOWLING AND FIELDING

Team	O	M	R	W	Avge	Best	5wI	10wM	Ct
Barbados	934.3	296	2133	71	30.04	6-56	2	–	22
Cavaliers	49	16	126	2	63.00	2-77	–	–	2
Commonwealth XI	87	12	295	12	24.58	4-69	–	–	5
A.E.R.Gilligan's XI	13	2	63	–	–	–	–	–	1
C.C.Hunte's XI	27	1	135	5	27.00	4-86	–	–	–
Jamaica XI	78.4	19	205	7	29.28	3-41	–	–	2
MCC	100	27	283	8	35.37	3-9	–	–	2
Nottinghamshire	2854.4	781	7202	281	25.62	7-69	9	1	111
Rest of the World XI	411	133	1364	50	27.28	5-39	1	–	18
	‡128.6	7							
South Australia	‡1006.1	118	3566	137	26.02	7-110	8	–	26

Team	O	M	R	W	Avge	Best	5wI	10wM	Ct
E.W.Swanton's XI	46	9	141	9	15.66	6-63	1	–	–
WEST INDIES	2930.2	887	7999	235	34.03	6-73	6	–	109
	‡502.1	88							
West Indians	1610.4	454	5094	216	23.58	9-59	9	–	106
	‡284	30							
Sir Frank Worrell's XI	93	14	336	10	33.60	4-59	–	–	3
TOTALS	**9234.5**	**2651**	**28942**	**1043**	**27.74**	**9-49**	**36**	**1**	**407**
	‡1921	**243**							

‡ Eight-ball overs

FIRST-CLASS HUNDREDS

	Score	For	Against	Venue	Season
1	104*	Barbados	British Guiana	Bridgetown	1954-55
2	219*	West Indians	Nottinghamshire	Nottingham	1957
3	101*	West Indians	MCC	Lord's	1957
4	104	West Indians	Somerset	Taunton	1957
5	183*	Barbados	Pakistanis	Bridgetown	1957-58
6	**365***	**WEST INDIES**	**PAKISTAN**	**Kingston**	**1957-58**
7	125	WEST INDIES	PAKISTAN	Georgetown	1957-58
8	109*	WEST INDIES	PAKISTAN	Georgetown	1957-58
9	108*	West Indians	Baroda	Baroda	1958-59
10	**142***	**WEST INDIES**	**INDIA**	**Bombay**	**1958-59**
11	198	WEST INDIES	INDIA	Kanpur	1958-59
12	161*	West Indians	Combined U	Nagpur	1958-59
13	**106***	**WEST INDIES**	**INDIA**	**Calcutta**	**1958-59**
14	154	Barbados	MCC	Bridgetown	1959-60
15	**226**	**WEST INDIES**	**ENGLAND**	**Bridgetown**	**1959-60**
16	147	WEST INDIES	ENGLAND	Kingston	1959-60
17	145	WEST INDIES	ENGLAND	Georgetown	1959-60
18	119	West Indians	Western Australia	Perth	1960-61
19	**132**	**WEST INDIES**	**AUSTRALIA**	**Brisbane**	**1960-61**
20	168	WEST INDIES	AUSTRALIA	Sydney	1960-61
21	103	MCC	Surrey	Lord's	1961
22	251	South Australia	New South Wales	Adelaide	1961-62
23	**153**	**WEST INDIES**	**INDIA**	**Kingston**	**1961-62**
24	104	WEST INDIES	INDIA	Kingston	1961-62

	Score	For	Against	Venue	Season
25	112	South Australia	Western Australia	Adelaide	1962-63
26	107*	South Australia	New South Wales	Adelaide	1962-63
27	196	South Australia	Queensland	Brisbane	1962-63
28	112	West Indians	Somerset	Bath	1963
29	**102**	**WEST INDIES**	**ENGLAND**	**Leeds**	**1963**
30	100*	West Indians	Yorkshire	Sheffield	1963
31	101	West Indians	T.N.Pearce's XI	Scarborough	1963
32	107	C.C.Hunte's XI	F.M.M.Worrell's XI	Kingston	1963-64
33	155	South Australia	South Africans	Adelaide	1963-64
34	122	South Australia	Queensland	Adelaide	1963-64
35	195	South Australia	Western Australia	Perth	1963-64
36	138	South Australia	New South Wales	Sydney	1963-64
37	124	South Australia	New South Wales	Adelaide	1963-64
38	124	South Australia	Victoria	Adelaide	1963-64
39	123	E.W.Swanton's XI	An Indian XI	Calcutta	1963-64
40	102	Commonwealth XI	Bengal Chief Minister's XI	Calcutta	1964-65
41	129	Jamaica XI	Cavaliers	Kingston	1964-65
42	183*	Barbados	Australians	Bridgetown	1964-65
43	204	Barbados	British Guiana	Bridgetown	1965-66
44	120	Jamaica XI	Worcestershire	Montego Bay	1965-66
45	153	West Indians	Nottinghamshire	Nottingham	1966
46	**161**	**WEST INDIES**	**ENGLAND**	**Manchester**	**1966**
47	163*	WEST INDIES	ENGLAND	Lord's	1966
48	174	WEST INDIES	ENGLAND	Leeds	1966
49	115	West Indians	Ceylon	Colombo	1966-67
50	165	Barbados	Guyana	Georgetown	1966-67
51	**113***	**WEST INDIES**	**ENGLAND**	**Kingston**	**1967-68**
52	152	WEST INDIES	ENGLAND	Georgetown	1967-68
53	100	Nottinghamshire	Middlesex	Lord's	1968
54	105*	Nottinghamshire	Kent	Dover	1968
55	132	West Indians	Western Australia	Perth	1968-69
56	130	West Indians	New South Wales	Sydney	1968-69
57	121*	West Indians	Combined XI	Launceston	1968-69
58	**110**	**WEST INDIES**	**AUSTRALIA**	**Adelaide**	**1968-69**
59	113	WEST INDIES	AUSTRALIA	Sydney	1968-69
60	104	Nottinghamshire	Surrey	Nottingham	1969
61	101	Nottinghamshire	Leicestershire	Nottingham	1969
62	116*	Barbados	Guyana	Georgetown	1969-70
63	115*	Nottinghamshire	Warwickshire	Nottingham	1970
64	160	Nottinghamshire	Surrey	The Oval	1970

	Score	For	Against	Venue	Season
65	103*	Nottinghamshire	Surrey	The Oval	1970
66	183	Rest of the World	England	Lord's	1970
67	144*	Nottinghamshire	Yorkshire	Sheffield	1970
68	114	Rest of the World	England	Leeds	1970
69	123*	Nottinghamshire	Kent	Folkestone	1970
70	**108***	**WEST INDIES**	**INDIA**	**Georgetown**	**1970-71**
71	135	Barbados	Indians	Bridgetown	1970-71
72	**178***	**WEST INDIES**	**INDIA**	**Bridgetown**	**1970-71**
73	132	WEST INDIES	INDIA	Port-of-Spain	1970-71
74	112	Nottinghamshire	Surrey	Nottingham	1971
75	151*	Nottinghamshire	Glamorgan	Swansea	1971
76	100	Nottinghamshire	Somerset	Weston-s-Mare	1971
77	134*	A World XI	Tasmania	Launceston	1971-72
78	254	A World XI	Australia	Melbourne	1971-72
79	**142**	**WEST INDIES**	**NEW ZEALAND**	**Bridgetown**	**1971-72**
80	100*	Nottinghamshire	Derbyshire	Ilkeston	1973
81	**150***	**WEST INDIES**	**ENGLAND**	**Lord's**	1973
82	128	Nottinghamshire	Derbyshire	Nottingham	1973
83	101*	Nottinghamshire	Warwickshire	Nottingham	1974
84	130	Nottinghamshire	Derbyshire	Ilkeston	1974
85	108	Nottinghamshire	Somerset	Nottingham	1974
86	132*	Nottinghamshire	Lancashire	Manchester	1974

FIRST-CLASS FIVE-WICKET ANALYSES

	Analysis				For	Against	Venue	Season
1	17	7	39	5	West Indians	Gloucestershire	Bristol	1957
2	15.5	6	31	5	West Indians	CC of India	Bombay	1958-59
3	22	4	63	5	West Indians	Queensland	Brisbane	1960-61
4	44	7	120	5	WEST INDIES	AUSTRALIA	Melbourne	1960-61
5	15.3	1	47	5	South Australia	Queensland	Brisbane	1961-62
6	23	3	72	6	South Australia	New South Wales	Adelaide	1961-62
7	32	9	63	5	WEST INDIES	INDIA	Kingston	1961-62
8	15	2	41	6	South Australia	Victoria	Melbourne	1962-63
9	21.2	–	69	5	South Australia	New South Wales	Adelaide	1962-63
10	16	4	48	6	South Australia	Western Australia	Perth	1962-63
11	44	6	110	7	South Australia	Victoria	Adelaide	1962-63
12	12.3	4	35	5	West Indians	Glamorgan	Cardiff	1963
13	31	10	60	5	WEST INDIES	ENGLAND	Birmingham	1963
14	28	8	48	5	West Indians	Leicestershire	Leicester	1963
15	26.4	4	81	6	South Australia	New South Wales	Adelaide	1963-64
16	17.5	7	71	6	South Australia	Victoria	Adelaide	1963-64
17	22	4	63	6	E.W.Swanton's XI	An Indian XI	Calcutta	1963-64
18	21.3	6	56	6	Barbados	British Guiana	Bridgetown	1965-66
19	9.2	4	11	6	West Indians	Derbyshire	Derby	1966
20	19.4	6	49	9	West Indians	Kent	Canterbury	1966
21	19.3	4	41	5	WEST INDIES	ENGLAND	Leeds	1966
22	26.3	9	83	6	West Indians	Indian Universities	Hyderabad	1966-67
23	14	4	25	5	Nottinghamshire	Middlesex	Nottingham	1968
24	15.5	5	31	5	Nottinghamshire	Somerset	Taunton	1968
25	41	13	90	6	Nottinghamshire	Essex	Nottingham	1968
26	22.3	3	69	7	Nottinghamshire	Kent	Dover	1968
27	33	9	89	5	Nottinghamshire	Surrey	Nottingham	1968
28	26	2	107	5	West Indians	South Australia	Adelaide	1968-69
29	33.6	12	73	6	WEST INDIES	AUSTRALIA	Brisbane	1968-69
30	40	18	42	5	WEST INDIES	ENGLAND	Leeds	1969
31	36	11	93	5	Nottinghamshire	Leicestershire	Nottingham	1969
32	20	11	21	6	Rest of the World	England	Lord's	1970
33	21	9	39	5	Nottinghamshire	Hampshire	Portsmouth	1970
34	25	10	44	5	Barbados	Combined Islands	Castries	1970-71
35	14	9	11	5	Nottinghamshire	Hampshire	Nottingham	1971
36	24	9	50	5	Nottinghamshire	Northamptonshire	Northampton	1971

TEST MATCH CAREER
MATCH RECORD

Season		Match	Venue	No	Runs	HO	O	M	R	W	Ct
1953-54	1	ENGLAND 5	Kingston	9	14	*	28.5	9	75	4	–
				9	26	c	1	–	6	–	–
1954-55	2	AUSTRALIA 2	Port-of-Spain	6	47	c	3	1	10	–	–
				6	8	*	–				–
	3	AUSTRALIA 3	Georgetown	6	12	c	16	10	20	3	1
				8	11	b	11	4	19	–	–
	4	AUSTRALIA 4	Bridgetown	2	43	c	11.5	6	30	1	–
				2	11	lbw	14	3	35	1	–
	5	AUSTRALIA 5	Kingston	7	35	*	38	12	99	1	–
				5	64	c	–				–
1955-56	6	NEW ZEALAND 1	Dunedin	3	27	ro	–				1
				–			4	4	–	–	–
	7	NEW ZEALAND 2	Christchurch	3	25	b	–				–
				–			–				1
	8	NEW ZEALAND 3	Wellington	2	27	c	14	11	3	1	–
				–			8.5	4	11	1	1
	9	NEW ZEALAND 4	Auckland	3	1	c	20	7	35	–	1
				6	1	ro	–				–
1957	10	ENGLAND 1	Birmingham	5	53	c	–				–
				3	14	c	30	4	77	–	–
	11	ENGLAND 2	Lord's	4	17	c	7	–	28	2	1
				5	66	c	–				–
	12	ENGLAND 3	Nottingham	2	47	b	21	6	60	1	–
				2	9	lbw	–				–
	13	ENGLAND 4	Leeds	2	4	c	32	9	79	1	–
				2	29	ro	–				–
	14	ENGLAND 5	The Oval	3	39	b	44	6	111	1	–
				3	42	b	–				–
1957-58	15	PAKISTAN 1	Bridgetown	3	52	c	–				–
				–			57	25	94	1	–
	16	PAKISTAN 2	Port-of-Spain	3	52	b	5.3	1	14	1	–
				6	80	lbw	22	8	41	2	1
	17	PAKISTAN 3	Kingston	3	365	*	5	1	13	–	1
				–			15	4	41	–	–
	18	PAKISTAN 4	Georgetown	2	125	b	16	2	47	–	–
				3	109	*	17	6	32	–	–
	19	PAKISTAN 5	Port-of-Spain	3	14	c	34	6	95	–	–
				3	27	b	–				–
1958-59	20	INDIA 1	Bombay	3	25	c	3	–	19	–	2
			(Brabourne)	3	142	*	3	–	8	–	–
	21	INDIA 2	Kanpur	3	4	c	24	4	62	2	–
				4	198	ro	21	10	29	0	–
	22	INDIA 3	Calcutta	6	106	*	6	–	32	1	2
				–			2	–	11	1	–

Season		Match	Venue	No	Runs	HO	O	M	R	W	Ct
	23	INDIA 4	Madras	4	29	c	18.1	8	26	4	1
			(*Corporation*)	4	9	c	18	8	39	2	–
	24	INDIA 5	Delhi	7	44	c	24	3	66	–	–
1958-59	25	PAKISTAN 1	Karachi	4	0	lbw	40	24	45	–	–
				6	14	lbw	9	5	12	–	–
	26	PAKISTAN 2	Dacca	9	29	lbw	8	4	7	–	–
				5	45	c	3	2	4	–	–
	27	PAKISTAN 3	Lahore	4	72	b	–				2
			(*Lawrence*)	–			6	1	9	–	–
1959-60	28	ENGLAND 1	Bridgetown	4	226	b	21	3	53	–	1
				–							–
	29	ENGLAND 2	Port-of-Spain	4	0	c	3	–	16	–	–
				4	31	lbw	–				–
	30	ENGLAND 3	Kingston	4	147	lbw	2	–	14	–	1
				4	19	ro	8	2	18	–	–
	31	ENGLAND 4	Georgetown	4	145	st	19	1	59	3	–
				–			12	1	36	1	
	32	ENGLAND 5	Port-of-Spain	4	92	b	20	1	75	3	4
				6	49	*	29	6	84	2	1
1960-61	33	AUSTRALIA 1	Brisbane	4	132	c	32	–	115	2	–
				4	14	b	8	–	30	–	1
	34	AUSTRALIA 2	Melbourne	5	9	c	17	1	88	1	2
				5	0	c	–				1
	35	AUSTRALIA 3	Sydney	4	168	c	5	2	14	1	1
				4	1	c	9	1	38	1	2
	36	AUSTRALIA 4	Adelaide	4	1	b	24	3	64	3	1
				4	20	ro	39	11	87	2	2
	37	AUSTRALIA 5	Melbourne	4	64	c	44	7	120	5	1
				5	21	c	13	2	32	–	1
1961-62	38	INDIA 1	Port-of-Spain	4	40	b	9.3	1	28	2	3
				–			15	7	22	4	–
	39	INDIA 2	Kingston	5	153	c	39	8	75	4	1
				–			17	3	41	1	1
	40	INDIA 3	Bridgetown	4	42	c	16	2	46	2	–
				–			17	10	14	–	3
	41	INDIA 4	Port-of-Spain	5	19	lbw	25	6	48	2	1
				5	16	*	47	14	116	3	1
	42	INDIA 5	Kingston	5	104	c	6	1	20	–	1
				4	50	c	32	9	63	5	–
1963	43	ENGLAND 1	Manchester	5	64	c	22	11	34	2	2
				–			37	4	122	2	1
	44	ENGLAND 2	Lord's	3	42	c	18	4	45	1	1
				5	8	c	4	1	4	–	–
	45	ENGLAND 3	Birmingham	6	19	b	31	10	60	5	–
				5	9	c	27	4	80	2	2
	46	ENGLAND 4	Leeds	5	102	c	6	1	15	–	–
				5	52	c	32	5	90	3	–
	47	ENGLAND 5	The Oval	5	26	ro	21	4	44	2	1
				–			33	6	77	3	1

Season	Match		Venue	No	Runs	HO	O	M	R	W	Ct
1964-65	48	†AUSTRALIA 1	Kingston	5	30	lbw	20.4	7	30	1	–
				6	27	c	17	2	64	1	–
	49	†AUSTRALIA 2	Port-of-Spain	5	69	ro	27.5	5	75	3	2
				5	24	lbw	–				–
	50	†AUSTRALIA 3	Georgetown	6	45	c	12	2	38	2	2
				6	42	c	19	7	39	2	2
	51	†AUSTRALIA 4	Bridgetown	6	55	c	37	7	143	1	1
				5	34	*	20	11	29	1	1
	52	†AUSTRALIA 5	Port-of-Spain	6	18	b	37	13	65	1	–
				6	8	b	2	–	7	–	–
1966	53	†ENGLAND 1	Manchester	6	161	c	7	1	16	–	3
				–			42	11	87	3	2
	54	†ENGLAND 2	Lord's	6	46	lbw	39	12	89	1	–
				6	163	*	8	4	8	–	–
	55	†ENGLAND 3	Nottingham	6	3	c	49	12	90	4	1
				6	94	c	31	6	71	1	4
	56	†ENGLAND 4	Leeds	6	174	b	19.3	4	41	5	–
				–			20.1	5	39	3	–
	57	†ENGLAND 5	The Oval	6	81	c	54	23	104	3	–
				7	0	c	–				–
1966-67	58	†INDIA 1	Bombay	6	50	b	25	9	46	3	1
			(*Brabourne*)	6	53	*	27	6	79	2	2
	59	†INDIA 2	Calcutta	7	70	c	28.5	16	42	3	–
				–			20	2	56	4	–
	60	†INDIA 3	Madras	7	95	c	27.2	7	69	2	1
			(*Chepauk*)	7	74	*	27	11	58	–	3
1967-68	61	†ENGLAND 1	Port-of-Spain	6	17	c	26	5	83	1	–
				7	33	*	–				–
	62	†ENGLAND 2	Kingston	6	0	lbw	31	11	56	1	1
				6	113	*	16.5	7	33	3	–
	63	†ENGLAND 3	Bridgetown	6	68	c	41	10	76	2	2
				6	19	b	–				–
	64	†ENGLAND 4	Port-of-Spain	6	48	c	36	8	87	–	–
				–			14	–	48	–	1
	65	†ENGLAND 5	Georgetown	5	152	c	37	15	72	3	–
				5	95	*	31	16	53	3	–
1968-69	66	†AUSTRALIA 1	Brisbane	6	2	c	14	5	30	1	3
				6	36	c	33.6	12	73	6	–
	67	†AUSTRALIA 2	Melbourne	6	19	b	33.3	4	97	4	1
				6	67	lbw	–				–
	68	†AUSTRALIA 3	Sydney	6	49	b	21		4	109	–	–
				6	36	c	–				–
	69	†AUSTRALIA 4	Adelaide	6	110	b	28		4	106	1	1
				7	52	c	22		1	107	1	–
	70	†AUSTRALIA 5	Sydney	4	13	c	28		4	94	2	–
				5	113	c	26		3	117	3	1
1968-69	71	†NEW ZEALAND 1	Auckland	6	11	c	19	1	87	2	2
				6	0	lbw	30	7	79	1	–

Season		Match	Venue	No	Runs	HO	O	M	R	W	Ct
	72	†NEW ZEALAND 2	Wellington	6	20	c	9	2	22	1	2
				6	39	c	8	2	22	–	–
	73	†NEW ZEALAND 3	Christchurch	6	0	b	8	3	21	–	–
				–			31	8	70	3	1
1969	74	†ENGLAND 1	Manchester	5	10	c	27	7	78	1	–
				5	48	c	3	1	1		
	75	†ENGLAND 2	Lord's	5	29	ro	26	12	57	2	–
				7	50	*	29	8	72	1	–
	76	†ENGLAND 3	Leeds	5	13	c	21	1	68	2	1
				6	0	b	40	18	42	5	1
1970-71	77	†INDIA 1	Kingston	5	44	c	30	8	57	2	1
				5	93	c	–				–
	78	†INDIA 2	Port-of-Spain	6	29	c	28	7	65	–	–
				5	0	b	15	5	16	–	–
	79	†INDIA 3	Georgetown	6	4	c	43	15	72	3	–
				5	108	*	5	1	14	–	–
	80	†INDIA 4	Bridgetown	5	178	*	20	9	34	2	–
				5	9	c	23	8	31	2	–
	81	†INDIA 5	Port-of-Spain	6	132	b	13	3	30	1	1
				5	0	b	42	14	82	2	2
1971-72	82	†NEW ZEALAND 1	Kingston	6	13	*	11	3	20	–	1
				–			13	5	16	–	–
	83	†NEW ZEALAND 2	Port-of-Spain	6	19	c	26	7	40	2	–
				6	9	b	20	3	54	1	–
	84	†NEW ZEALAND 3	Bridgetown	5	35	c	29	6	64	4	–
				7	142	c	–				–
	85	†NEW ZEALAND 4	Georgetown	7	5	c	42	15	76	–	–
				–			–				–
	86	†NEW ZEALAND 5	Port-of-Spain	8	28	c	11	5	17	2	1
				6	2	b	29	12	45	1	–
1973	87	ENGLAND 1	The Oval	7	10	ro	22.1	13	27	3	1
				6	51	c	11	3	22	–	–
	88	ENGLAND 2	Birmingham	6	21	b	30	6	62	3	–
				6	74	b	7	1	21	–	–
	89	ENGLAND 3	Lord's	6	150	*	8	–	30	–	4
				–			4	1	7	–	2
1973-74	90	ENGLAND 1	Port-of-Spain	6	23	c	14	3	37	2	–
				–			34	15	54	3	–
	91	ENGLAND 2	Kingston	6	57	c	33	11	65	3	–
				–			34	13	73	1	–
	92	ENGLAND 3	Bridgetown	7	0	c	18	4	57	1	1
				–			35	21	55	1	–
	93	ENGLAND 5	Port-of-Spain	5	0	c	31	16	44	1	–
				6	20	b	24.2	9	36	2	–

* not out. † captain.

TEST MATCH CAREER

BATTING SUMMARY BY SERIES

Series		M	I	NO	HS	Runs	Avge	100	50	0
1953-54	E	1	2	1	26	40	40.00	–	–	–
1954-55	A	4	8	2	64	231	38.50	–	1	–
1955-56†	NZ	4	5	–	27	81	16.20	–	–	–
1957†	E	5	10	–	66	320	32.00	–	2	–
1957-58	P	5	8	2	365*	824	137.33	3	3	–
1958-59†	I	5	8	2	198	557	92.83	3	–	–
1958-59†	P	3	5	–	72	160	32.00	–	1	1
1959-60	E	5	8	1	226	709	101.28	3	1	1
1960-61†	A	5	10	–	168	430	43.00	2	1	1
1961-62	I	5	7	1	153	424	70.66	2	1	–
1963†	E	5	8	–	102	322	40.25	1	2	–
1964-65	A	5	10	1	69	352	39.11	–	2	–
1966†	E	5	8	1	174	722	103.14	3	2	1
1966-67†	I	3	5	2	95	342	114.00	–	5	–
1967-68	E	5	9	3	152	545	90.83	2	2	1
1968-69†	A	5	10	–	113	497	49.70	2	2	–
1968-69†	NZ	3	5	–	39	70	14.00	–	–	2
1969†	E	3	6	1	50*	150	30.00	–	1	1
1970-71	I	5	10	2	178*	597	74.62	3	1	2
1971-72	NZ	5	8	1	142	253	36.14	1	–	–
1973†	E	3	5	1	150*	306	76.50	1	2	–
1973-74	E	4	5	–	57	100	20.00	–	1	2
TOTALS		**93**	**160**	**21**	**365***	**8032**	**57.78**	**26**	**30**	**12**

† Away series

BATTING SUMMARY BY OPPONENTS

Opponents	M	I	NO	HS	Runs	Avge	100	50	0
Australia	19	38	3	168	1510	43.14	4	6	1
England	36	61	8	226	3214	60.64	10	13	6
India	18	30	7	198	1920	83.47	8	7	2
New Zealand	12	18	1	142	404	23.76	1	–	2
Pakistan	8	13	2	365*	984	89.45	3	4	1
TOTALS	**93**	**160**	**21**	**365***	**8032**	**57.78**	**26**	**30**	**12**

TEST MATCH CAREER

BATTING SUMMARY BY VENUE

Venue	M	I	NO	HS	Runs	Avge	100	50	0
Bridgetown	9	14	2	226	914	76.16	3	3	1
Georgetown	7	12	3	152	853	94.77	5	1	–
Kingston	11	18	5	365*	1354	104.15	5	4	1
Port-of-Spain	17	31	4	132	954	35.33	1	4	4
In West Indies	**44**	**75**	**14**	**365***	**4075**	**66.80**	**14**	**12**	**6**
Adelaide	2	4	–	110	183	45.75	1	1	–
Brisbane	2	4	–	132	184	46.00	1	–	–
Melbourne	3	6	–	67	180	30.00	–	2	1
Sydney	3	6	–	168	380	63.33	2	–	–
In Australia	**10**	**20**	**–**	**168**	**927**	**46.35**	**4**	**3**	**1**
Birmingham	3	6	–	74	190	31.66	–	2	–
Leeds	4	7	–	174	374	53.42	2	1	1
Lord's	5	9	3	163*	571	95.16	2	2	–
Manchester	3	4	–	161	283	70.75	1	1	–
Nottingham	2	4	–	94	153	38.25	–	1	–
The Oval	4	7	–	81	249	35.57	–	2	1
In England	**21**	**37**	**3**	**174**	**1820**	**53.52**	**5**	**9**	**2**
Bombay	2	4	2	142*	270	135.00	1	2	–
Calcutta	2	2	1	106*	176	176.00	1	1	–
Delhi	1	1	–	44	44	44.00	–	–	–
Kanpur	1	2	–	198	202	101.00	1	–	–
Madras	2	4	1	95	207	69.00	–	2	–
In India	**8**	**13**	**4**	**198**	**899**	**99.88**	**3**	**5**	**–**
Auckland	2	4	–	11	13	3.25	–	–	1
Christchurch	2	2	–	25	25	12.50	–	–	1
Dunedin	1	1	–	27	27	27.00	–	–	–
Wellington	2	3	–	39	86	28.66	–	–	–
In New Zealand	**7**	**10**	**–**	**39**	**151**	**15.10**	**–**	**–**	**2**

Venue	M	I	NO	HS	Runs	Avge	100	50	0
Dacca	1	2	–	45	74	37.00	–	–	–
Karachi	1	2	–	14	14	7.00	–	–	1
Lahore	1	1	–	72	72	72.00	–	1	–
In Pakistan	**3**	**5**	**–**	**72**	**160**	**32.00**	**–**	**1**	**1**
HOME	44	75	14	365*	4075	66.80	14	12	6
AWAY	49	85	7	198	3957	50.73	12	18	6
TOTALS	**93**	**160**	**21**	**365***	**8032**	**57.78**	**26**	**30**	**12**

TEST MATCH CAREER
HUNDRED PARTNERSHIPS (43)

SECOND WICKET (3)

			E	A	NZ	I	P
C.C.Hunte (260), G.St A.Sobers (365*)	Kingston	1957-58	–	–	–	–	446†
G.St A.Sobers (125), C.L.Walcott (145)	Georgetown	1957-58	–	–	–	–	269
C.C.Hunte (114), G.St A.Sobers (109*)	Georgetown	1957-58	–	–	–	–	135

THIRD WICKET (4)

			E	A	NZ	I	P
R.B.Kanhai (217), G.St A.Sobers (72)	Lahore	1958-59	–	–	–	–	162
E.D.A.St J.McMorris (73), G.St A.Sobers (147)	Kingston	1959-60	133*	–	–	–	–
R.B.Kanhai (55), G.St A.Sobers (145)	Georgetown	1959-60	115	–	–	–	–
G.St A.Sobers (147), S.M.Nurse (70)	Kingston	1959-60	110	–	–	–	–

FOURTH WICKET (12)

			E	A	NZ	I	P
G.St A.Sobers (226), F.M.M.Worrell (197*)	Bridgetown	1959-60	399†	–	–	–	–
R.B.Kanhai (150), G.St A.Sobers (152)	Georgetown	1967-68	250	–	–	–	–
G.St A.Sobers (365*), C.L.Walcott (88*)	Kingston	1957-58	–	–	–	–	188*
C.L.Walcott (110), G.St A.Sobers (64)	Kingston	1954-55	–	179	–	–	–
G.St A.Sobers (132), F.M.M.Worrell (65)	Brisbane	1960-61	–	174	–	–	–
R.B.Kanhai (158*), G.St A.Sobers (93)	Kingston	1970-71	–	–	–	173	–
C.A.Davis (125*), G.St A.Sobers (108*)	Georgetown	1970-71	–	–	–	170*	–
C.A.Davis (79), G.St A.Sobers (178*)	Bridgetown	1970-71	–	–	–	167	–
B.F.Butcher (117), G.St A.Sobers (69)	Port-of-Spain	1964-65	–	160	–	–	–
R.B.Kanhai (92), G.St A.Sobers (102)	Leeds	1963	143	–	–	–	–
C.C.Hunte (182), G.St A.Sobers (64)	Manchester	1963	120	–	–	–	–
G.St A.Sobers (142*), O.G.Smith (58)	Bombay	1958-59	–	–	–	119	–

FIFTH WICKET (12)

Partnership	Venue	Year	E	A	NZ	I	P
S.M.Nurse (137), G.St A.Sobers (174)	Leeds	1966	265*†	–	–	–	–
C.A.Davis (105), G.St A.Sobers (132)	Port-of-Spain	1970-71	–	–	–	177	–
B.F.Butcher (209*), G.St A.Sobers (94)	Nottingham	1966	173	–	–	–	–
G.St A.Sobers (142*), B.F.Butcher (64*)	Bombay	1958-59	–	–	–	134*	–
S.M.Nurse (74), G.St A.Sobers (67)	Melbourne	1968-69	–	134	–	–	–
G.St A.Sobers (168), S.M.Nurse (43)	Sydney	1960-61	–	128	–	–	–
R.B.Kanhai (104), G.St A.Sobers (81)	The Oval	1966	122	–	–	–	–
G.St A.Sobers (145), F.M.M.Worrell (38)	Georgetown	1959-60	121	–	–	–	–
G.St A.Sobers (198), B.F.Butcher (60)	Kanpur	1958-59	–	–	–	114	–
C.H.Lloyd (78*), G.St A.Sobers (53*)	Bombay	1966-67	–	–	–	102*	–
F.C.M.Alexander (57), G.St A.Sobers (80)	Port-of-Spain	1957-58	100	–	–	–	–
G.St A.Sobers (66), E.de C.Weekes (90)	Lord's	1957	–	–	–	–	101

SIXTH WICKET (10)

Partnership	Venue	Year	E	A	NZ	I	P
G.St A.Sobers (163*), D.A.J.Holford (105*)	Lord's	1966	274*†	–	–	–	–
C.A.Davis (183), G.St A.Sobers (142)	Bridgetown	1971-72	–	–	254	–	–
G.St A.Sobers (198), J.S.Solomon (86)	Kanpur	1958-59	–	–	–	163	–
G.St A.Sobers (106*), J.S.Solomon (69*)	Calcutta	1958-59	–	–	–	160*	–
G.St A.Sobers (161), D.A.J.Holford (32)	Manchester	1966	127	–	–	–	–
G.St A.Sobers (113), S.M.Nurse (137)	Sydney	1968-69	–	118	–	–	–
G.St A.Sobers (57), B.D.Julien (66)	Kingston	1973-74	112	–	–	–	–
G.St A.Sobers (153), F.M.M.Worrell (58)	Kingston	1961-62	–	–	110	–	–
G.St A.Sobers (113*), D.A.J.Holford (35)	Kingston	1967-68	110	–	–	–	–
G.St A.Sobers (178*), M.L.C.Foster (36*)	Bridgetown	1970-71	–	–	–	107*	–

SEVENTH WICKET (2)

Partnership	Venue	Year	E	A	NZ	I	P
G.St A.Sobers (150*), B.D.Julien (121)	Lord's	1973	155*†	–	–	–	–
G.St A.Sobers (153), I.L.Mendonça (78)	Kingston	1961-62	–	–	127	–	–

* not out/unbroken partnership   † West Indies record partnership (then)

TEST MATCH CAREER

BOWLING AND FIELDING SUMMARY BY SERIES

Series		O	M	R	W	Avge	Best	5wI	10wM	Ct
1953-54	E	29.5	9	81	4	20.25	4-75	–	–	–
1954-55	A	93.5	36	213	6	35.50	3-20	–	–	1
1955-56†	NZ	46.5	26	49	2	24.50	1-3	–	–	4
1957†	E	134	25	355	5	71.00	2-28	–	–	1
1957-58	P	171.3	53	377	4	94.25	2-41	–	–	2
1958-59†	I	119.1	33	292	10	29.20	4-26	–	–	5
1958-59†	P	66	36	77	0	–	–	–	–	2
1959-60	E	114	14	355	9	39.44	3-59	–	–	7
1960-61†‡	A	191	27	588	15	39.20	5-120	1	–	12
1961-62	I	223.3	61	473	23	20.56	5-63	1	–	11
1963†	E	231	50	571	20	28.55	5-60	1	–	8
1964-65	A	192.3	54	490	12	40.83	3-75	–	–	8
1966†	E	269.4	78	545	20	27.25	5-41	1	–	10
1966-67†	I	155.1	51	350	14	25.00	4-56	–	–	7
1967-68	E	232.5	72	508	13	39.07	3-33	–	–	4
1968-69†‡	A	206.1	37	733	18	40.72	6-73	1	–	6
1968-69†‡	NZ	105	24	301	7	43.00	3-70	–	–	5
1969†	E	145	47	318	11	28.90	5-42	1	–	2
1970-71	I	219	70	401	12	33.41	3-72	–	–	4
1971-72	NZ	181	56	332	10	33.20	4-64	–	–	2
1973†	E	82.1	24	169	6	28.16	3-27	–	–	7
1973-74	E	223.2	92	421	14	30.07	3-54	–	–	1
TOTALS		**2930.2**	**887**	**7999**	**235**	**34.03**	**6-73**	**6**	**–**	**109**
		‡502.1	**88**							

BOWLING AND FIELDING SUMMARY BY OPPONENTS

Opponent	O	M	R	W	Avge	Best	5wI	10wM	Ct
Australia	286.2	90	2024	51	39.68	6-73	2	–	27
Australia‡	397.1	64							
England	1461.5	411	3323	102	32.57	5-41	3	–	40
India	716.5	215	1516	59	25.69	5-63	1	–	27
New Zealand	227.5	82	682	19	35.89	4-64	–	–	11
New Zealand‡	105	24							

Opponent	O	M	R	W	Avge	Best	5wI	10wM	Ct
Pakistan	237.3	89	454	4	113.50	2-41	–	–	4
TOTALS	**2930.2**	**887**	**7999**	**235**	**34.03**	**6-73**	**6**	**–**	**109**
	‡502.1	88							

† Away series ‡ Eight-ball overs

TEST MATCH CAREER

BOWLING AND FIELDING SUMMARY BY VENUE

Venue	O	M	R	W	Avge	Best	5wI	10wM	Ct
Bridgetown	359.5	125	761	19	40.05	4-64	–	–	9
Georgetown	280	94	577	20	28.85	3-20	–	–	5
Kingston	398.2	116	879	27	32.55	5-63	1	–	8
Port-of-Spain	643.1	182	1434	41	34.97	4-22	–	–	18
In West Indies	**1681.2**	**517**	**3651**	**107**	**34.12**	**5-63**	**1**	**–**	**40**
Adelaide	113	19	364	7	52.00	3-64	–	–	4
Brisbane	87.6	17	248	9	27.55	6-73	1	–	4
Melbourne	107.3	14	337	10	33.70	5-120	1	–	6
Sydney	89	14	372	7	53.14	3-117	–	–	4
In Australia	**‡397.1**	**64**	**1321**	**33**	**40.03**	**6-73**	**2**	**–**	**18**
Birmingham	125	25	300	10	30.00	5-60	1	–	2
Leeds	171.4	42	374	19	19.68	5-41	2	–	2
Lord's	143	42	340	7	48.57	2-28	–	–	8
Manchester	137	35	338	8	42.25	3-87	–	–	8
Nottingham	101	24	221	6	36.83	4-90	–	–	5
The Oval	185.1	55	385	12	32.08	3-27	–	–	3
In England	**862.5**	**223**	**1958**	**62**	**31.58**	**5-41**	**3**	**–**	**28**
Bombay	58	15	152	5	30.40	3-46	–	–	5
Calcutta	56.5	18	141	9	15.66	4-56	–	–	2
Delhi	24	3	66	0	–	–	–	–	–
Kanpur	45	14	91	2	45.50	2-62	–	–	–
Madras	90.3	34	192	8	24.00	4-26	–	–	5
In India	**274.2**	**84**	**642**	**24**	**26.75**	**4-26**	**–**	**–**	**12**

Venue	O	M	R	W	Avge	Best	5wI	10wM	Ct
Auckland	69	15	201	3	67.00	2-87	–	–	3
Christchurch	39	11	91	3	30.33	3-70	–	–	2
Dunedin	4	4	0	0	–	–	–	–	2
Wellington	39.5	19	58	3	19.33	1-3	–	–	3
In New Zealand	**151.5**	**49**	**350**	**9**	**38.89**	**3-70**	**–**	**–**	**10**
Dacca	11	6	11	0	–	–	–	–	–
Karachi	49	29	57	0	–	–	–	–	–
Lahore	6	1	9	0	–	–	–	–	2
In Pakistan	**66**	**36**	**77**	**0**	**–**	**–**	**–**	**–**	**2**
HOME	1681.2	517	3651	107	34.12	5-63	1	–	40
AWAY	1355 ‡397.1	392 64	4348	128	33.98	6-73	5	–	69
TOTALS	**3036.2 ‡397.1**	**909 64**	**7999**	**235**	**34.03**	**6-73**	**6**	**–**	**109**

‡Eight-ball overs

TEST MATCH CAREER HIGHLIGHTS

#1: Kingston, Jamaica, Mar/Apr 1954 – v England (5th)
Made his debut at the age of 17 years 245 days (still the second-youngest to represent West Indies) and took the first of his 235 wickets when he dismissed Trevor Bailey, his first biographer.

#17: Kingston, Jamaica, Feb/Mar 1958 – v Pakistan (3rd)
He converted his first three-figure score in Test cricket into what was to remain the highest score at this level for 36 years, compiling an undefeated 365 in 614 minutes – 183 minutes fewer than Len Hutton had batted in setting the previous record of 364. He hit 38 fours, completed 1000 runs in his 29th innings and, at 21 years 216 days,

remains the youngest to score a triple hundred at this level. His partnership of 446 with Conrad Hunte was then the second-highest for any wicket in Tests. They were the fourth pair to bat throughout a complete day of Test cricket.

#18: Georgetown, British Guiana, Mar 1958 – v Pakistan (4th)
Scored a hundred in each innings (125 and 109 not out) to bring his aggregate in his last three innings to 599 for once out. He added 269 for the second wicket with Clyde Walcott.

#20: Bombay, India, Nov/Dec 1958 – v India (1st)
Scored 142 not out and shared and unbroken fifth-wicket stand of 134 with Basil Butcher to establish a partnership record by two batsmen using runners – both had sustained leg injuries.

#21: Kanpur, India, Dec 1958 – v India (2nd)
Run out for 198 after batting for 340 minutes and hitting 28 fours, he set a sixth-wicket partnership record for this series by adding 163 with Joe Solomon.

#22: Calcutta, India, Dec 1958/Jan 1959 – v India (3rd)
Scored 106 not out to register his sixth hundred in as many Tests.

#23: Madras, India, Jan 1959 – v India (4th)
Completed 2000 runs in his 39th innings.

#27: Lahore, Pakistan, Mar 1959 – v Pakistan (3rd)
Shared a series record third-wicket partnership of 162 with Rohan Kanhai.

#28: Bridgetown, Barbados, Jan 1960 – v England (1st)
Frank Worrell (197 not out in 682 minutes) and Sobers (226 in 647 minutes) played the then two longest innings against England and their partnership of 399 in 579 minutes remains the West Indies

record for any wicket in this series and a national fourth-wicket record in all Tests. It was then the longest partnership in Test cricket. They were the first pair to bat through two days play of a Test, although a rest day intervened and the final hour of their first day was lost to rain.

#33: Brisbane, Australia, Dec 1960 – v Australia (1st)
Contributed his tenth hundred (132) to the first tied Test, reaching his fifty in 57 minutes and completing 3000 runs in his 55th innings.

#37: Melbourne, Australia, Feb 1961 – v Australia (5th)
Bowled unchanged for 41 eight-ball overs during the first innings, mostly in front of a crowd of 90,800, then the record attendance for any day of Test cricket.

#39: Kingston, Jamaica, Mar 1962 – v India (2nd)
Scored 153, partially with a runner because of cramp, and hit four sixes.

#46: Leeds, England, Jul 1963 – v England (4th)
Scored his 14th hundred and completed 4000 runs in his 77th innings.

#48: Kingston, Jamaica, Mar 1965 – v Australia (1st)
Captaining West Indies for the first time, he took his 100th wicket and became the first to complete the double of 4000 runs and 100 wickets.

#54: Lord's, England, Jun 1966 – v England (2nd)
His unbroken partnership of 274 with David Holford, his cousin, remains the West Indies sixth-wicket record in all Tests.

#56: Leeds, England, Aug 1966 – v England (4th)
Scored his third hundred of the rubber (174), including 103 runs between lunch and tea on the second day. His highest Test innings in England took 240 minutes, contained 24 fours and took him beyond

5000 runs in 95 innings, 2000 runs against England, 500 runs in the rubber and 1000 first-class runs for the tour. His partnership of 265 in 240 minutes with Seymour Nurse was the West Indies fifth-wicket record in all Tests until 1998-99. He then took his 50th wicket against England and ended England's first innings with a spell of 3 for 0 in seven balls.

#57: Kennington Oval, England, Aug 1966 – v England (5th)
Won his fifth toss of the rubber. Although he was dismissed first ball on the final day, his contribution to West Indies' 3-1 victory was massive: 722 runs (average 103.14), 20 wickets and ten catches.

#65: Georgetown, Guyana, Mar/Apr 1968 – v England (5th)
Scored 152 and 95 not out. In his 111th innings he became the first to score 6000 runs for West Indies.

#66: Brisbane, Australia, Dec 1968 – v Australia (1st)
Mostly using his orthodox slower style, he returned his best analysis in Tests: 33.6-12-73-6.

#79: Georgetown, Guyana, Mar 1971 – v India (3rd)
His 22nd hundred in 138 innings took his aggregate beyond 7000 runs, the third batsman to reach this mark after Walter Hammond and Colin Cowdrey.

#80: Bridgetown, Barbados, Apr 1971 – v India (4th)
Scored his third hundred in successive first-class innings against India, having made 135 for Barbados in the intervening match. When he claimed his 200th victim he became the second player after Richie Benaud to complete the double of 2000 runs and 200 wickets.

#82: Kingston, Jamaica, Feb 1972 – v New Zealand (1st)
Became the first fielder to hold 100 catches for West Indies.

#84: Bridgetown, Barbados, Mar 1972 – v New Zealand (3rd)
Shared a series sixth-wicket record partnership of 254 in 363 minutes with Charlie Davis and exceeded Colin Cowdrey's world record Test match aggregate of 7459 runs. His final aggregate of 8032 runs remained the record for Test cricket until Geoffrey Boycott surpassed it in 1981-82.

#86: Port-of-Spain, Trinidad, Apr 1972 – v New Zealand (5th)
Became the first captain to win all five tosses in a rubber on two occasions. Made the last of his 85 consecutive Test appearances to establish the world record until 1982-83. His tally of 39 consecutive Tests as captain (9 wins, 10 defeats and 20 draws) remained the record until 1989.

#89: Lord's, England, Aug 1973 – v England (3rd)
Shared an unbroken stand of 155 in 113 minutes with Bernard Julien which remains the West Indies seventh-wicket record against England. His undefeated 150 in 288 minutes from 227 balls was the last of his 26 hundreds in official Tests. Only Sir Donald Bradman (29) had then scored more.

#91: Kingston, Jamaica, Feb 1974 – v England (2nd)
In his 157th innings he became the first to score 8000 runs in Test cricket.

#93: Port-of-Spain, Trinidad, Mar/Apr 1974 – v England (5th)
In his final Test he became the first West Indian to take 100 wickets against England.

SOBERS'S PLACE IN TEST MATCH RECORDS

(Updated to 1 January 2002)

BATTING RECORDS

8000 RUNS

Runs			M	I	NO	HS	Avge	100	50
11174	A.R.Border	A	156	265	44	205	50.56	27	63
10122	S.M.Gavaskar	I	125	214	16	236*	51.12	34	45
9475	S.R.Waugh	A	144	227	41	200	50.94	27	44
8900	G.A.Gooch	E	118	215	6	333	42.58	20	46
8832	Javed Miandad	P	124	189	21	280*	52.57	23	43
8540	I.V.A.Richards	WI	121	182	12	291	50.23	24	45
8231	D.I.Gower	E	117	204	18	215	44.25	18	39
8114	G.Boycott	E	108	193	23	246*	47.72	22	42
8032	**G.St A.Sobers**	**WI**	**93**	**160**	**21**	**365***	**57.78**	**26**	**30**

LEADING AVERAGES

(Qualifications: 25 innings; avge 55.00)

Avge			M	I	NO	HS	Runs	100	50
99.94	D.G.Bradman	A	52	80	10	334	6996	29	13
60.97	R.G.Pollock	SA	23	41	4	274	2256	7	11
60.83	G.A.Headley	WI	22	40	4	270*	2190	10	5
60.73	H.Sutcliffe	E	54	84	9	194	4555	16	23
59.23	E.Paynter	E	20	31	5	243	1540	4	7
58.67	K.F.Barrington	E	82	131	15	256	6806	20	35
58.61	E.de C.Weekes	WI	48	81	5	207	4455	15	19
58.45	W.R.Hammond	E	85	140	16	336*	7249	22	24
57.96	S.R.Tendulkar	I	89	143	15	217	7419	27	30
57.78	**G.St A.Sobers**	**WI**	**93**	**160**	**21**	**365***	**8032**	**26**	**30**
56.94	J.B.Hobbs	E	61	102	7	211	5410	15	28
56.68	C.L.Walcott	WI	44	74	7	220	3798	15	14
56.67	L.Hutton	E	79	138	15	364	6971	19	33
55.85	A.Flower	Z	57	100	19	232*	4524	12	25

800 RUNS IN A SERIES

Runs		Series	Season	M	I	NO	HS	Avge	100	50
974	D.G.Bradman	A v E	1930	5	7	–	334	139.14	4	–
905	W.R.Hammond	E v A	1928-29	5	9	1	251	113.12	4	–
839	M.A.Taylor	A v E	1989	6	11	1	219	83.90	2	5
834	R.N.Harvey	A v SA	1952-53	5	9	–	205	92.66	4	3
829	I.V.A.Richards	WI v E	1976	4	7	–	291	118.42	3	2
827	C.L.Walcott	WI v A	1954-55	5	10	–	155	82.70	5	2
824	**G.St A.Sobers**	**WI v P**	**1957-58**	**5**	**8**	**2**	**365***	**137.33**	**3**	**3**
810	D.G.Bradman	A v E	1936-37	5	9	–	270	90.00	3	1
806	D.G.Bradman	A v SA	1931-32	5	5	1	299*	201.50	4	–

350 RUNS IN A MATCH

456	G.A.Gooch	333	123	E v I	Lord's	1990
426	M.A.Taylor	334*	92	A v P	Peshawar	1998-99
380	G.S.Chappell	247*	133	A v NZ	Wellington	1973-74
375	A.Sandham	325	50	E v WI	Kingston	1929-30
375	B.C.Lara	375	–	WI v E	St John's	1993-94
365	**G.St A.Sobers**	**365***	–	**WI v P**	**Kingston**	**1957-58**
364	L.Hutton	364	–	E v A	The Oval	1938
354	Hanif Mohammed	17	337	P v WI	Bridgetown	1957-58
351	B.C.Lara	221	130	WI v SL	Colombo	2001-02

300 RUNS IN AN INNINGS

375	B.C.Lara	WI v E	St John's	1993-94
365*	**G.St A.Sobers**	**WI v P**	**Kingston**	**1957-58**
364	L.Hutton	E v A	The Oval	1938
340	S.T.Jayasuriya	SL v I	Colombo	1997-98
337	Hanif Mohammad	P v WI	Bridgetown	1957-58
336*	W.R.Hammond	E v NZ	Auckland	1932-33
334*	M.A.Taylor	A v P	Peshawar	1998-99
334	D.G.Bradman	A v E	Leeds	1930
333	G.A.Gooch	E v I	Lord's	1990
325	A.Sandham	E v WI	Kingston	1929-30
311	R.B.Simpson	A v E	Manchester	1964
310*	J.H.Edrich	E v NZ	Leeds	1965
307	R.M.Cowper	A v E	Melbourne	1965-66
304	D.G.Bradman	A v E	Leeds	1934
302	L.G.Rowe	WI v E	Bridgetown	1973-74

YOUNGEST PLAYERS TO SCORE A TRIPLE HUNDRED

Years	Days					
21	**216**	**G.St A.Sobers**	**365***	**WI v P**	**Kingston**	**1957-58**
21	318	D.G.Bradman	334	A v E	Leeds	1930

25 HUNDREDS

100			200	Opponents I	E	A	SA	WI	NZ	I	P	SL	Z
34	S.M.Gavaskar	I	4	214	4	8	–	13	2	–	5	2	–
29	D.G.Bradman	A	12	80	19	–	4	2	–	4	–	–	–
27	S.R.Tendulkar	I	2	143	5	6	3	1	3	–	1	6	2
27	S.R.Waugh	A	1	227	9	–	2	6	2	2	2	3	1
27	A.R.Border	A	2	265	8	–	–	3	5	4	6	1	–
26	**G.St A.Sobers**	**WI**	**2**	**160**	**10**	**4**	–	–	**1**	**8**	**3**	–	–

UNOFFICIAL TEST MATCHES

(FOR REST OF THE WORLD)

Season	Match	Venue	No	Runs	HO	O	M	R	W	Ct
1970	†ENGLAND 1	Lord's	6	183	c	20	11	21	6	1
			–			31	14	43	2	1
	†ENGLAND 2	Nottingham	6	8	b	20.5	3	49	2	1
			6	18	c	18	7	24	–	–
	†ENGLAND 3	Birmingham	6	80	b	20	11	38	3	1
			5	7	lbw	51.5	20	89	4	2
	†ENGLAND 4	Leeds	6	114	c	20	11	24	–	–
			7	59	c	34	9	65	–	–
	†ENGLAND 5	The Oval	6	79	b	15	5	18	1	1
			6	40	*	42	15	81	3	–

* not out. † captain.

Index